CARY GRANT
Haunted Idol

By the same author

SIR JAMES GOLDSMITH:
The Man and the Myth

CAUGHT IN THE ACT:
Children in Trouble
(*with Marcel Berlins*)

Cary Grant

HAUNTED IDOL

Geoffrey Wansell

COLLINS
8 Grafton Street, London WI
1983

William Collins Sons and Co Ltd
London · Glasgow · Sydney · Auckland
Toronto · Johannesburg

Wansell, Geoffrey

Haunted idol: a biography of Cary Grant.
1. Cary Grant   2. Moving picture actors and
actresses – United States – Biography
I. Title
791.43'028'0924   PN2287.G675   ''

ISBN 0 00 216371 3

Photoset in Linotron Baskerville by
Rowland Phototypesetting Ltd
Bury St Edmunds, Suffolk
Made and printed in Great Britain by
William Collins Sons and Co Ltd, Glasgow

For Daniel

Contents

Illustrations

Cary Grant

between pages 254 and 255

Preface

There are a thousand Hollywoods. There is the one that everybody sees: the dream factory with its silent, white-walled studios, its carefully watered mansions in Bel Air and Beverly Hills, and the crowds outside the Chinese Theater beckoned by a great wooden sign in the hills; but there are other Hollywoods. There is the Hollywood of towering apartment blocks, where Ramon Novarro was battered to death and Mae West finally died virtually alone at the age of eighty seven; the Hollywood where knots of old men stand on the sidewalks living on their memories. There is the new Hollywood of manicured young men in designer jeans climbing casually into convertibles and checking that their hair is in place in their driving mirrors, the Hollywood of deals struck in aerobics classes, of meetings in romper-rooms and jacuzzis. But in the end there is only one Hollywood that really counts: the Hollywood of legend.

That is the eternal Hollywood, where the stars have never stopped shining, and their names have never been forgotten. Some may have disappeared into rest homes and private clinics, to die miserable or too soon; but many, many survive, living quietly behind their high walls, lingering in the flesh as well as in the memory.

Astaire and Rogers, Dietrich and Davis, Stewart, Colbert and Hepburn, all epitomize this unforgettable Hollywood, where glamour and style mattered more than reality; and all of them are still alive. But no one survivor of this dying breed seems to capture the nonchalant, effortless charm of the old Hollywood as well as Cary Grant.

On the screen he was unmistakable. In more than seventy

9

films he always seemed to play himself: the ageless, elegant, witty sophisticate with whom many of the cinema's most beautiful women fell hopelessly in love. Dietrich, Hepburn, Dunne, Rogers, Bergman, Monroe and Kelly all collapsed at his feet. Perhaps more than any other star he captured what Hollywood meant in its golden days: an indelible personality with a style and class all his own.

To be a star may be the ambition of millions, but it is the penalty of a few. Cary Grant paid a perilous price for his celebrity; he became entombed in the legend he had so effectively created. For although he will remain forever one of the cinema's greatest stars, he has spent most of his career trying to forget his haunted childhood, to erase the poverty of his upbringing by a relentless pursuit of wealth, and to overcome the paralysing fear of women instilled in him by his doting but mentally unstable mother.

When I started to write this biography two years ago I hardly guessed the difference between the public and the private Grant. All I knew was that none of the interviews or books that I had read about him prepared me for the nervous, haunted man I actually met when I went to interview him early in 1981. I decided then to try to put the record straight and find out what lay behind the flawless mask he had so painstakingly created, to discover why he was both hypnotized and terrified by his own creation; and to present, as well as any biographer can do, the real Cary Grant.

Prologue

'Fame has also this great drawback, that if we
pursue it we must direct our lives in such a
way as to please the fancy of men, avoiding
what they dislike and seeking what is pleasing
to them.'

Spinoza

The room in the London flat was small, drab, and almost unbearably hot. There were thick net curtains to keep out the bright winter sunshine, and even the two glowing table lamps seemed only to add to the gloomy air of reticence and suspicion. There were no glittering chandeliers, no huge vases of flowers, not even a bottle of champagne; there was just the slight scent of fear. It was the room of a man intent on hiding himself from the world – though I did not know then how true that first impression would turn out to be. It was, above all, a most unlikely setting for one of the world's most cherished and enduring movie stars.

'Hel-lo, I'm Ca-ry Grant,' he said, in his unmistakable voice, and he smiled his unforgettable smile.

It was January 1981 and he had just turned seventy-seven. His hair now was white rather than the luminous black that had shone out of the screen in the 1930s, but in most other ways he was still as his fans remembered him: 6ft 2in tall, immaculately dressed, and with a suntan as perfect as ever. Only his handshake was cautious, like that of a small child who has never found his courage with strangers.

'De-light-ed to meet you,' he said, but his eyes did not quite match his words. There was something elusive, private about him. Millions of movie-goers may have felt they knew him as a friend, as 'the fairy tale hero' (the description is film critic Pauline Kael's) who always played himself. But did this character, one of the cinema's most perfect creations, bear any resemblance to the man sitting opposite me? There seemed little to connect the two.

I knew that Cary Grant disliked discussing the past (he

had never given either a television or a radio interview). 'He will only talk about his interest in Fabergé, that is the only reason he is seeing you,' I had been sternly warned before meeting him. 'And he will not be tape recorded in any circumstances.' Even now, talking to him, I found him hard to understand. How could anyone who had been a star for half a century, and appeared with almost every great leading lady the cinema had ever produced, not look back on the pleasure he had brought to millions with the greatest delight and pride?

By coincidence Mae West, one of his first co-stars, had just died in Hollywood. They had appeared together in her first major film, *She Done Him Wrong*, in 1933, and it had launched her international career. Almost without thinking I said:

'You must be very upset about Miss West's death.'

There was silence.

'I don't think about it.'

A pause. Then:

'Is there any-thing I can get you. Cof-fee, tea? Can't drink much coffee myself these days.'

The words were as faultlessly and as effortlessly enunciated as in his best screen dialogue; the courtesy as complete as ever.

'Having starred with her . . .'

Cary Grant did not shudder visibly, but it struck me that it was as if someone had stepped on his grave.

'I never think about it. Never.'

The spell was broken by the appearance of the young English public relations officer, Barbara Harris, who had become his constant companion. They were not married then, but her affection for this man, who was fifteen years older than her father and forty-seven years older than herself, was very apparent. Brown-haired, calm, and with the clear, soft complexion of an English rose, she was preparing to leave for the Passport Office, and Cary Grant relaxed, comfortable in the presence of the living here-and-now.

'You've never written your autobiography,' I said. 'You must have been asked many times.'

'Don't think anyone would be int-er-ested, and I don't want to waste my time writing about the past, or talking about it now, I'm too busy living.'

I knew quite well that he had said the same thing before, countless times, in newspaper interviews. 'I've only got a few thousand hours left, I'm not going to waste them.' And 'Nobody is ever truthful about his own life.' I had heard and read it all. It was as though he was choosing to conceal things from himself, as though the memory of his appearance on thousands of movie screens over more than thirty years had come to appal him. Perhaps that was why he had been fascinated by psychotherapy, and why he had experimented with the drug LSD. Certainly, when I told him that I had been in Jungian therapy for a year and asked about his own experiences, Cary Grant, for the first time, seemed to become himself.

'I've tried all sorts of things in the States, and I've been to a couple of places in England. One of them was very good, a country house where you can spend a week taking LSD and discovering about yourself. It made me realize things I never knew. It's made an enormous difference to me.' As he said this, he looked down, a frail man rather than a movie star. It was another contradiction, another tell-tale sign that his screen personality was a fortress he had constructed to protect him from the world.

In the hour and a half that followed we talked about the parts of his life before he realized the price of fame: about the English music hall, still flourishing in his youth; about the acrobatic troupe he had joined as a boy from Bristol; about vaudeville in the United States; and finally about why he had given up acting, at the moment when he was the biggest box office star in the world, in order to become a businessman.

'It's no surprise. Actors have always been businessmen. Do you know a more complicated business than films? Or any other where a man can earn $3m for ten days work?'

He dated his change of heart about the movies to the birth of his only child, his daughter Jennifer, in 1966.

'She's the greatest production of my life. I decided I wanted to spend all my time with her, and I couldn't do that if I was making films.'

Gradually he retired behind the façade of his practised charm until, as I left, we shook hands again, a little more calmly but no less cautiously than before, and I walked down the stairs and out into the bright watery sunlight of the cold London street. The soft heavy scent of the room was still with me, and in my mind was the thought that, bewildering as it might seem, Cary Grant did not seem to have enjoyed being a star.

As I walked back through Mayfair I remembered another meeting, also in London. It had been January in Chelsea two years before, and I had waited for half an hour in another small, stuffy flat while Dyan Cannon, who had been Cary Grant's fourth wife, prepared herself for our interview.

'I feel so different now,' she had shouted through the half-open door to her bedroom. 'My hair has just got to be right.'

Dyan Cannon had not been keen to talk about her life as the former Mrs Cary Grant.

'I'm me, an actress in my own right,' she had said firmly, as she swept into the flat's chintz drawing-room to hug their daughter Jennifer, the bright-eyed twelve-year-old who had been sitting quietly beside me on the sofa.

Less than a fortnight after seeing Cary Grant I happened to interview Stewart Granger, another English actor who had gone to find fame in Hollywood. He had just published the first volume of his autobiography, and parts of it were about Grant, who had been a friend of his in the 1950s and who had introduced him and Granger's former wife, Jean Simmons, to the reclusive millionaire Howard Hughes. Without prompting Granger suddenly said: 'Cary is exactly the opposite of what he appears to be, you know. He isn't carefree or debonair at all.'

At that moment I decided to write a biography of the haunted star I had met in that hot, stuffy room, and to try to unravel the enigma at the heart of his life and career.

It did not prove an easy process. I wrote to him in Beverly Hills but received a polite reply from his lawyer and close friend, Stanley Fox, advising me that Cary Grant did not want any book written about him. That was hardly a surprise, but I wrote back again saying that I believed any biographer had a duty to treat his subject fairly and cour-teously, and that I wanted to allow Grant to give his own interpretation of his life, as a balance to the views of others. There was a silence.

In May 1982, that unmistakable voice returned. Grant himself telephoned me in London.

'I know who I am,' he said, sounding as apprehensive as ever, 'and I know what people say about me. I even know what my enemies think of me. So I have no intention of collaborating or authorizing you to write this book.' Then, suddenly, as if the screen personality he had so brilliantly created still hynotized him, and he wanted to discover what I thought of it, he added: 'But I will talk to you.'

I went to California and spent three months tracing his old colleagues, searching through dusty studio archives, talking to people in the movie business. My activities were punctuated by a string of telephone calls from Grant.

'You're only writing this book because you think I'm going to die,' he announced one day. 'Don't try to tell me you aren't.' In fact by that time I was convinced that Cary Grant would live as long as his remarkable mother, who had survived almost to her ninety-sixth birthday.

'I think you'll go on for years,' I told him.

He clearly did not believe me.

'It's because you're trying to write the definitive book, that's the only reason you're doing this.'

'The only people who'll talk to you will be those whose autographs I've refused to sign, or the ones I've sacked,' he declared on another occasion.

That was not true. His own friends had already begun to volunteer information. But the phone calls continued.

'I've told Doris Day she could say what she wanted about me.'

'Jimmy Stewart told me he was going to speak to you.'

Then, after a few days' interval:

'No-one's ever talked to my friends before. We should meet, but I don't want to appear to be authorizing you.'

I returned to London to start writing and the telephone rang again.

'Sorry I didn't see you when you were here. Perhaps when I'm in London in May or June, perhaps then.'

I explained that I quite understood, and that I hoped he'd had a happy birthday.

'I'm eighty next year, you know. I've every intention of getting to that birthday.' He sounded almost astonished by the thought, but pleased.

'I spend every birthday and New Year at home, it's a time for reflection, I find. But now I'm going on a cruise. I feel a little tired, I've been working too hard.'

Sitting in London 6,000 miles away I thought to myself that talking to his old friend Howard Hughes must have been much like this. The same disembodied, elusive voice on the telephone, the strange fascination at what the world thought and yet apparently an intense disregard for it.

And so I began to discover the haunted human being behind this ageless, debonair, and effortlessly charming star of the movies' golden age. One of the last of Hollywood's acknowledged aristocrats. He has counted among his friends Noël Coward and Cole Porter, Louis Mountbatten and Aristotle Onassis, Robert Kennedy and Ronald Reagan. He is still a welcome guest at Buckingham Palace and the White House, as well as at Frank Sinatra's estate in Palm Springs. Marlene Dietrich, Katharine Hepburn, Jean Harlow, Irene Dunne, Carole Lombard, Ginger Rogers, Ingrid Bergman, Grace Kelly, Sophia Loren and Audrey Hepburn have been among the leading ladies of his seventy or so films.

Just as the typescript was finished Grant's voice returned on the telephone.

'I've been in London for a few days, but lousy all the time.'

I said I quite understood, and asked how he planned to spend his birthday.

'No dinners, no television, no interviews. I'm just going to sit at home. I've turned down all the requests. Birthdays are a time for meditation and reflection. Don't you think?'

It was the reaction of a man obsessed with his right to privacy, yet afraid of being forgotten.

Cary Grant may not talk about the past, but he has preserved it meticulously in his home. In a fireproof vault hidden behind a secret panel and protected by a series of alarms, he has carefully accumulated memories of his lifetime: the school blazer he wore as a child, the box of cap badges he collected as a boy scout, the contracts and the fan letters, the film stills and the press cuttings of a career which began while Marie Lloyd was still alive and finished several years after Marilyn Monroe's death. There he keeps his five marriage certificates and the photographs of his wives, his passports and his birth certificate, his father's waistcoat pocket-watch and his mother's rings. He has hoarded them like a miser's gold. Strange to think that hidden from the world – and indeed, in so far as he can manage it, from himself – is a small, sensitive boy who began life in Bristol under the name of Archibald Alec Leach, the only child of an obsessed and doting mother.

PART ONE
Archibald Alec Leach

'I became an actor for the usual reason –
a great need to be liked and admired.'

Cary Grant

I

'A Proper Little Gentleman'

'She never told her love,
But let concealment, like a worm i' th' bud,
Feed on her damask cheek. She pin'd in
    thought;
And with a green and yellow melancholy
She sat like Patience on a monument,
Smiling at grief.'

William Shakespeare, *Twelfth Night*

Elsie Maria Kingdon was a Victorian by birth and by disposition. She favoured prim, high-necked blouses, mutton chop sleeves, starched petticoats and hard work. She did not care for alcohol, tobacco or, all that much, for men. A short wiry young woman, blessed with beautiful olive skin, sharp brown eyes and a slightly cleft chin, she seemed shy, almost innocent, to those who did not know her. Those who did, knew that her dutiful manner concealed a waspish temper and a frightening determination.

Elsie stayed at home to look after her parents while her four older brothers left to make their way in the world. Then, at twenty-one, she felt it was time to create her own family. The man she chose to be her partner in this task was Elias Leach, a tailor's presser by trade, the son of a local potter. Her own father, a shipwright, was a cut above his future son-in-law and there were those who whispered that his daughter was a bit of a snob. But when she and Elias went to the altar in their local parish church, on Saturday, 30 May 1898, she felt sure she would be able to make something of him.

23

Elsie and Elias Leach moved into a respectable small terraced house they had rented a mile or so north of the centre of Bristol. Their lighting was all by gas. What heating there was came from small coal fires in every room, and the black range in the kitchen. But the house was in the neat St Paul's district of the town, and there was a perfectly respectable parlour in which they could entertain their relatives to tea. The new Mrs Leach took care to see that her brocade and anti-macassars were clean, her dark table polished and her piano topped with its framed photographs to give the correct impression of stability and pride that every family insisted upon in those dying days of Queen Victoria's reign. Elsie also insisted that every Sunday she and her husband should attend their local church.

To their friends the Leaches looked a perfectly matched couple: he a tall, blithe and handsome young man of twenty-five, with a fine, if rather fancy moustache, and a benevolent sense of humour; she a little frailer with black hair, a splendid selection of hats and a proud, slightly wistful look.

The reality was less romantic. As their only son later remembered: 'My father had an inwardly sad acceptance of the dull life he had chosen,' while his mother's appearance failed to reveal what he called 'her will to control – and her deep need to receive unreservedly the affection she sought to control'.

When she realized she was pregnant only a few weeks after her marriage, Elsie felt triumphant, and began to prepare for motherhood with the studied intensity she brought to everything in her life. In the bottom drawer of the tall wooden chest in her bedroom she began to assemble baby clothes, and a cot was installed in the house at No. 30, Brighton Street.

For his part Elias Leach pressed as many trousers, coats and waistcoats at Todd's Clothing Factory as his employer would allow him to, determined to provide for his new family. Yet no matter how much overtime he worked, it never seemed quite enough for his single-minded young wife. At home Elsie Leach contented herself with the thought that no matter what happened to her husband, the child she was about to bear would be a credit to her. She would see to that. But she also knew that no matter how fiercely determined a mother might be, no child born in 1899 was guaranteed life. The death rate among infants was still appallingly high, and at the back of Elsie's mind there was a tiny nagging fear – a fear which did not entirely abate when the child, a boy, christened John William Elias, was born at home on 9 February 1899.

Elsie felt exceptionally close to her first son, who was born the day after her own twenty-second birthday, and for the first few months of his life she spent every waking moment with him. He suffered from coughs and occasional bouts of fever, but she would always nurse him back to health, sitting beside his cot at night as he fought to catch his breath, feeding him carefully and never leaving his side. When her husband came home from work he would find her sitting with the child in her arms, willing him to live.

But in the months that followed, the convulsions and fever did not abate, and when Dr Powell called to see Elsie on 7 February 1900, he told her firmly that there was nothing more she could do. Staying up night after night had only exhausted her. The best thing for both of them was that she should rest.

Elsie Leach never revealed what went through her mind that evening as she climbed into bed beside her husband and went to sleep. The memory was to become too painful. That night her son John died of tubercular meningitis. It was the day before her twenty-third birthday and just two days before his first.

Elsie Leach was probably never the same after that night, but she conducted herself with calm dignity as she arranged for her son's funeral in the local churchyard, and she wore the black shawl of mourning with the bearing her brothers expected of her. She did not allow herself to give way too much to tears. She had already decided that she would have another child.

Grief and the morbid fear that her son's death had been

her fault were emotions that Elsie could not ever reveal to her husband in the privacy of the parlour in the new terraced house to which they had moved in Hughenden Road. She pushed the memory of her son's death more and more deeply within her, hoarding it just as she hoarded his tiny clothes. To Elias, his wife seemed less and less the frail, feminine woman he had married, more and more the stiff embodiment of the now dead queen, made strong by death and duty. He left her to her solitude. Walking down the hill towards Portland Square each morning, past the pony-drawn milk carts with their churns on the back, and the ladies in wide-brimmed hats and long skirts, he looked forward to the cheerful freedom of his work.

Finally, in the late spring of 1903, only a few months after King Edward VII's often postponed coronation, Elsie Leach told her soft-voiced husband that she believed she was pregnant again.

'It's not before time,' she added firmly, 'and I can only say that I'm glad.'

'So am I. So am I,' Elias told her, his sad face for once wreathed in smiles.

It was what his wife wanted. It was what every couple wanted, a child to make the home complete.

Elsie's meticulous preparations began again. The back bedroom was cleaned, and the baby clothes assembled. As autumn turned to winter the cot was brought out to be reassembled from its pieces. White linen sheets were tied around it, and a proper canopy erected over it to keep out draughts. The room was not repainted blue or pink, but it was made spotlessly clean. This time Elsie was going to see to it that her child survived.

One cold wet January day in 1904, only a fortnight before her twenty-seventh birthday, Elsie Leach felt the first pains of labour. She made sure that her cousins had called the doctor and the midwife, and had run down to the factory to tell Elias. Then she retired to the upstairs front bedroom, and settled herself calmly in the brass bedstead for her ordeal.

As the night progressed the room grew hotter and hotter as more and more coal was heaped on to the small open fire in its black leaded grate. She did not notice it. Shortly after one o'clock the following morning, 18 January, with the rain blowing against the double-sashed windows, the midwife delivered the child. To his mother's intense satisfaction it was a boy whose eyes, when he first opened them, were exactly the same colour as her own, a dark engaging brown.

Elias Leach was suitably proud. He insisted on everyone sharing a small glass of whisky 'to wet the baby's head' and to 'keep out the cold'. In the neat room upstairs Elsie Leach retired gratefully to sleep, the small boy in her arms. The effects of the chloroform the doctor had given her to dull the pain had not quite worn off.

It was six weeks before she would allow her husband to record their son's birth. She was superstitiously afraid that a fatal weakness might strike him down as it had done her first born. She had no wish to incur the wrath of a God who had rewarded her patience and nightly prayers with the gift of a second son by announcing his arrival too soon. So it was not until 29 February 1904, that Elias Leach journeyed down to the Bristol Register Office in Quaker's Friars to register the birth before the Superintendant Registrar, Mr D. E. Bernard. He told him that the boy's name was to be Archibald Alec Leach.

Though events which would change the whole face of the world were soon to take place, on the Broad Quay of Bristol in 1904 sailing ships were still unloaded and horse-drawn cabs still carried the sugar merchants to their counting-houses and customs sheds. For Mrs Leach, provincial England seemed to be settling back into a calm it had last known under Disraeli. She was simply determined that her son would survive. Archie, as he was known, was to be her testament. Everything else might fail her, but she would see to it that he never did. She would keep him with her at all times, supervise his activities, choose his clothes, and make sure that the friends he made lived up to her expectations.

This child would be the only reason for her life. She had already decided that there would be no more.

For Archibald Alec Leach it was a claustrophobic upbringing. As the black-haired baby grew into a small, sad-eyed little boy Elsie Leach's fascination with him deepened into an obsession. She saw to it that her son was kept in a baby's dress with his hair falling around his shoulders in ringlets long after he had grown out of the stark upright bassinet in which she wheeled him round Bristol. The white, girlish dresses confused more than one unsuspecting passerby as he started to run across the little common at the end of their street, and at times his mother would add to the confusion by calling him Alexandra. She had even suggested that Alexandra might be a suitable middle name before his christening at the local parish church, and it was only partly a joke.

It was not that she wanted her son to be a girl, it was more that she wanted a doll, a dependent being who would be unable to exist without her love and attention. In return she required him to worship her alone. The intensity of their relationship scarred the boy's attitude to women throughout the rest of his life – the irony was that he was to spend more than fifty years being pursued by some of the most beautiful women in the world.

Elias Leach, who preferred his friends to call him Jim, worked longer and longer hours at the clothing factory in Portland Square and took to coming home a little later in the evenings after a drink or two in the local pub. Even his small son noticed that his father's face seemed to turn sad after a Sunday spent at home, and the atmosphere in their meticulously neat terraced house seemed to descend regularly into gloom.

'My father progressed too slowly to satisfy my mother's dreams,' he said years later. 'The lack of sufficient money became an excuse for regular sessions of reproach, against which my father learned the futility of trying to defend himself.'

Their bickering left an indelible impression on the boy. He blamed himself for his parents' quarrels and vowed later in life never to let himself fall into similar financial difficulties. Yet at the same time he longed to have his mother all to himself. It was her praise and her reaction that he needed, no matter how much sympathy he instinctively felt for his father.

When Archie was four the family moved house again. Elias himself was not particularly keen to do so, and the boy seemed happy enough, but Elsie was anxious that everyone should realize that her son was going to be something special in the family, that they should move up. She had already started to teach him to sing and dance. Before long he was having piano lessons.

In the afternoons she would take him for walks on the Downs, then towards the River Avon and the superb Georgian terraces of Clifton where she herself had been born. The walks were an experience the boy never forgot: they filled him with dreams of the affluence and success which were what his mother wanted for him. She longed to return to the elegant crescents of Clifton, and he shared that longing to the full. More than sixty years later he saw to it that she did so, but for the moment both concentrated on making young Archie every bit as much of a 'little gentleman' as the sons of the solicitors and merchants who lived there.

Not that the frail boy, whose right shoulder had developed slightly lower than his left and who had also become left-handed, did not sometimes defy his mother. He could 'be the very devil with his temper', she told her friends, and his cousins would remember him as proud and wilful, stubborn and inventive. He was given to petulance, and to the small deceits of an only child.

'My earliest memory,' he later confessed, 'is of being publicly bathed in a portable enamel bathtub, in the kitchen before the fire at my grandmother's house, where my mother was, I suppose, spending the day. It was quite an old house which either had no bathroom or, more likely, was unheated and too cold for me to be there. I was just a squirming mass

29

of protesting flesh, protesting against being dunked and washed all over in front of my grandmother.'

Bristol had always been a Godfearing town, and its traditions of strict churchgoing and hard work had not been abandoned. Children in such a town were taught to be polite to strangers, to respect authority, and 'to speak only when spoken to'. Elsie Leach also impressed upon her son that his father was not 'made of money', that money 'didn't grow on trees', that he must 'brush the mud off your shoes before you come into the house' and look after his clothes because 'they're not made of iron'. When he stood in the hall before going out, waiting for Elsie to straighten the folds of his coat and smooth his long hair, the boy felt simultaneously proud and vexed, wanting to be independent and yet desperate to please her. He felt then, as he would feel many times in the future, very special, that he was his mother's little prince. It was their shared secret. Besides, his father could frighten him. Elias Leach would sometimes take him out into their leafy garden, where he had made a swing in the branches of an apple tree, and push him higher and higher on it until he became terrified. His father wanted him to be 'a real boy' who got into trouble and whose knees got dirty, but the garden swing did not effect the transformation; it only made his son frightened of heights.

There were brief moments when all came right. In the fine June of 1909, the year in which the King's horse Minoru won the Derby and the Epsom crowd yelled 'Good Old Teddy', the Leach family sat together in their garden under the apple tree and had Sunday lunch from a trestle table. The boy would bob up and down in his seat, his father would remark how well the lilies of the valley he had planted had done, and how nice the fuchsias looked, while his mother would relax visibly in the afternoon sun of that last summer of Edwardian England. Archie Leach remembered later: 'They were the happiest days for the three of us.'

But in general the relations between Elsie and Elias became more and more distant, and Archie felt afraid and different from the other children he met every afternoon on the common. They used to tell him, 'If you pick daisies you're a pansy' and 'If you pick dandelions you'll dampen the bed' (which was true – he did wet his bed from time to time). He felt apart from the others, alone in his own world.

One night that autumn Archie Leach woke up in his small cold bedroom to hear the sound of singing from downstairs.

'As I walked along the Bois de Boulogne with an independent air . . . You could hear the girls declare' – it was his father's voice – 'He must be a millionaire' was chorused by several other voices he did not recognize. He wriggled down under the sheets. Then he heard his mother's firm tone:

'Do be quiet, you'll wake the boy.' 'I will indeed lass,' and then the sound of footsteps approaching up the stairs. His beaming father opened the dark wood door to his bedroom and said softly, 'Are you awake, lad? Have we wakened you?' Archie sat up in bed and nodded.

'Never mind, you come and show us what you can do.' And with that his father picked him up, wrapped him in one of the blankets and carried him downstairs into the hot stuffy front room. The smell of smoke in the air almost made him cough.

He was put down on the table, and looked round nervously. He recognized some of his uncles and aunts, but not everyone. Then suddenly, conscious of the angry look on his mother's face, he looked down.

'Now lad, show 'em how well you know your poem,' his father told him.

The boy still looked down, his bare feet strangely pink against the white linen table cloth beneath him.

'Go on, lad, you know – "Up in a Balloon".'

Archie Leach still said nothing, only too conscious that he should not have been out of bed at all, least of all 'performing' as his mother used to call it.

Suddenly he saw her lunge towards him and try to pull him off the table into her arms. His father stopped her.

'No, no, Elsie, the lad's all right,' he said soothingly. 'He'll enjoy it.'

But Elias Leach did not take the chance that his wife might try to snatch the boy away again. He took his son into his arms and raised him so that his head almost touched the gas mantle hanging from the ceiling.

'Come on, Archie, you know.'

Faintly at first, and with a slight lisp, the boy began to recite the first poem he had ever learnt, 'Up in a Balloon so High'. As he went on he looked round at the faces of the adults in the smoky room, and his confidence grew. For the first time he realized the excitement of being praised, felt a foretaste of the thrill of applause. As he settled back later between the sheets of his bed, clutching the apple he had been given as a present, he felt exultant. And in the last moments before he dropped off to sleep he murmured the first words of the poem to himself again: 'Up in a Balloon so High'.

He hoped his mother had not thought he had spoken it too badly.

At last the boy escaped the smocks and dresses of his first four years and found himself dressed instead in dark shorts with thick woollen socks almost up to his bare knees. He was to go to his first school. The new Education Act laid down that a child should start school at five, but Elsie Leach wanted better. *Her* son must begin at once, so an apprehensive Archie Leach was marched off to the Bishop Road elementary school at the age of four and a half. A tall building, with the tiled walls and high ceilings of the time, it stood in the shadow of the town's prison. Archie recalled years later how frightened he felt when first shown into his classroom with its uncovered floorboards and rows of double wooden desks. He was instructed to use his chalk and slate, and reminded that lack of attention would bring a wooden ruler down hard across his knuckles. The sensitive spoiled boy was terrified.

There were compensations, however. Between lessons he found for the first time that he was not alone, that he could join in with other boys of his own age and play football.

'Very gradually I grew accustomed to associating with other children,' he said years later, 'or, rather, mostly with other boys. Little boys. In fact I was, to my surprised delight, invited to play goalkeeper in the football team – a rather scrubby group who hadn't sufficient bravery to play with the girls during recreation time, and kicked a soccer ball around instead.' This was not so very surprising, for football was in the air, and the city of Bristol had two new football teams in the recently formed English Football League. Their games were attracting bigger and bigger crowds each Saturday afternoon.

'We had no goalposts, just chalk lines marked on a jagged stone wall at each end of the playground to denote where they should be,' the former Archie Leach went on. 'Whenever the ball struck the wall between those lines, that was considered a goal. I whacked into that wall countless times, skinning bare knuckles and knees, and snagging my clothes, desperately trying to stop the other side scoring – until it dawned on me why no one was eager to be goalkeeper, and why, probably, they had invited me.' The shy, neat boy with his shoes polished and his hair parted on the left could not escape the feeling of being alone even in the hubbub of the school playground. 'If that ball slammed past me, I alone – no other member of the team but I alone – was held, to my mystification, responsible for the catastrophe.' He felt alone as he stood there waiting for the ball to fly towards him, but he also felt, as he was always to feel, special.

If he managed to keep the ball from banging into the wall behind him, and stop the opposing team scoring a goal, he was cheered and hugged by his own team. As he said almost sixty years later: 'Right then and there I learned the deep satisfaction derived from receiving the adulation of my fellow little men. Perhaps it began the process that resulted in my search for it ever since. No money, no material reward is comparable to the praise, the shouts of well done, and accompanying pat on the back of one's fellow man.'

At home, however, there was no applause and little laughter. Elsie Leach did not want her son to be praised by anyone except herself. He was still to be controlled, as every child should be. He was to wear Eton collars made of stiff celluloid, raise his cap politely, to polish his shoes, and not get dirty in any circumstances. Most important of all, he was to do precisely what Elsie wanted.

Elias Leach worked on at Todd's Clothing Factory. He described his wife as a 'good woman' to his friends at work, and added, 'She looks after the boy properly,' even if he privately thought that she tended to be a bit too strict. On Saturdays the boy would run down the road to meet him when he came home from work and search eagerly through his pockets as they walked up the hill together for the present his father usually brought him at the end of the week. Sometimes the two of them played games on the parlour table in the evenings, pushing coloured counters down the snakes or up the ladders and hurrying them into the safe squares of the Ludo board.

The boy's pocket money was sixpence a week, but he rarely got it. His mother would fine him twopence for each mark he made on the stiff white linen table cloth she put on the dining table for Sunday lunch, and he could be clumsy. Terror of spilling the slightest drop of food or water on to the cloth remained so fixed in his mind that for years afterwards he would refuse even to own a dining table.

There were diversions. By 1912 more than two hundred companies in England had registered with the Board of Trade as film exhibitors, and had started more than three and a half thousand cinemas. The grand music halls were still filled every day with audiences glad to wallow in their warm affectionate atmosphere, but seats in them were more expensive and the entertainment more adult. For Archie Leach, as for most of his schoolfriends, it was the new, cheaper cinemas that provided their weekly entertainment.

Inevitably – in their case – his parents took him separately. Elias Leach favoured the comparatively humble Metropole, a vast barn-like building with hard seats and bare floorboards where the audience hissed as they watched silent serials like *The Clutching Hand*, with its beautiful new heroine,

Pearl White. This cinema smelt of raincoats and wellington boots, and the boy remembered for years afterwards being given a bag of peppermints or a bar of chocolate by his father before they went inside for the afternoon.

'We lived and loved each adventure,' he was to say 'and each following week I neglected a lot of school homework conjecturing how that hero and heroine could possibly get out of the extraordinary fix in which they'd been left.' Indeed so hooked was he that he would go to Pringles Picture Palace to see another serial on Saturday afternoons as well as Mack Sennett's new short comedies. 'The unrestrained wriggling and lung exercise of those Saturday matinées, free from parental supervision, was the high point of my week,' he later recalled.

Elsie Leach, however, felt her son was a cut above such common pleasures. She preferred to take him to Bristol's more expensive Claire Street Cinema, where the customers took tea and cakes in wicker armchairs in the balcony while they watched the films. There he was instructed in the correct use of a pastry fork and expected to sit up straight and pay attention. It was a bleak contrast to the joy of Saturday afternoons at the Metropole, when his father and he started stamping and shouting to warn the unsuspecting heroine that the villain was creeping up behind her.

By the time the King died from a sudden massive heart attack in May 1910, Archie had begun to realize that his parents were not at all happy. 'I remember the grief of my father and mother the morning King Edward VII died, and saw them sharing a common bond of sympathy,' he was to say. 'A rare moment.' That night, as if to presage the momentous changes that would soon overtake the world, the Prime Minister, H. H. Asquith, watched Halley's comet shoot through the sky for the first time in a hundred years. Within a few months, the streets of Britain's cities were plunged into rioting. Soon the railwaymen, the sailors, the firemen, the dockers and the miners were all on strike, protesting that the real value of their wages had been falling steadily for the past decade. In some places the violence was so intense that the army was called in to restore order: but not before two men were shot dead in Liverpool and another two killed in Llanelli in Wales. Bristol itself did not entirely escape as the nervous local police kept vigil over the pickets at the dock gates.

Things were never to be quite the same again, and for Elias Leach the mood was infectious. He too wanted to make sure that life in future would be different. In 1912, at the age of forty, he decided to leave his wife.

It was the most momentous decision he had ever taken. For it was not just his wife he would be leaving, but also his son, his house, his job and his home. Though he had cycled around the vales of Gloucestershire and Wiltshire over the past twenty years, he had never lived anywhere but in the town where he had been born. And now, while Home Secretary Winston Churchill was proclaiming that workers deserved 'time to look about them, time to see their homes in daylight, to see their children, time to think and read and cultivate their gardens – time, in short to live,' Elias Leach was telling his wife that he was moving eighty miles away to Southampton.

He did not tell her that he had also found a woman with whom he thought he might be able to be happy. He simply explained that he had been offered a job in a new factory making khaki army uniforms and would be a fool not to take the chance to better himself. It was the same story he told his friends at work, and they saw no reason to doubt it. In any case, it was partly true. The clothing firm were sorry to see Elias Leach leave. He had worked there for more than twenty years, and the seamstresses and cutters collected enough money to buy him a pocket-watch for his waistcoat, engraved with his name, as a parting gift. But Elsie Leach was less perturbed at her husband's decision. She had already taken to greeting his late return from the factory each evening in silence. After watching him eat his supper without a word, she would leave him alone while she retired upstairs to bed in the still, sombre house.

'Odd, but I don't remember my father's departure from

36

Bristol,' his son was to say later. 'Perhaps I felt guilty at being secretly pleased. Or was I pleased? Now I had my mother to myself.'

But within six months Elias Leach was forced to return to Bristol, and to the home he thought he had left for good. The cost of his two houses and his two lives had proved to be more than the increased salary he earned in Southampton could sustain. The caution that the newly cheerful, moustached man had thrown to the winds turned to dust as he crept back under the thumb of his wife. His son never forgot the humiliation his father had to suffer as the price for his return. Long after Elias's death, Archie kept that engraved pocket-watch locked in a drawer in his Hollywood home.

As the cold winter of 1913 began and Archie celebrated his ninth birthday, Elias Leach sank into a gloom from which he was not to recover for more than a year. He would sometimes lift his small son on to his knee in front of the parlour fire but nothing seemed to cheer the sad-faced man as he smoked his pipe. On the other side of the fire his wife sat with her hands firmly clasped on her lap, particularly when she was in a temper. And she was often in a temper.

At ten years old, taller now and with the confidence of a boy eager to find his own feet, Archie would go to the tuckshop opposite his school when classes ended at four o'clock and buy jam tarts with his pocket money. 'Or Five Boys Chocolate that was made by Fry's in Union Square in Bristol and then go home for tea,' he recalled. After sandwiches or a poached egg he would go back out into the street in the summer evenings to play cricket or football with the other boys in the neighbourhood. He had become an untidy child, the neatness his mother had tried to instill scuffed off by the rebelliousness of childhood, his quietness replaced by an enthusiasm for hitting and kicking balls as far as possible, even at the cost of breaking a window. The subdued, self-conscious child who had gone to school at four and a half had become boisterous and restless.

'I was not turning out to be a model boy,' he said later.

'It depressed me to be good, according to what I judged was an adult's conception of good. The worst thing I ever did as a child,' the actor confessed not long after his mother died, 'and it was dreadful, was to set fire to a little girl's dress with a match. It was a Bengal Light. She ran off screaming to her mother who put her out! But I didn't set fire to her on purpose.'

In spite of his rebelliousness Archie and his mother remained suffocatingly close. After months of pleading she finally agreed that he should have his first pair of long trousers: white flannels, very much the fashionable thing for any young man in 1913 to wear in the summer time. He was to take the tickets at the merry-go-round at the annual church bazaar on Redland Green, and this, it was agreed, might be a proper occasion for a new pair of trousers. But his delight at escaping from shorts that left his knees bare was not to last. Ever conscious of the need to save money, Mrs Leach had decided to make his flannels herself rather than buy them.

'How can I be expected to get these to fit you properly if you will insist on fidgeting about,' she expostulated briskly, while she tucked the white cloth around his legs.

The boy stood in the kitchen, as still as he could, while she finished with her pins.

'What on earth you want white flannels for I will never understand,' she muttered, smoothing the flannel through her fingers.

He did not explain – she would never understand, he told himself – that he had fallen in love for the first time. The object of his affections was the local butcher's daughter, and he had not in fact seen her for several weeks now, since the day when he had walked past her house to deliver a message to his grandmother. It was out of his way, but he could not resist the temptation, because he knew she usually played in her front garden when she came home from school. And there she was, sure enough, looking at him, not saying a word. Equally speechless, and totally transfixed, he walked slowly past her – and collided with a new iron lamp post.

The plump, pretty girl's laugh reached him as he collapsed on the kerb, but when he was able to raise his head again she was gone. His passion had not dimmed, however, and he hoped there was a chance she might be tempted to visit the merry-go-round and see his new white trousers.

'There, satisfied are you?' his mother said finally, inspecting her work with the sharp-eyed look he knew well. 'They seem all right to me.'

The boy did not know what to say. The trousers felt strange; and yet he liked the idea that he was no longer a child. Would he see the girl again as the Wurlitzer organ played and the carousel's wooden horses rose and fell behind his ticket booth?

But it was a dream. 'Those home-made trousers didn't seem to fit or appear as well, nor was the flannel of the same quality as the shop-bought, ready-made version of white flannels I saw on other boys,' he remembered later. 'I was crestfallen.'

Secretly he could not rid himself of the suspicion that his mother had made his trousers ill-fitting on purpose. He would never admit it. Instead the boy who was later to become one of the best-dressed men in the world simply vowed to own some well-cut white flannels of his own one day. But Elsie Leach, unnoticed by her son, was undoubtedly growing stranger. She seemed to be getting even more obsessively fastidious, and developed a habit of locking every door in the house. She took to hoarding food and to asking no-one in particular, 'Where are my dancing shoes? What's happened to my dancing shoes?' At other times she would sit motionless in front of the fire, staring at the coals, with the gas mantle turned down so low that only a halo of light hung around her. Archie did notice that she washed her hands again and again, scrubbing them brutally with a bristle brush. What he could not know was that the fragile balance of her mind, for so long precariously maintained by his dependence on her, was beginning to fail. But Elias did know, and in the spring of 1914, when his son was occupied playing with his marbles, and with the thought of becoming one of Lord Baden-Powell's new boy scouts, he decided that it had fractured beyond recall. After consulting his own doctor and the local magistrates, but without telling his son, Elias Leach committed his wife, Elsie Maria, to the local mental institution at Fishponds.

Elias never shared the same house with Elsie again in the remaining twenty-one years of his life; nor was he ever to discuss with his son why he had taken this painful step. One bright cold Friday morning he arranged for the hospital's staff to collect Elsie from their home, and he quietly stayed away from the factory that day to travel with her. After settling her in, he quietly went back to work. Now, especially, he could not afford to lose a day's pay.

At school his son had no idea what was happening, and no inkling that his mother would not be there to get him his supper when he returned home shortly after five o'clock. As the gas-lit streets were growing dark, the cobbles glistening in the damp air, Archie Leach ambled slowly up the hill to the claustrophobic terraced house. Even as he rang the bell and waited for his mother to open the door he had no idea that the woman who had dominated his life during the past ten years would not be part of his life again for the next twenty. He was never to know whether she had left the house that morning quietly, or screaming at the top of her voice. No matter how much he tried to suppress it, he would never shake off the despair that her absence bred in him, and the feeling of guilt that it might have been his fault. The memory of that day would be with him for the rest of his life.

Two of Archie's cousins were lodging in part of the house, and when there was no reply at his own front door, he set off to see if they could tell him where she was. They told him she had gone off to the local seaside town of Weston-super-Mare for a short holiday, but would be back soon. His father's answer was equally bewildering.

'Gone away for a rest, lad,' he said, when he returned home from work.

'Where to?'

'Not far lad, she needed it.'

'When will she be back?'

'Not long.'

Elias Leach busied himself with the new task of looking after his son. Over the weeks ahead he would say to him from time to time, 'Your mother's well, sends you her love.' But he would never tell the ten-year-old boy with the olive skin, cleft chin, and brown eyes anything else.

Gradually he realized that his mother would never return to him, and as he climbed between the cold, slightly damp sheets in his bedroom night after night, he asked himself why she had left him. What had he done wrong?

'No sense in worrying yourself, lad,' his father would murmur occasionally, but the boy could not shake off the fear and the guilt his new loneliness left in him. Nor could he escape the feeling that it was dangerous to trust anyone, particularly any woman, again. As he was to put it bleakly half a century later:

'I was not to see my mother again for more than twenty years. By which time my name was changed and I was a full grown man living in America. I was known to most people in the world by sight and by name, yet not to my mother.'

The ghosts that were to haunt Archibald Alec Leach for the rest of his life had begun to take shape.

2

What Other Life Could There Be?

'I can remember, I can remember,
The months of November and December
Were filled for me with peculiar joys
So different from those of other boys.
For other boys would be counting the days
Until end of term and holiday times,
But I was acting in Christmas play
While they were taken to pantomimes.
I didn't envy their Eton suits,
Their children's dances and Christmas trees.
My life had wonderful substitutes
For such conventional treats as these.
I didn't envy their country larks,
Their organized games in panelled halls:
While they made snow-men in stately parks
I was counting the curtain calls.'

Noël Coward, *The Boy Actor*

The sadness that enveloped the boy seemed to drive him deeper and deeper into himself. The pain of his mother's loss sharpened the lonely restlessness he had always felt. He took to wandering through the streets of Bristol and sitting for hours at the town's quayside to watch the ships easing out into the Channel towards the Atlantic on the evening tide, their sails slapping in the breeze. Then he would walk home in the dusk.

Finally, as the early spring of 1914 turned to summer, he ran away from home. He took his wooden scooter, and pushed off down the Gloucester Road towards the River Avon. But his nerve failed. He came home again after dark having failed to stow away on a schooner; but he did not forget the experience. Next time, he would plan his flight more carefully.

His rebelliousness continued. One afternoon he was marched down to the local police station by an angry neighbour who had caught him throwing sticky India rubber balls at unsuspecting passersby. But he also joined Bristol's first troop of boy scouts shortly after it started in the Young Men's Christian Association Hall in St James's Square. The troop would assemble for parade on Wednesday evenings, and meet again on Saturday afternoons for the manoeuvres known as 'exercises'. Once a month there would be a church parade on Sunday morning when the troop of about forty boys, aged between ten and seventeen, would attend one of the local churches and form up afterwards in their uniforms of green woollen jumpers and short brown shorts. The boys carried broomsticks proudly over their shoulders as they marched through the streets.

His fellow scouts later remembered Archie as 'rather small for his age and somewhat untidy and dishevelled in appearance' although his patrol leader in Hounds Troop, Bob Bennett, said: 'He was just an ordinary bloke who seemed cheerful enough, although he was a bit of a loner.' Most of the boys in the troop would stick together, once the parades were over, to go to the pictures. But, says Bennett, 'He'd disappear off.'

The boyish camaraderie which the movement inspired, with its strongly patriotic tone, did make a great impression on him, however, and when War was suddenly declared on 4 August – 'bursting like a bombshell upon the ordinary people' in the words of a future Prime Minister, Harold Macmillan – Archie was as keen as the others to be pressed into service. The sixteen-year-olds were soon to be encouraged to leave for France, but the younger ones were given duties at home. Archie Leach and his troop became junior Air Raid Wardens.

Before the sombre casualty lists of men killed in the trenches of Flanders began to dim the jingoism of an England where three-quarters of a million men volunteered to fight for their country in the first seven weeks of the war, Archie Leach and his father were forced to leave their home. His two cousins had moved out and Elias Leach found that he could no longer afford to keep himself and his son there. He and the boy went to live with his own mother in Picton Street, a narrow lane, between two rows of tiny terraced houses, barely wide enough to allow a horse and cart to pass, and where the sun hardly ever seemed to penetrate the shadows. Archie and his father shared the downstairs front room and the upstairs back bedroom, while his grandmother lived in the bigger front bedroom upstairs. They shared the kitchen with its black range and wooden upright chairs, the kettle boiling over the coal fire.

'I didn't see a great deal of her,' Archie said later, 'and I took care of my needs as best I could; sharing with her and father each Saturday and Sunday breakfast and midday dinner, and scrounging around in the kitchen, or stone larder, for other meals on my own.' He would never lose this habit of scavenging for food. Perhaps the move convinced him he had to leave Bristol as quickly as he could. In any event, even without his mother's high-pitched exhortations ringing in his ears every day, he suddenly started to study for the school scholarship examinations. In the first months of 1915 he won one of the Liberal Government's 'free places' to the Fairfield Secondary School, not far from his home.

Fairfield was a respectable Victorian school less than a mile from the centre of Bristol in the middle of a new estate of decent terraced houses, cramped on one side by a line of Brunel's Great Western Railway. Since 1906 it had been obliged by the government to offer 'free' places to children whose parents could not otherwise have afforded to send them there. It was hardly the dignified 'Academy' that Archie Leach described in the later years of his life. Nevertheless there were special ties, caps and blazers to be worn in the school colours of plum with blue and yellow stripes, gym clothes to be bought, and bicycle shed fees to be paid. 'I economized wherever I could but just the required books each term were really more than my father could afford,' he recalled. When he finally went to the school in September 1915 he bargained for secondhand copies of any books he needed, and sold them again as soon as he had used them, so as to keep his father's expenses to a minimum. But in the process, 'my aspirations for a college education slowly faded. It was obviously too expensive to consider.'

Alongside the knowledge that there was little hope of his going to one of England's universities came the realization that, like most other boys of his age, he was probably destined for the trenches of France. School for him, and all the boys who saw their cousins and uncles going away to war, seemed a supreme irrelevance, and his heart was not in his books.

In particular he hated mathematics – algebra, geometry and trigonometry – and he was also roundly loathed by his Latin mistress for his idleness. But he did not mind geography – 'because I wanted to travel' – and got on fairly well at history, art and chemistry, although even they hardly captured his imagination.

For most of the time he was simply a mischievous, wilful boy with a rebellious and insolent streak that brought him into regular contact with his headmaster's cane. When he was caught he had the ability to open his dark brown eyes and raise a single eyebrow quizzically, as if in proof of his innocence. As he stood waiting for his punishment, wearing a scruffy pullover, twisting his ink-stained hands behind his back and with his socks pushed down to his ankles, he just seemed to be desperate to be noticed. A frail boy with sad eyes and an almost girlish face, he looked like a belligerent fawn.

Back at the gloomy house in Picton Street he was also growing more and more aware of his father's melancholy. 'He was a dear sweet man,' Archie would remember, 'and I learned a lot from him. He first put into my mind the idea of buying one good superior suit rather than a number of

45

inferior ones. Then even when it is threadbare people will know at once it was good.' But even that comradeship could not conceal Elias Leach's despair.

The shadow of Elsie still hung over them both. And as it did so the scruffy boy, whose scout patrol once forcibly washed his neck after his dirtiness had lost them a troop competition, developed, like her, an obsession with being clean. As if struggling to purge himself he began to wash as he had never washed before.

'I washed myself constantly, a habit I carried far into adulthood in a belief that if I scrubbed hard enough outside I might cleanse myself inside: perhaps of an imagined guilt that I was in some way responsible for my parents' separation.'

He was also to tell a magazine nearly half a century later: 'I thought the moral was – if you depend on love and if you give love you're stupid, because love will turn around and kick you in the heart.'

The journey into adolescence had begun, and it brought with it a vanity that was to remain with the boy throughout his life. When another boy knocked him over accidentally in the school playground that winter he was shocked at the damage. 'My front tooth snapped in half. Straight across.' He had fallen face forward on to the icy ground. Anxious not to let his father discover what had happened, and to preserve the features that he was aware were beginning to attract some attention among the girls at the school, he decided to have the remaining piece of his broken front tooth pulled out at the local dental hospital. The price of an extraction there was low enough for him to pay for it out of the pocket money he had started saving. For weeks after the extraction he kept his mouth closed as much as possible, while the gap between his front teeth slowly began to close, and as a result he perfected the rather tight-lipped smile that became famous. But he never had a second front tooth fitted.

As the war dragged on and in 1917 he came to the end of his second year at Fairfield School, so the prospect grew that he would be called up into the army. To prepare himself for this he volunteered to do war work during his summer holidays. Many of his fellow boy scouts did the same, but Archie had another reason: he wanted to get away from home. 'I was so often alone and unsettled at home,' he remembered later, 'that I welcomed any occupation that promised activity.'

He got it. He was given work as a messenger in Southampton Docks where, incidentally, his father still had friends from his own stay in the town three years before. There the thirteen-year-old boy started to help thousands of young men on to the ships waiting to take them to France. He could not fail to notice the look of apprehension on their faces as they climbed the long wooden gang-planks and he handed them a lifejacket.

When he returned to Bristol he found he could not slip back into the life he had led before. The image of the men lying on the floor of the sheds, or sitting with their packs and rifles behind them, playing cards or singing, stayed in his mind. He took to missing the games of cricket he usually played, and instead haunted the docks and wharves of the River Avon, as he had done when his mother had first disappeared. The sadness he had felt then still clung to him like a shroud. 'Once I even applied for a job as a cabin boy, but was turned down – not only because I was too young, but because I couldn't bring permission from my parents,' he said later.

Yet it was not to be the ships carrying sugar, cocoa, tobacco or coffee that would finally help him escape, but a part-time assistant teacher in the school's chemistry laboratory, who invited him to go backstage one Saturday afternoon at the Bristol Hippodrome. The jovial, middle-aged man had just installed the theatre's new electrical switchboard and lighting systems to replace the original gas lamps. As the boy, so often sullenly wrapped up in himself, followed the man through the stage door and along the narrow tiled corridors

47

that led past the dressing-rooms towards the stage, he realized there was another life.

'I suddenly found myself in a dazzling land of smiling, jostling people wearing and not wearing all sorts of costumes and doing all sorts of clever things.' The sickly smell of the greasepaint mixed with the faint aroma of sweat hung in the air. The warmth, colour and friendliness of it all captivated him. 'That's when I knew. What other life could there be but that of an actor?' He knew he wanted to join it at once. It was what he had longed for without even knowing it existed. Actors travelled and toured. They were classless, cheerful and carefree. But most of all they could present to the world the face they chose, and no-one wanted to know how they felt. The audience adored them for what they appeared to be, not what they were. To the insecure Archie Leach, who had been presenting a brave face to the world for as long as he could remember, this idea was a revelation.

He took to hanging about the Hippodrome at every opportunity, until the electrician introduced him to the manager of another of the town's theatres, the Empire. While the Hippodrome specialized in spectaculars in the style of its famous counterpart in London, the Empire offered a more traditional music hall, spiced with the new fashion for revue. The shows – with titles like *Jingles* and *Spangles* – were filled with comedians, magicians, singers and chorus girls. At the Empire he was allowed to help the men work the new arc lights mounted at each side of the stage. Unpaid but utterly content to have found somewhere to go, he felt at home at last, as he changed the coloured carbon filters and made himself as useful as he could. He was spellbound, so stagestruck that on one evening he allowed an arc light he was holding to reveal the mirrors secretly assisting the famous illusionist, The Great Devant. He was fired on the spot. Undeterred, he went back to the Hippodrome.

He ran messages again, and was finally rewarded with a job as a call boy in the early evenings, summoning the performers when the time was due for them to appear. He was delighted, although, as he confessed later, 'I was most annoyed I couldn't do the Wednesday matinée because of school.' He was paid ten shillings a week, and when he finished work he would walk home. 'I didn't want to spend my earnings on a train.'

In fact, he did start doing Wednesday matinées and missing school as a result. There was no-one at home to reprimand him. His father went out before him in the mornings and came back home after him in the evenings. His grandmother did not know where he went. No-one seemed to care what he did, except at the theatre. It became the home he no longer had.

One evening at the Hippodrome he met Bob Pender, a stocky cheerful man of forty-six who ran a troupe of boys specializing in slapstick comedy, known as Pender's Knock-about Comedians. The boys acted comic sketches in mime. They ran and fell, balanced and tumbled, jumped and walked on stilts. More than twenty years later Pender recalled, 'A young fellow came up to me and said he wanted to go on the stage.' It was Archie Leach.

What the boy did not tell Pender was that he was still only thirteen, and therefore not quite old enough officially to leave school. When the jovial man told him that there might be a chance of his joining the act if he could get his parents' permission, because so many of the troupe were leaving to go off to the war, he remembered the lesson of his application to be a cabin boy. 'Before I knew it I was writing a letter purportedly from my own father to Mr Pender, and I conveniently neglected to explain that I was not yet four-teen,' he said later. Within ten days a reply came back from Pender inviting him to Norwich, where the troupe were performing, for an interview. But Elias Leach never saw that letter, even though it had been addressed to him – his son had intercepted it at the front door. Even better, Pender had sent him the rail fare.

That night Archie Leach could not sleep. Unable to decide whether or not he should go, he packed and then unpacked, until finally just before six o'clock in the morning he made up his mind. He stole quietly out of the house, knowing that his father would probably not miss him for days. As he closed the door behind him and walked through the empty streets towards the railway station, he knew one part of his life was ending.

As the terrible war ground on, the music halls of England were filled with people only too anxious to take their minds off its horrors from time to time. Warm, cheerful and bathed in an affection for happier times, the songs of Harry Lauder and Marie Lloyd, of Florrie Forde and Vesta Tilley, the jumble of jugglers and acrobats, conjurors and unicyclists, made them a haven of refuge. Sophisticated audiences in London might prefer the new musical shows like *Chu Chin Chow*, but for most ordinary people the music halls were the only escape, both from the war and from their families at home. They also provided a sense of belonging, shared by audiences and many performers alike, and certainly by the boy who had run away from his home in Bristol to join them.

Bob Pender had spent his life in the boisterous, uninhibited world of music hall. When he was a child his father had toured with a portable wooden theatre, and by the time he was fourteen he was playing a monkey on the music-hall stage. He used to say proudly: 'And I did that act for fourteen years.' By the time he was nineteen he had started his own troupe of boys to play in pantomime sketches. He may never have enjoyed the success of Fred Karno, but he was every bit as successful as most of the other knockabout troupes then touring the halls, like Charlie Manon's Knockabout Comedians or Joe Boganny's Lunatic Bakers.

Pender knew very well how attractive the music hall could be to boys who were unhappy at home, so he and his wife Margaret, who had been a dancer at the Folies-Bergère, were distinctly sceptical about the nervous boy who presented himself at the Theatre Royal in Norwich shortly after ten o'clock one cold winter's morning in 1917. Privately Pender was prepared to bet that the letter he had received had been written by Archie rather than by his father, but he also knew that his troupe urgently needed some new blood. 'After looking me over carefully they agreed that if it was still all right with my father they would apprentice me to their troupe,' Archie recalled. 'They gave me a short handwritten contract stipulating that I was to receive my keep and ten shillings pocket money a week.'

The next morning the new recruit began to learn how to be an acrobat, an art he never forgot. Together with a dozen other boys , most of them older than himself, he was taught the essence of tumbling and the basis of the acrobatic dances he would need in the act. He was taught how to fall convincingly, how to balance and how to take an imaginary blow. Pender's sketches did not need words, they simply needed boys who could turn a back flip without a moment's hesitation. When the morning's rehearsals were over the new boy was expected to stand at the back of the theatre or, if he was lucky, in the wings, and watch the act. He had to know what he might have to do if he suddenly had to go on – as there was always a chance he would.

'So I practised making up and thickly covered my face with greasepaint that took hours to apply in imitation of what I took to be the prevailing theatrical mode,' he was to say later. He did not enjoy this experience, indeed he would eventually prefer to avoid wearing any make up at all, and feel embarrassed in the company of actors and actresses who insisted on doing so. But at this stage he was intent on diving head first into the traditions of the theatre.

At the end of the week the troupe moved forty miles south to the slightly larger town of Ipswich in Suffolk for the next week of twice-nightly performances. The routine of practice and watching the act each night continued, but Archie still had not appeared on stage.

One evening between the two shows the theatre's stage door-keeper told him that there was a man waiting to see him. 'Says he's your father,' the old door-keeper told him. It was.

Before father and son could say anything to each other the stocky figure of Bob Pender emerged from his dressing-

51

room, and shook hands with Elias Leach. Although the boy did not know it, the meeting was not unexpected, for Pender had taken the precaution of writing another letter to Elias Leach to make sure he felt happy about his son's new apprenticeship. He had invited him to come and see them.

In fact, though Archie was too shaken to notice it, there were great similarities between the two men. They were almost exactly the same age, and both were given to wearing bowler hats, waistcoats and rather flamboyant wing collars and ties. They were also both subscribers to the teachings and practices of the fraternal order of Free and Accepted Masons, the largest secret society in the world. Bob Pender had not known that when he wrote about his latest recruit, but once he caught sight of the insignia hanging from Leach's watch chain he was able to feel relieved. Between Masons, he knew, there was unlikely to be disagreement.

Without telling the by now pale-faced boy what they intended to do, the two men left the theatre together for a drink. Standing in the wings on the edge of the empty stage, Archie looked across at the drawn curtains and wondered whether he would ever see them again. He need not have worried. After some discussion it was agreed between the two men that he had better finish his education – but he would soon be fourteen and there would be nothing to keep him in class after the end of that school year. 'If he leaves I'd be happy to take him back,' Pender concluded.

Elias Leach took his son back to Bristol on the train the following morning, travelling across London between the great stations of Liverpool Street and Paddington by the newly electrified underground train. The newspaper placards were announcing food rationing; there was no end in sight to the war. Back at school, Archie revelled in being a celebrity. He demonstrated the cartwheels, handsprings and backflips he had learnt with the troupe, and carefully concealed the fact that he had never actually appeared in front of an audience. Gradually, however, his mind returned to wandering in its familiar loneliness. He could not forget the release and fantasy of the Pender troupe. 'I did my unlevel best to flunk at everything,' he said. 'The only class I attended with any interest and alacrity was the twice-weekly instruction in the gymnasium.'

For the rest of the time he played truant and caused disruption. The singing teacher actually threw a bunch of keys at him during one lesson, so appalling was his misbehaviour, and again, but now with greater regularity, he began to appear in front of the school's formidable headmaster, Augustus Smith. 'And he could lay it on,' the boy recalled later; but the canings and reprimands had no effect. He had inherited his mother's stubbornness.

Finally, in March 1918, matters came to a head. One afternoon Archie and another boy, a close pal of his, sneaked into the girls' lavatories while the rest of the school were studying, and were discovered there by one of the women teachers. Once again Archie Leach found himself in front of his dreaded headmaster. It was to be the last time.

'The following morning when the school filed in for morning prayers,' he wrote later, 'my name was called and I was marched up the steps on to the dais and taken to stand next to Gussie Smith, where, with a quivering lip that I did my best to control, I hazily heard such words as "inattentive . . . irresponsible and incorrigible . . . discredit to the school" and so forth, and through a trance-like mixture of emotions realized I was being publically expelled in front of the assembled school.'

The now rather tall boy – he had grown four inches in the past year – walked across the playground, took his bicycle from the shed and went home. He was just fourteen. Three days later he was back on the train and rejoining the Pender troupe.

His father had not put up any resistance to the idea. For one thing, he had been expecting it. For another, to have the financial burden of his son off his hands meant that he had a little more money for himself. Although he would never divorce his mentally ill wife he had begun to realize that he could not stop living a normal life just because she was no longer there. He had again found someone with whom to share his life, a woman who would be his wife in all but name.

For his part his son was glad finally to be escaping from the wintry shadow of his mother. He had never seen her again since the day four years before when he had come back from school to discover she had gone. There had not even been a letter from her, even though his father had told him from time to time that she was asking after him. He still felt desolate at her loss, and he had no idea at all where she was. So he grabbed greedily at the opportunity to find a new family who would welcome his presence, anxious to indulge the feeling she had fostered in him of being a special boy, yet aware that she would not be there to cut him down to size, to deny him the praise and admiration he longed for. He returned to the Penders and the music hall.

Three months later, in August 1918, Pender and his troupe came back at the Bristol Hippodrome, and this time their latest recruit was performing on the stage with them. The act still relied on pantomime, as it had always done, but that did not detract from the pleasure Elias Leach felt at seeing his son perform. With the war nearing its end (the German advance had just collapsed), there was a chance, he hoped, that the boy would not end up in the mud of Flanders as so many had done in the past four years; and besides, he seemed to have found something he liked to do.

Before the second house at the Hippodrome that night Elias Leach had another drink with Bob Pender and merely asked if his son could stay at Picton Street while the troupe were in Bristol. Pender agreed. After the final curtain that night Leach and his son walked home in the warm night air together through the centre of the city, back to the gloomy house they no longer shared.

'We hardly spoke,' the boy was to write, 'but I felt so proud of his pleasure and so much pleasure in his pride, and I remember we held hands for part of that walk.'

At the end of the week Archie Leach went back to lodging with the Penders, and back on the road touring the music halls. The warmth and affection that he craved were still there, and most important of all, Pender's troupe provided him with an identity. They taught him the pantomime art of timing, of knowing how to get a reaction from an audience, but they also taught him that he did not need to be alone.

When they were in London, playing the Gulliver circuit of music halls, most of the boys lived with the Penders in their house in south London, a district traditionally beloved of music hall performers. Sleeping in dormitories like pupils at an English boarding school, they were subject to a not dissimilar regime. Lights were put out strictly at 10 p.m., and the boys had to be washed, dressed and ready for breakfast at 7.30 the next morning. Hardly the bawdy, bohemian 'actor's life' of popular imagination.

When the Armistice was signed – in a railway carriage at Réthondes – on 11 November 1918, Bob Pender's boys were in Preston in the north of England, still performing their elaborate clowning acts but now as part of a show in which the newly popular moving pictures were introduced as an attraction. Archie remembered later that the theatre was almost empty that night – but not as a result of celebrations in the streets. The terrible post-war 'flu epidemic was beginning to claim its first victims. Before it abated a quarter of the population would have caught the disease and a hundred and fifty thousand would have been killed by it. By Christmas even the Pender boys were affected, though it did not stop them performing. By now they had split into two groups of eight boys each. The more experienced troupe spent the holiday period playing the great industrial city of Liverpool, while the less experienced, which included Archie, were performing on the pier of a small seaside town not far away in North Wales, Colwyn Bay.

In the next eighteen months, while the English music hall struggled to regain its pre-war vitality in the face of competition from revue and musicals, from Bernard Shaw's 'farcical play' *Pygmalion*, which was still running in London, and from the increasingly popular moving pictures, Archie Leach ruthlessly taught himself to be a performer, and to conceal his own personality as he did so.

'At each theatre I carefully watched the celebrated head-line artists from the wings, and grew to respect the diligence it took to acquire such expert timing and unaffected confidence, the amount of effort that resulted in such effortlessness,' he was to say later. 'I strove to make everything I did at least appear relaxed. Perhaps by relaxing outwardly I thought I could eventually relax inwardly; sometimes I even began to enjoy myself on stage.'

The determination to succeed paid handsome dividends. Not long after the King and Queen had attended their second Royal Command Performance for variety artists at Sir Oswald Stoll's mighty London Coliseum, where they had seen Harry Tate, the inimitable comedian of the car sketch, and Grock, the famous clown, Pender told his youngsters that he had booked the troupe for New York. They were to join a Charles Dillingham show at the Globe Theater on Broadway, but there was one drawback – he could only take eight boys. One whom he chose was Archie Leach, now a close friend of his own younger brother Tommy, who was also to be included.

The sixteen-year-old Archie realized that there was now nothing to keep him in England. He still did not know where his mother was, and his father seemed to be creating another life for himself. Standing on the deck of the magnificent SS *Olympic* as she nosed carefully out of Southampton Water in July 1920, he had no tears in his eyes. As he watched the chalk cliffs of the Needles fall away slowly behind him, he knew he might not see them again. He also knew that he did not much care.

When she was launched in 1911 the White Star Line's SS *Olympic* had been called 'the world's wonder ship'. The first-class stairway was panelled in mahogany, and had a wooden symbol representing Honour and Glory inlaid at the main landing. The first-class dining-room had Louis Seize chairs and close carpeting. At 46,000 tons she was bigger and faster than the Cunard Company's famous *Mauretania*, and exactly the same size as her sistership, the doomed *Titanic*, which had sunk on her maiden voyage in April 1912. Since that disaster the *Olympic* had been specially fitted with double sides and 'additional watertight bulk heads extending from the Bottom to the Top of the Vessel', but somehow its passengers always seemed just a little nervous. To the officers and crew, the gaiety on board seemed almost frenzied.

Perhaps it was the gaiety, forced or not, that drew actors to the ship, and especially film actors. The *Olympic* had taken Charlie Chaplin and the Fred Karno company to New York for the start of their second tour of the United States. Marlene Dietrich, Clara Bow, Pola Negri and Maurice Chevalier had travelled first class on it, although in a few years many of them were to transfer their affections to the French liner *Ile de France*, and then, later again, to the beautiful SS *Normandie*.

Archie Leach, however, was not travelling first class but like Chaplin before him, second. Nevertheless he would occasionally glimpse some of the liner's more celebrated passengers on their morning walks around the deck. Among them were the world's most famous honeymooners, Douglas Fairbanks and Mary Pickford, who had just launched the United Artists Company in Hollywood and had also been married in a blaze of publicity a few weeks before. They captivated the boy from Bristol. 'They were gracious and patient in face of constant harassment by people with cameras and autograph books whenever they went on deck,' he remembered. 'Once I even found myself being photographed with Mr Fairbanks during a game of shuffleboard and as I stood beside him I tried to tell him my adulation.' The athletic actor smiled and accepted the compliment, thanking the boy for his kindness.

The star's generosity stuck in Archie Leach's mind, and so did his deep sun tan, which he then and there determined to imitate. That morning he began a regime he kept up for the rest of his life – a regular period of sitting in the sun to make sure he looked as healthy, and as relaxed, as Fairbanks. It was not to be the only parallel between the two men's careers: twenty-two years later the boy would have almost as celebrated a honeymoon with the 'richest girl in the world', Barbara Hutton.

As he played deck tennis, watched the daily tug of war, and listened to the band while the ship sailed sedately across the summer calm of the Atlantic, Archie could hardly believe his luck. As the *Olympic* entered harbour he stayed up all night along with the rest of the troupe, to watch the sun rise over Eiffel's magnificent Statue of Liberty and – with wonder tinged with terror – saw the new towers of Manhattan start to shimmer in the early daylight. He had no idea what lay in store for him as the great four-funnelled liner edged into the pier at the West Side to a deafening clamour of hooting. Bustling, breathless, dirty, down-at-heel and yet endlessly electric, here at last was the city where reputations were made at a stroke, and where every barman, newspaper seller, and shoeshine man on Broadway and 42nd Street had only one topic of conversation – show business.

Originally Bob Pender and his troupe had been booked to play the Globe Theater but soon after they had made their way down the canvas-covered gangplank they learnt there had been a change of plan. The eight boys, together with their eternally cheerful boss, now resplendent in a dog-tooth check suit with his wife Margaret beside him flaunting her best fox fur, set off instead towards the majestic Hippodrome on Sixth Avenue. Called 'the largest theatre in the world', it could seat nearly four and a half thousand people and played two shows a day six days a week, with a matinée on Sundays. The immense stage concealed forty-eight dressing-rooms, each named after a State of the Union. Best suited to exhibition acts like the Penders, who relied on pantomime and not dialogue, 'the Hipp' as it was called, was now to house Charles Dillingham's new spectacle *Good Times*, with a cast of almost a thousand and a backstage company of eight hundred.

Archie was befriended, as he had been since his earliest days as a nervous recruit in Norwich, by the company's rotund, benevolent comic, Don Barclay. He also celebrated his new-found independence in America by falling in love. As he would do many times in the future he chose a girl utterly unlike his small, dark-eyed and wiry mother. Gladys Kincaid, as she was called, was blonde, blue-eyed and generously endowed, but she was also capable of inducing in him startling fits of depression. When the time came for the show to close, Archie was in a state of despair. 'I dreaded the bustle of packing backstage that last night,' he remembered afterwards, 'just as I have at the finish of every show or film I've been associated with ever since.' He certainly did not want to drag himself away from the stage door. While the other boys waited impatiently outside, he languished inside, longing for a last look at the girl who had become the focus of his adolescent passion.

'When she appeared I remember standing there tongue-tied and fuddle-headed while people milled around us and those nitwits outside kept putting their heads round the door yelling, "Hurry up" and "Come on".'

They were to stand there for what seemed like an hour before both blurted out: 'I do hope we see each other again' at precisely the same moment. They had never even held hands, although he had given her a multicoloured woollen sweater for Christmas. She rushed out of the stage door, leaving him looking bashfully after her. They never met again. But the seventeen-year-old Archie mooned about for weeks.

It was the spring of 1921, a time of prohibition and speakeasies, of King Oliver and a young Louis Armstrong, when young women with short skirts and bobbed hair wished they could shimmy like their sister Kate. Jack Dempsey was the world heavyweight champion, Big Bill Tilden the greatest tennis player of the day and Warren Harding had just been inaugurated President. It was the beginning of an era to which F. Scott Fitzgerald had just given a name: the Jazz Age.

A quarter of the American population were going to the silent movies every week, and the vaudeville houses were suffering as a result. Not that B. F. Keith's theatres, for which Pender had booked his troupe next, were doing badly. They were the major circuit in American vaudeville, and had their own fierce rules and regulations to keep them such. Groucho Marx, who played them with his brothers, used to recall: 'They fined you for everything'; and many others were frightened by the sign which used to hang backstage at every theatre, stating: 'Don't say "slob" or "son of a gun" or "Holy Gee" on the stage unless you want to be cancelled peremptorily.'

For the next year Pender, his wife and their eight English boys toured Keith's east coast circuit. They played in theatres from Cleveland to Boston, Chicago to Milwaukee, and Washington to Philadelphia, happily sharing the same bills as the Foy family or Eddie Cantor, unaware that vaudeville would ever come to an end.

The pinnacle of the Keith circuit was the Palace in New York. In the ten years since it had opened on its ugly site on Broadway at 47th Street it had become a vaudeville legend. Jack Benny, who played it as part of a double act known as Benny and Woods, described it as 'The theatre every actor was nervous about,' because it was acknowledged as the top of the vaudeville tree. Performers would arrange to meet on the pavement outside its entrance, on what became known as the Palace Beach, and the restaurants and cafés on the block were called 'the corn exchange for comedians'. When the Pender troupe played the Palace in June 1922 they knew they had conquered vaudeville. What they did not know was that they were about to split up.

Bob Pender and his wife had decided to take a holiday before starting another tour. No-one went to vaudeville in the summer anyway, and traditionally the weeks until Labour Day in early September were the time to work out a new act. Archie Leach and Tommy Pender, who was still in the troupe, both felt the time had come to break out from the Pender dormitory. They told Pender they were homesick and wanted to go back to England and, generous as ever, he gave them their fare home. 'It cost me £40, and I rearranged the troupe before going to Minneapolis, and from there we went to Hollywood for a season,' he later said rather wryly.

But the two had no intention of returning to England. They had decided to work on their own. With no prepared act they set themselves up as an unofficial Pender troupe, relying on the stilts, tumbling and slapstick routines that they were accustomed to. Even this did not seem to upset their old boss, who was by then in California. The stocky man with the ready smile and the loud check suits had been on the road as an entertainer since he was born. He was now almost fifty and the endless routine of hotels, lodging houses and flats and the early morning railway journeys to the next town on the tour had taken its toll. So what did he care? Later that year, while his younger brother and Archie Leach were still doing a version of the act he had created in New York, he sailed back to England. Within two years he gave up the music hall altogether and retired to run a small toy shop in the English resort of Southend-on-Sea, down the Thames from London. He died there in 1939.

Vaudeville was dying too, even before Bob Pender retired, but if Archie Leach noticed it he had no intention of trying for anything else, for the moment anyway. He was simply determined to survive.

3

Tall, Dark Handsome
– and Silent

'There were no more wise men; there were no
more heroes.'

F. Scott Fitzgerald, *This Side of Paradise*

Coney Island in the summer of 1922 was everything the
greatest amusement park in the world should be: clean, well
organized and fun. The rides were the fastest, the Ferris
wheel the tallest and the new rollercoaster the most frightening in the world. There was no traffic on the main streets,
and the policemen who patrolled it were rarely troubled. It
was the place where every family in New York knew they
could be sure of a good time. Since the subway had reached it
two years before, the boardwalk looking across the sand
towards the Atlantic ocean had been packed, especially on
Saturdays and Sundays.

In fact it was Coney Island that provided Archie Leach's
first job after he left the Pender troupe. One evening that
summer, as prosperity was beginning to return to America,
he had been invited to a dinner party in Park Avenue. The
fact that he was eighteen now, tall and darkly handsome,
had meant an increasing number of invitations. His face
may have been a little fleshy and his nose a little wide, but it
made not the slightest difference; Archie Leach was attractive enough to grace any dinner table. That evening he was
seated beside George Tilyou, whose family owned and
operated the Steeplechase Park on Coney Island.

'I remember seeing a man walking on stilts along Broad-

Mrs Leach's only child, Archie:
the lonely boy from Bristol who was
separated from his mother at the age of
ten. They did not meet again for more
than twenty years.

Bob Pender's Troupe of Knockabout
Comedians: as they were when Archie
Leach ran away to join them in the
English music hall.

way advertising something or other, and I heard myself suggesting to Mr Tilyou that perhaps I could do the same for him,' he recalled later. Within a week he found himself walking up and down outside Steeplechase Park on six-foot-high stilts wearing a bright green coat with red braid, a bright green cap and exceptionally long black trousers.

'I got three dollars on weekdays, but after the first Saturday and Sunday I struck for five dollars a day. He wouldn't give it to me at first, but I took him outside and showed him that the weekend crowds were so terrific that I was knocked down regularly, and that was worth five dollars.' Before long Tilyou had doubled that to five dollars for weekdays and ten dollars each for the weekends, a total of forty-five dollars a week. Archie supplemented his income by doing a deal with the proprietor of a hot dog stand. 'I got five hot dogs a day just for walking by his stand. So then I fixed up a deal with a restaurant and an ice cream place and I got all the food I wanted free.'

The only drawback was that his stilts provided a target for the children who toured the park looking for less conventional amusement. 'I used to walk in fear, constantly afraid some hoodlums would dash between my legs, knock me down and break my knees, so that I wouldn't be able to find a job that fall.' He was often upended half a dozen times a day, but he stuck it out. Any job was better than none. Then, fortunately, a new opening presented itself in vaudeville. The director of the New York Hippodrome, R. H. Burnside, was preparing for the autumn season another spectacle on the lines of Dillingham's *Good Times*, which he planned to call *Better Times*. The new version of the Pender troupe – including Tommy Pender and Archie Leach – began to practise together again and in September they returned to the theatre they had started at two years before for another season, calling themselves The Walking Stanleys. This time Archie Leach was a little more confident with the chorus girls in the cast. He started to go out with one of them, who lived with her family in Brooklyn.

'One night,' he recalled forty years later, 'we attended a

late party in someone's apartment. Prohibition was in force so naturally we drank. I drank hard apple cider, thinking it least likely to affect me; and in no time at all was laid to rest in a spare bedroom, where I was hazily joined, thanks to the manoeuvring of some well-meaning friends, by the lady in question. We awakened to find ourselves falteringly, fumblingly and quite unsatisfactorily attempting to ascertain whether those blessed birds and bees knew what they were doing.' It was the first time he had ever tried to make love to a girl but, as he recalled, 'I cannot add it was an occasion for song.'

For the next few weeks he tried to do what he thought a suitor should do and escort the girl home to her parents' house in Brooklyn every evening after the show, but gradually the problems of finding a way of getting back into Manhattan again persuaded him to give up. Instead, he took to having supper with some other former members of the Pender troupe to talk about what sort of act they could put together after *Better Times* closed. For Archie Leach women were not such a serious business as making a living.

Burnside's spectacle at the Hippodrome closed in the first months of 1923. It was the last time any New York producer would ever try to mount anything so extravagant, and it forced the former members of the Pender troupe to put their plans for a new act into action. After trying out their new mime show, with its familiar mixture of tumbling, stilt-walking and slapstick farce, they got a booking with the Pantages circuit.

The experience came as a considerable shock after the comparative luxury of the Keith circuit on the east coast. Alexander Pantages, the circuit's founder, had started out as a waiter in a concert hall on the west coast of America during the Klondike Gold Rush in 1896, and after teaming up with a burlesque producer called Jack Flynn, who supplied the chorus girls, he had started opening vaudeville theatres. The first two were next door to each other in Seattle. This circuit was principally on the west coast from Washington down to California and in western Canada. Working his theatres could mean up to five shows a day on Saturdays and Sundays, with four on every other day. But Alexander Pantages gave Archie Leach one great gift. On this tour he got his first sight of the town that would become his home: Hollywood.

When Horace Henderson Wilcox had first bought the hundred and twenty acres of cactus and palm trees, orange groves and poinsettias north-west of Los Angeles in 1887, he had wanted to found a religious community based on sober principles; he was, after all, a Kansas prohibitionist. His wife, Daeida, had first called the place Hollywood, but it did not develop in quite the way Wilcox had hoped.

In 1906 the American Biograph and Mutoscope Company had set up in the sunshine of central Los Angeles, eight miles away down a rough country road, and in 1907 the director of some of the early one-reel films, Francis Boggs, had turned up from Chicago with a handful of actors from Colonel Selig's motion picture company. Selig had decided to send them to California because the state boasted it had three hundred and fifty sunny days a year. With Hobart Bosworth, a former Broadway actor who had lost his voice, in the starring role, Boggs made *The Power of the Sultan* on a vacant lot next to a Chinese laundry. Four years later the first studio to settle in Hollywood itself was opened on Sunset Boulevard by the Centaur Company, run by two English brothers, William and David Horsley. Within a few months fifteen other companies from the east coast had joined them in Hollywood, partly to take advantage of the fine weather but also because of the cheap rents.

By 1919, after Hollywood had incorporated itself into Los Angeles as a result of a paralysing drought (the city provided it with water) four out of every five films made anywhere in the world were being made in southern California. The electricity and coal shortages during the Great War had sent more and more film companies hurrying across the continent, and by the time Douglas Fairbanks and Mary Pickford arrived back in the town from their honeymoon trip on the

SS *Olympic* in 1920 they were at the centre of the world-wide industry.

Cecil B. DeMille, Jesse Lasky and Sam Goldwyn had made *The Squaw Man,* D. W. Griffith had directed both *The Birth of a Nation* and *Intolerance,* Mack Sennett had launched the Keystone Cops, and Charles Chaplin had created 'the little fellow' well before Archie Leach's train pulled into Los Angeles station early in 1924. The city was already a modern Babylon, a place of scandal and excess, where rumour fuelled the wildest fantasies. There were no art galleries or museums, few bookshops and no traditional theatres to give a young Englishman a sense of home. But, like so many of the other hopefuls who had flocked there, Archie Leach wanted a new life, not memories.

'I saw palm trees for the first time in my life,' he was to recall. 'I was impressed by Hollywood's wide boulevards and their extraordinary cleanliness in the pre-smog sunshine. I didn't know I would make my home there one day. And yet, I *did* know . . .

'There is some prophetic awareness in each of us. I cannot remember daring consciously to hope I would be successful at anything: yet, at the same time, I knew I would be.'

It was nearly eight years, however, between this first visit and his return.

For the moment he was still playing four shows a day as a silent comedian for Pantages; still climbing on to his stilts when the act demanded it; and still not speaking a word. As the troupe slowly worked their way up the California coast into Canada and then started back eastwards again, Archie began to want to do more than that. As the columnist Hedda Hopper pointed out later: 'He figured out that performers who talked got more money so, just like that, he decided to talk.'

For years afterwards he suffered a nightmare about his search for a speaking part that summer. In the dream he would remember: 'I am standing on the lighted stage of a vast theatre facing a silent, waiting audience. I am the star, and I am surrounded by a large cast of actors, each of whom knows exactly what to do and say! And I can't remember my lines! I can't remember them because I've been too lazy to study them. I can find no way to bluff it through, and I stand there inept and insecure. I make a fool of myself. I am ashamed.'

When he began to tour the Broadway booking agents' offices looking for speaking parts in plays the question he was asked was usually the same. 'You ever spoken lines?' the girls behind the small wooden railings would ask in a slightly bored voice. Tall, athletic-looking, and rather flashily handsome, he was striking enough to make them look up, but he could not deny his inexperience. Nor could he control the insecurity he had always felt. He tended to answer meekly: 'None at all, I'm afraid.'

There were occasional jobs, however. In one company he was supposed to portray 'The Spirit of the Theatre' by dressing in a leotard and emerging from a trapdoor in the centre of the stage at the opening of the show, to explain what the audience were about to see. One night he duly came up through the trapdoor without much difficulty, but as he was descending again as the cue for the show to start, the trapdoors shut prematurely. He spent the first act with his head sticking up above the floor of the stage with the chorus line kicking around him, because the stage manager had no intention of bringing down the curtain just to rescue a walk-on player.

There were also some slapstick routines which called on him to use the tumbling he had refined with the Pender troupe, and he still got one or two bookings as a mime because of his slightly bow-legged walk, which had earned him the nickname 'Rubber Legs' in some vaudeville houses. In between bookings he returned to Coney Island, once as a lifeguard, more usually as a 'barker', encouraging the customers to try the thrills of the Red Mill, sample the delights of the Tunnel of Love or – on one occasion – to pay to gawp at a bearded lady. He also spent some time on Sixth Avenue selling handpainted ties which a young Australian, John Kelly, had been making in his flat in Greenwich Village.

Kelly, who was to go on to Hollywood and become famous as the designer Orry-Kelly, said later: 'He was a very likeable kid who had rather a thick English accent, although he was losing it fast. He lived in my apartment in Greenwich Village for a time. He was trying to act but he was godawful and other friends of mine thought so too.'

Gradually Archie began to play the straight man more and more often, going out on tour with any comedian who would take him, or working around New York for the minimum rate of $62.50 between the two of them. As he put it later: 'Eventually I played practically every small town in America [and] as the "straight man" I learned to time laughs. When to talk into an audience's laughter. When to wait for the laugh. When not to wait for the laugh. In all sorts of theatres, of all sizes, playing to all types of people; timing laughs that changed in volume and length at every performance.' It may not have been quite the 'speaking' he had thought of when he left the Pantages tour but it taught him his technique. He also started watching the great straight men work – George Burns, who was starting out with his wife, Gracie Allen; and Zeppo Marx, part of 'the greatest comedy act in showbusiness', as the Marx Brothers called themselves.

Eventually his old friend Don Barclay turned up, and suggested that Archie should become his partner in a mind-reading act. At a beach cottage in Long Island the two men tried out their routine, using the children next door as their audience. As it happened, these children were well used to the ways of vaudeville as their father, Walter Winchell, was still working in it.

'Gentlemen,' Barclay would say from the midst of the audience. 'This is a serious test of thought transmission. Professor Knowall Leach will endeavour to call anyone in the audience by name.' The comic would then ask selected victims their name before shouting to his partner on the stage:

'This gentleman's from Buffalo.'

'Bill,' the straight-faced stooge would shout back.

'Now here's a stickler, Professor. For the love of . . .'
'Pete.'
'No, no, the other kind.'
'Mike.'
'This girl is an upper and a lower, Professor.'
'Bertha.'
'And here's one not deaf but dumb.'
'Dora.'
'Dumber than that.'
'Belle.'

Then Barclay would vary the routine slightly. He would shout to his partner:

'Where is this man's father?'

There would be a pause.

'At this minute your father is in Denver, Colorado.'

The member of the audience would then shout: 'No, he's not, he's in Memphis.'

Another slight pause. Then the puzzled Professor would say from the stage: 'Your mother's husband may be in Memphis, but your father's in Denver.'

Years later Barclay would say: 'Archie always felt that was bad taste. But bad taste or not it always got a big laugh.'

In the summer of 1927 the two men took their double act on the road. They started in Toledo, Texas, but got no further than Newark, New Jersey, where the theatre manager told Barclay to get another straight man or the act was cancelled. Sadly they broke up, hardly ever to see each other again, and a disheartened Archie Leach took the train back to New York. It was an experience he preferred to forget.

The speakeasies were still there and the young men still paraded in their snap brimmed hats and spats, but the Broadway Archie Leach came back to in the summer of 1927 had changed. Audiences were no longer desperate to relieve the thought of war with laughter at the vaudeville theatres. Now they preferred a more sophisticated gaiety. The loud jackets and baggy trousers of vaudeville were giving way to the white tie and tails of musical comedy. Archie Leach could hardly know it, but the change was to make him a star.

It was certainly, now, no handicap to be English. Gertrude Lawrence, Beatrice Lillie and Jack Buchanan had already taken New York by storm in André Charlot's *London Revue of 1924*, while Noël Coward's *The Vortex* had been breaking box office records for five months. It seemed as though almost any young Englishman who looked dashing in tails had a chance of success. Romance, too, was in the air. The most popular songs from *No, No, Nanette* were still echoing in the nightclubs. 'Tea for Two' and 'I Want To Be Happy' seemed somehow to capture the spirit of the times. This was not England recovering from the General Strike; it was the America of Fred and Adèle Astaire, glittering in George Gershwin's *Lady Be Good*. It was the country of Valentino and Theda Bara, not John Galsworthy and George Bernard Shaw. The ladies in the theatres wanted their leading men to be tall, dark, and handsome – and, preferably, as mysterious as the Red Shadow in Romberg's *The Desert Song*.

The twenty-three-year-old Archie Leach was undeniably tall; with his brooding eyes and olive skin he was unquestionably handsome, and his hair was every bit as dark as Valentino's. His face may have been fleshier than Coward's or Astaire's, but it had an almost Mediterranean voluptuousness that theirs lacked. Archie realized that if he could master their clipped, elegant and fundamentally English style it would add to his appeal. As a step towards this, he started dressing more conservatively. His suits became a little better cut, his shirts white and his ties restrained. He took to standing with one hand in his pocket, adopting a studiedly nonchalant stare, in an awkward parody of Coward himself. It looked graceless at first, but he knew that to succeed he had to become someone else and he was not to be put off.

As his transformation gathered pace he was invited to more and more parties as an escort for unattached ladies. Manhattan hostesses knew he would light their cigarettes with a studied movement of the wrist, and take their arm at precisely the right moment, although perhaps a little too cautiously. Like one of the young men in Margaret Kennedy's new novel, *The Constant Nymph*, he took to being brittle, charming and always 'frightfully' gay. It was a mask he became steadily more reluctant to take off.

When he wasn't invited out to dinner he took to spending his spare time at Rudley's Restaurant on 41st Street and Broadway, where a circle of actors and writers gathered daily. At a corner table there was always gossip about jobs. Preston Sturges was a member of the Rudley's table; so were Moss Hart, George Murphy, Edward Chodorov and Humphrey Bogart, then still assisting the independent producer, William A. Brady. Later Moss Hart described the Archie Leach of those years as 'disconsolate', and Edward Chodorov was to say: 'He was never a very open fellow, but he was earnest and we liked him.'

Still relying on the discipline he had used since childhood, he kept quiet most of the time, learning as much as he could from the conversation around him, eager for any intellectual education and even spiritual leadership. Not that he neglected vaudeville. It still provided him with a steady, if not handsome, living. He played dates here and there at small theatres and private clubs and he would sometimes do Sunday night benefits. One Sunday evening his partner was too drunk to stand up and the desperate stage manager persuaded Archie to go on by himself. He sang two songs, told a couple of jokes, did a short acrobatic dance, and retired gratefully to the wings. But the experience convinced him that he could probably survive alone, and that he might have a future in musical comedy, if he could learn to sing.

One of his friends, Max Hoffman, was already in musical comedy. Hoffman was a not particularly successful juvenile but he was a friend of Reggie Hammerstein, the stage director whose elder brother was the lyric writer, Oscar Hammerstein II, composer of the lyrics for Jerome Kern's *Showboat*, Rudolf Friml's *Rose Marie* and Sigmund Romberg's *The Desert Song*. One night Reggie Hammerstein spent some time persuading the young Leach that he had a future in musical comedy. It was unusual for Archie to take the advice of anyone of his own age, but he was a little in awe of a young man whose grandfather had owned the famous Victoria Theatre and whose uncle Arthur was about to open another theatre that would bear the family's name. The arguments, moreover, sounded all the more attractive when linked with the high salaries musical comedy performers commanded. As he put it years later: 'I went into musicals because frankly they paid more money than the drama in New York.'

Archie began to take singing and voice lessons, and in the evenings the two young men would discuss the best way for him to get his first part in a musical. In September 1927 the obvious opportunity presented itself. The young stage director took his friend to meet his uncle Arthur, who had just announced that he was to stage *Golden Dawn*, a new operetta, with lyrics by Oscar. The story might be hackneyed, but there was a good juvenile part which could suit the newly trained Archie Leach. 'It was the nicest thing anyone ever did for me.'

Arthur Hammerstein did not object to the idea of Archie; as the character he would be playing was supposed to be an Australian prisoner-of-war, it would not matter too much if Broadway audiences were slightly bemused by Archie's English accent. Hammerstein's main worry was whether his leading lady, Louise Hunter, was a big enough name to pull in the crowds at the box office, and whether Paul Gregory, the somewhat erratic leading man, would turn up at the theatre on time regularly to star opposite her.

Late in October Hammerstein sent *Golden Dawn* out on the road for a month of previews. Two weeks in Boston were followed by two weeks in Philadelphia; then would come the Broadway opening on the last day of November.

Boston was not a success. Oscar Hammerstein and Otto Harbach fiddled with the lyrics and amended the story every day, so that everyone became increasingly confused. In

Philadelphia things went better. The show seemed to be working, and the cast relaxed a little. By the end of the second two-week run they were even beginning to feel they had a chance of being in a hit. But Archie was taking no risks on the prospect of a long run. He was carefully saving as much as he could from the salary of $250 a week that Hammerstein was paying him. He did not intend to end up in Bristol as a bum.

Golden Dawn opened on 30 November 1927 to distinctly cool reviews. The critics praised it as a 'lavishly mounted' spectacle but thought that it failed to 'realize its promised potential' and that the cast had to struggle with the 'material they had to work with'. Archie Leach was noticed as a 'pleasant new juvenile' and a 'competent young newcomer', and there were one or two other bright spots. In any case the public did not seem to read the reviews. The name Hammerstein was enough. *Golden Dawn* held on for more than five months, then quietly closed after its hundred and eighty-fourth performance, not a bad start to Archie's new career. At the corner table in Rudley's the regulars took to calling him 'Kangaroo' and 'Boomerang', and maintained that he actually sounded Australian because he was struggling so intently to improve his English accent. Archie took the hint. When looking for work he began calling himself Australian. No-one need know that he was a lonely boy from Bristol, less carefree and debonair in the privacy of his apartment than he liked to appear to his friends.

He was distinctly cheered when Arthur Hammerstein offered him a new part. This was in *Polly*, a musical version of *Polly with a Past*, the American comedy written by George Middleton and Guy Bolton, in which Ina Clair had made a great success seven years before. Archie was to play the role which Noël Coward had taken in London, but as soon as rehearsals started he began to worry, and to worry in public. He fussed interminably – his clothes weren't right; there wasn't enough for him to do; the 'business' he was supposed to use to make the audience laugh with wasn't funny enough; his lines didn't work. It was the meticulous, niggling fussing

73

of a privately insecure man who desperately wanted to succeed; it became one of his hallmarks.

On this occasion, in fact, it was not unjustified. *Polly* may have boasted the considerable talents of Fred Allen, one of vaudeville's best dead-pan comics, as well as the coyly pretty Inez Courtney, but it did not really work as a musical. Neither did Archie himself shine. As the critic in Wilmington, Delaware, put it when the show was on its six weeks' provincial tour before New York: 'Archie Leach has a strong masculine manner, but unfortunately fails to bring out the beauty of the score.' Later he admitted ruefully: 'My musical comedy inexperience was too evident to go unnoticed, and I was taken out of *Polly* and replaced before it opened on Broadway.' Once there, it opened to a deadening silence and closed after fifteen performances. His sacking had shocked him, but the show's failure softened the blow, and so did the six weeks' money at $250 a week.

The possibility of making even more money had just presented itself. Marilyn Miller, who had started as one of the chorus girls in Florenz Ziegfeld's hugely successful Follies, wanted a replacement for her leading man in the musical comedy *Rosalie* and she thought that the 'promising young juvenile' from *Golden Dawn* might be just right. A leading lady who had a clear idea for the new leading man she wanted was not unfamiliar to Ziegfeld. Twenty years of 'glorifying the American girl', as his publicity called it, meant that he had heard most things from the ladies in his productions. But for once he was not all that averse to the proposal, all the more so as Archie would cost him a good deal less than the comedian Jack Donahue, whose part he would be taking over; and would certainly not want anything like the $2,500 a week being paid to Marilyn Miller herself. So the autocratic Ziegfeld asked his arch-enemy Arthur Hammerstein to release Archie from his contract. Hammerstein was not amused. To Ziegfeld he said that there was not the slightest chance of his letting him have Archie Leach. But to Archie he said, 'I'm selling your contract to someone else.' The man he sold it to was J. J.

Shubert who, with his brother Lee, to whom he was reputed never to speak, was Broadway's biggest theatrical producer.

Ironically nothing could have been better for Archie's career. Within a few weeks the Shuberts had cast him in a new musical with Jeanette MacDonald and had agreed to pay him $350 a week. For a man who had been in only two previous productions, and had been summarily fired from one of them, this was no small stroke of fortune. But even then Archie took no chances. He agreed the salary with the Shuberts himself before he set foot inside the theatre to rehearse. He was still determined never to be penniless. 'I had great disdain for working for the Shuberts. I wanted to be with Ziegfeld, you see, so that I had no fear of Mr J. J. because they were beneath me,' he recalled later. When it had opened in Atlantic City the musical had been called *Snap My Garter*, but the confident new juvenile told J. J. Shubert, 'That sounds like a burlesque show,' and the impresario changed the title to *Boom, Boom*.

Even the Broadway musicals were under threat. Talking pictures had begun to take away the audiences that the theatres relied on. Al Jolson had already uttered his first words on the screen: 'You ain't heard nothing yet'; and every other film studio was rushing to climb on the Vitaphone bandwagon. The newly merged Metro-Goldwyn-Mayer was already making the first all-singing, all-dancing, all-talking musical and calling it *Broadway Melody*. It opened in February 1929, only three weeks after *Boom, Boom*, and overshadowed everything.

Still, Jeanette MacDonald remembered later: 'The heavy in our show was a dark-eyed, cleft-chinned young Englishman, who in spite of his unmistakeable accent, was cast as a Spaniard. We did a fandango together, during which he tossed me over his arms. He was absolutely terrible in the role, but everyone liked him. He had charm.' So much for Archie's performance. Of the show itself the *New Yorker's* critic declared: 'It can teach one more about despair than the most expert philosopher.' After seventy performances at the Casino Theatre, it closed, but it did bring the Latin-looking Archie Leach and the sometimes petulant Jeanette MacDonald one benefit. During the run Paramount Publix Pictures decided they should both be given a screen test at their Astoria studios in New York. Paramount had built its reputation on bringing stage stars to Hollywood ever since its chairman Adolph Zukor had persuaded Minnie Maddern Fiske to leave New York in 1916 and star in *Tess of the D'Urbevilles*.

In the hysteria after the opening of *Broadway Melody*, the audition was an opportunity neither of the two young players wanted to miss. Riding across the East River towards Queens and the studios they agreed it was 'torture' but that it was worthwhile. In Archie's case it did not prove to be so at first. The studio told him he would never make a movie star: his neck was too thick and his legs were too bowed. But they liked Jeanette MacDonald and swept her off to Hollywood where her first film, *The Love Parade*, was directed by Ernst Lubitsch as his first experiment with sound, and had Maurice Chevalier as her co-star. To console himself Archie Leach went out and bought himself a Packard Phaeton, a very large and quite expensive car, designed for touring, with an open top and a 143-in wheelbase which made it difficult to steer it round corners. He had hardly ever sat behind the wheel of a car before and certainly could not drive this one, but whatever Paramount thought he did not intend to be ignored.

The Shuberts kept on his contract, and put him into *A Wonderful Night*, a reworking of Johann Strauss's *Die Fledermaus*, starring Gladys Baxter and Mary McCoy, and again written by Fanny Todd Mitchell. It opened at the Majestic on 31 October 1929, two days after the blackest day of the Wall Street crash. Archie played Max Gunewald, a dressy, vain, superficial and romantic young man, basically the same as the character he had played before. One New York critic called him 'woefully unfunny', although he went on to say that the rest of the men in the cast were no better. Another suggested that he 'sometimes manages to miss the proper note entirely', while a third added: 'Archie Leach, who feels that acting in something by Johann Strauss calls for distinction, is somewhat at a loss as to how to achieve it.' Not that the notices mattered all that much: miraculously, the show struggled on for a hundred and twenty-five performances, playing to largely empty houses, before the Shuberts put it out of its misery.

So far Archie's career had mainly consisted of being fired, not getting the part, and struggling in mediocre musicals. He was, however, surprisingly undismayed. He was living with three other young men in an apartment in Greenwich Village, sporting a fashionable racoon coat – which he would never give away or sell – and learning to drive the Packard. It seemed a good life for a young man of twenty-five. Yet one thing was wrong. He was not at all comfortable in the company of young women of his own age. With his female partners in the theatre he was calm enough, superficially charming though also reserved and, some thought, pompous. Outside the theatre, however, he was gauche, moody and given to adolescent bouts of showing off.

Years later he said sadly: 'That was my trouble. Always trying to impress someone. Now wouldn't you think that with a new, shiny, expensive open car, and an open-neck shirt, with a pipe in my mouth to create a carefully composed study of nonchalance, sportiveness, savoir-faire and sophistication, I would cut quite a swath amongst the ladies? Nothing of the sort. In all those years in the theatre, on the road, and in New York, surrounded by all sorts of attractive girls, I never seemed able to fully communicate with them.'

A romance with a girl in Boston fizzled out. Others he tried to court seriously ended up telling him he was conceited and self-satisfied. He felt more comfortable with men. He liked to joke with them after the show was over, drink with them in the Broadway bars. No matter how attractive he may have seemed to the women on the other side of the footlights, he was more than a little afraid of the sex as a whole.

Soon the Shuberts were employing him again in the touring company version of the musical *The Street Singer* opposite Queenie Smith. For the next nine months he toured through the provincial towns where unemployment was just beginning to put able-bodied young men out on to the streets. His baritone voice, however unsatisfactory, was at least keeping him out of the clutches of the depression yet, as he strolled awkwardly through the performances, he was tortured by the sense of being a fake. Archie Leach was beginning to feel trapped by the debonair personality he had adopted to survive.

Defensive and moody, he could be awkward with his fellow performers; distant for days at a time and then given to sudden bursts of charm, as if he was never sure whether anyone liked him for himself. In the afternoons he would take bus rides round whichever city he found himself in, just as he had once done in London and New York, or he would drive into the country in his Packard, to be alone. And he saved his money carefully. On the road with *The Street Singer* in the first months of 1931 the Shuberts were paying him $450 a week, more than ten times the wage of the average working man in America – that is, if the man was lucky enough to be working. President Hoover was already admitting that more than ten million Americans were out of a job. In the drought-ridden southern states a quarter of the farmers had lost their homesteads, and had begun the tragic trek west in the hope of finding work in the orange groves of California. For them a Packard Phaeton and a racoon coat were impossible dreams, but Archie Leach's salary enabled him to live well, and to begin to erase the memory of the cold, gloomy rooms in his grandmother's cheerless house – even if sometimes the damp mean smell in her pantry came back to him. On tour he subdued the recollection with elaborate meals in the company of the most beautiful young women in the show's chorus. Diffident as he was, and occasionally helplessly tongue-tied, he felt this was expected of him, the sort of thing a twenty-six-year-old leading man should be seen doing.

On 5 November 1930, Ernst Lubitsch and Maurice Chevalier were both nominated for the new Academy Awards for their work on *The Love Parade*, the film Jeanette MacDonald had left New York to make after his screen test with her the year before. The musical had also been nominated as the best picture of the year, only to lose to Lewis Milestone's brilliant anti-war film *All Quiet on the Western Front*. Only a few months after this chastening reminder to Archie Leach that other people's careers had fared better than his own, the tour of *The Street Singer* came to an end, in the spring of 1931.

Because he still had his contract to pay, J. J. Shubert proposed to Archie that he spend the summer in St Louis, where the brothers were responsible for running the open-air Municipal Opera in Forest Park. Rather than let go of a comforting salary, Archie Leach accepted; but times were hard and hardly had the season begun when the Shuberts asked every member of the company to take a cut in salary. The dancer Frank Horn, who became his secretary for more than twenty years and who was in the St Louis company, recalled later that 'Everybody did – except Archie Leach. He asked for a rise. So when his contract expired, he was through.'

Through or not he completed the season of eighty-seven performances, playing everything from *Music in May* to *Rio Rita*, from *The Street Singer* and *A Wonderful Night* to *Irene* and *Countess Maritza*. He always played the handsome juvenile, and managed to look dashing if not always to display much talent. Indeed, with his dark hair and olive skin he cut something of a romantic figure in the comparatively quiet Missouri town, so much so that the *Daily Variety*'s Midwestern correspondent was inspired to write a glowing piece about him. The press mention caught the eye of another Broadway producer, William Friedlander, who was on the verge of casting a new musical play, *Nikki*. He not only sent someone to St Louis to see this attractive young man, but asked the Shuberts if he might borrow him.

Written by John Monk Saunders for his wife, Fay Wray,

who played the female lead, *Nikki* opened at the Longacre Theater New York on 29 September 1931 under the happiest auspices. Loosely based on a magazine story about flyers left in Paris after the First World War, it had earlier that year been made into a popular film, entitled *The Last Flight*, by First National Pictures, with Richard Barthelmess in the role of Cary Lockwood which would now be taken by Archie Leach. But that was a film. As a musical, this thin mixture of romance and forgettable melodies did not endear itself to audiences for whom the theatre was now an expensive luxury. Although Friedlander moved it to the George M. Cohan Theater in a desperate bid to keep it going, *Nikki* closed on 31 October 1931 after just thirty-nine performances.

Archie next accepted an offer to make a one-reeler film called *Singapore Sue*, at Paramount's Astoria studios, opposite the Chinese character actress Anna Chang. It was the first time he had been inside the studio since his abortive screen test two years earlier. As one of four American sailors visiting Chang's café in Singapore, Archie smiled and murmured his few words of dialogue. On the screen, dressed in white tropical uniform, he looked almost oriental himself, with his heavy sallow features and ripe lips topped by a wide, false smile; but the short's director, Casey Robinson, who later went to Hollywood himself as a screen writer, was sufficiently impressed to write, 'a note to the important executives at Paramount, none of whom I knew at the time, urging them to screen the short, not for my work but for that of a young actor whom I felt to be a sure-fire future star.' But the short was not screened until the middle of the following year, and by that time its voluptuous-looking leading man had reached Hollywood by another route.

Fay Wray, Archie's co-star in *Nikki*, was packing for California. She had been offered the part of the beauty that hypnotises the beast in the film which RKO Radio were planning from Edgar Wallace's story *King Kong*. Like many other actresses she had decided to leave Broadway behind her, as her husband had already done. 'Why don't you come out on a visit,' she said to Archie, almost in passing.

Together with his friend, the composer Phil Charig, Archie had originally planned to take a golfing holiday in Florida. The regular salary he had been receiving over the past year meant that he had more than enough money to live on and he wasn't anxious to jump back into another Shubert contract. Billy Grady of the William Morris Agency, always known by his nickname of 'Square Deal' and later to become casting director of MGM had advised him in the same sense and had also told him: 'You must become a leading man. Why don't you go to California?'

So Archie and Phil Charig went to California instead of Florida, setting out in mid-November 1931 to drive the three thousand miles across the continent. The Packard was crammed with so many suits they could hardly squeeze into it themselves, but they were in no particular hurry. After ten days, driving some of the time with the tiny glass windscreen folded down to help them get a tan in the wind, they arrived in Hollywood, settled themselves into a suite at the Château Elysée, where Katharine Hepburn had stayed when she had first arrived, and set out to discover what California had to offer to two handsome young men.

Billy Grady had arranged for Archie to see the Hollywood agent Walter Herzbrun, who in turn introduced him to Marion Gering, a former Broadway stage director who was now directing films. Two evenings later Gering invited Archie to dine with himself and his wife at the home of the production chief of Paramount, the fearsome B. P. Schulberg, who had not only helped to launch the Famous Players Company with Adolph Zukor in 1912, but had also started the film careers of both Clara Bow, the 'It' girl, and Gary Cooper, by then the studio's biggest star. Given to massive fits of temper, Schulberg was reputed to receive a salary of $500,000 a year from Zukor. The dinner was intimate and, inevitably, sumptuous.

'I'm going to make a screen test of my wife tomorrow,'

81

Gering murmured to Archie after the main course had been cleared away. 'She thinks she'd like to be in movies and B.P. agreed I could do it. Why don't you make it with her?' said Schulberg peremptorily, addressing Archie from the head of the table. 'She'll need someone to act against. You only have to feed her the lines. Nothing too difficult.'

Archie Leach smiled and replied that he would be delighted. As he left Schulberg's house to drive back to the hotel he resolved to make sure the test caught his right profile and that he would also see to it that the lighting did not make his neck look too thick. He suspected it would not be difficult to upstage the lady he was helping. As the Packard rolled down Sunset Boulevard towards the new shopping arcade, 'At the Crossroads of the World', he found himself smiling again.

The test, which took place at Paramount Publix's studios on Marathon Street, right in front of the Hollywood Cemetery, involved for Archie nothing more than the reading of a few lines and a series of entrances and exits. Throughout the morning he remembered to relax and to keep his eye on the camera so that it would catch him in the best light. By comparison the pretty but rather flustered Mrs Gering was a good deal less in control. Less than a week later Schulberg called him.

'How would you feel about a contract? We could start you at $450 a week with options for five years. Standard, everybody signs it.'

Archie Leach had taught himself never to agree to anything too quickly. 'I'd like to think about it.'

'Do that. Only one other thing. You'll need to change your name.'

At that moment the only son of Elsie Maria Leach realized that it was possible to forget his unhappy past, to put it aside as if it had never happened, and to become someone new. He could begin his life again six thousand miles away from the chill, haunted memories of home. He and his father wrote to each other from time to time, but Elias had set up house with another woman and had said she was expecting a child. As for his mother, she was a subject they never discussed. Now Archibald Alec Leach knew exactly what he was going to do. He was going to cease to exist.

PART TWO
The Matinée Idol

'I see Hollywood as a precarious sort of
Streetcar. Call it Aspire. There's only room for
so many, and every once in a while, if you look
back, you'll see that someone has fallen off.
When Tyrone Power got on it meant someone
was left sprawled out on the street. Ronald
Colman sits up with the motorman. Gary
Cooper is smart, he never gets up to give
anybody his seat.'

Cary Grant

4

'Hello, I'm Cary Grant'

'The movies. It's everything, money, fame,
adventure – the thrill of a lifetime.'

Robert Armstrong to Fay Wray in *King Kong*

No matter how gay the stars seemed, and no matter how
hard the studios tried to reassure the world, Hollywood at
the end of 1931 was distinctly nervous. Gone were the
carefree days of the late 1920s, when even the taxi drivers
had acted like millionaires, and Garbo, Chaplin and Swan-
son had gathered at the Cocoanut Grove to hear Paul
Whiteman and The Rhythm Boys with Bing Crosby.
Movies were no longer 'depression proof'. They were beginning to lose money. The mighty Warner Brothers, in spite of
its success with *The Jazz Singer* and the first talking pictures,
was contemplating an estimated loss of eight million dollars.
Even tiny RKO, which had just won the Academy Award
for Best Picture of the Year with its elegant western *Cimarron*,
starring Richard Dix and Irene Dunne, had slipped more
than five and a half million into the red. And it looked as
though things were going to get worse.

At Paramount, Adolph Zukor, its chairman and creator,
was less worried than most. His company was about to
report a profit of six million dollars and his stars had done
well at the fourth Academy Awards Ceremony in November. Jackie Cooper and Fredric March had been nominated,
while the director Norman Taurog had been honoured for
his work on the studio's film *Skippy*. Even more satisfying to
Zukor was the fact that Josef von Sternberg and Marlene

Dietrich had also won him a string of nominations for *Morocco*, the first film on which they had worked together in America. It had been not only as visually dazzling as Sternberg's *The Blue Angel* but had also given Zukor a foreign star to rival Garbo, Louis B. Mayer's prize at Metro-Goldwyn-Mayer. One film magazine had carried out a poll of its readers in which they were asked: 'Who will be the greater star of tomorrow: Dietrich or Garbo?' A majority chose Dietrich.

But Mayer and Zukor were the only studio heads in Hollywood whose companies were comfortably in profit, and they both knew what those profits depended on – the appeal of their stars. Mayer could boast Clark Gable, Marie Dressler, Norma Shearer and Joan Crawford, but Zukor had Dietrich's co-star in *Morocco*, Gary Cooper, as well as Fredric March, Claudette Colbert and Carole Lombard. Always anxious to improve his stable, he had also recently approached Tallulah Bankhead and Herbert Marshall; and Zukor saw no reason why Archie Leach might not prove useful, if he agreed to change his name.

Universal had just proved the importance of a good name with the success of their film *Frankenstein* whose star, Boris Karloff, was an Englishman whose real name was William Henry Pratt. MGM had insisted that Lucille LaSueur become Joan Crawford and had promoted a fan magazine contest for the new name. Fox had encouraged Jane Peters to become Carole Lombard and Zukor's Frank Cooper had had the good sense to change his first name to Gary after a small town in Indiana. Schulberg himself had suggested to Luis Alonso that he might call himself John Adams, though the actor had finally settled for Gilbert Roland. So when he told the cautious but enthusiastic Archie Leach that if he accepted the studio's contract he would have to find a new name, the ruby question was, which one?

The first suggestion came from his friend, Fay Wray, and her husband, John Monk Saunders. 'They said it might be nice if I used the name by which I'd been known in their play, Cary Lockwood,' he recalled later. The studio liked the first part but objected to the second. 'There's already a Harold Lockwood in pictures,' Schulberg said firmly, when Archie presented his idea the next morning. 'We need something short, sharp and easy to remember, like Gable or Cooper.' And without a pause he produced a typewritten list of alternatives. One of the names on it was Grant.

'That's the name we'll put on your contract,' he told Archie. 'It should be ready shortly.'

Schulberg and his colleagues had another reason for liking the name, which they did not tell their new player: it could be confused with Gary Cooper. They already had it in mind to use the fledgling Grant as a dark-haired version of Cooper, their most popular leading man, and to star him in the roles that Cooper turned down. They also hoped that Cooper might be made just a little nervous by Grant's arrival, for the hard-working, hard-headed, 6ft 2in ex-cattlerancher had had them seriously worried. He had gone off in a huff on safari in Africa and was refusing to come back to Hollywood unless Zukor and Schulberg agreed to his right to decide which pictures he made and with whom. As he put it later: 'I had made twelve pictures in an year for Paramount, I hardly had time to eat. I really hadn't had a vacation since I started there five years before so I just went to Africa and vowed to stay there forever if need be. They knew I meant it.'

He had barely been out of town for four weeks when Paramount signed Cary Grant. As the fan magazine *Photoplay* noted not long afterwards; 'Cary looks enough like Gary to be his brother. Both are tall, they weigh about the same, and they fit the same sort of roles.' Bringing in a newcomer as a potential threat to an established star was nothing new in Hollywood. Metro had brought in James Craig as a threat to Clark Gable, and Robert Young as a threat to Robert Montgomery. It was insurance. If things worked out with the original star, the substitute could be paid off without too much fuss and bother. But no studio would risk having a confrontation with its major star unless it was prepared to replace him.

It was some time before Archie understood this state of affairs. As he signed 'Cary Grant' on his new contract in January 1932 he was more occupied with the thought of becoming another person in exchange for his $450 a week. He understood at once that what mattered in the picture business was the image any actor presented on the screen. Hollywood was the dream factory, where the lucky inhabitants could live out their fantasies. No-one was anything other than what he appeared – and, even more important to Archie, no-one ever questioned the past. In Hollywood, it did not exist.

The studios knew that the glamour of their top players was an essential ingredient in the success of their films. It was axiomatic in Hollywood that the cinema-going public did not want to know that its favourite hero was drunk more often than he was sober, or that the heroine it currently worshipped had become addicted to morphine, and the job of each studio's lavishly-staffed publicity department was to see that the image never slipped. As a result, this hypocrisy left the field wide open to the petty racketeers, the drug pedlars and blackmailers who swarmed into the town. It had already cost Mabel Normand, Wallace Reid, and Alma Rubens their careers and their lives.

For Archie Leach, however, the glamorous mask was a deliverance. As the motion picture fan magazines were soon to report, Cary Grant was 'suave, distinguished, graceful in every move he makes before the camera. The word "polished" fits him as closely as one of his own well-fitting gloves.' He was also 'handsome' and 'virile', 'blushed "fiery red" when embarrassed', and possessed the 'same dreamy, flashy eyes as Valentino'. Not a bad hop from Picton Street. Nevertheless he took some pains to protect his new personality. As a reporter noted during his first few months at Paramount: 'Anything he says about himself is so offhand and perfunctory that from his own testimony you get only the sketchiest impression of him.' And Elisabeth Goldbeck wrote in *Motion Picture* magazine: 'Seldom have I seen a man so little inclined to pour out his soul, and you have to scratch around and dig in order to discover even the bare facts of his life from him.'

He betrayed only one small sign of his buried past. After the contract was signed he bought a small Sealyham terrier, which he called Archie Leach. It was the only recognition he would allow himself that he had not always been Cary Grant.

As the effects of the depression cut deeper and deeper into cinema attendances, so Hollywood relied more and more heavily on its stars. MGM's production genius, Irving Thalberg, took the first major step early in 1932 by putting five of the studio's biggest names into a film version of Vicki Baum's successful novel and play, *Grand Hotel*. Greta Garbo and John Barrymore were to lead a cast which also included Joan Crawford, Wallace Beery and Lionel Barrymore. The gamble paid off. *Grand Hotel* won the year's Academy Award as Best Picture, and took more than two and a half million dollars in box-office receipts from audiences fascinated both by Crawford's hotel secretary and by Garbo's mercurial ballerina.

But the studios also realized that they must offer something else – a hope of better times and a reassurance to their public that things could turn out all right in the end, even if they looked bleak now. It was this optimistic philosophy that lay at the heart of Frances Marion's beautiful script for MGM's *The Champ*, and it was one with which Schulberg at Paramount heartily agreed. As if to underline this policy, Schulberg decided to launch Grant in as optimistic a film as he could find. His choice was George Marion Junior's adaptation of Avery Hopwood's Broadway play, *Naughty Cinderella*, to be directed by Frank Tuttle and retitled *This Is the Night*.

His role hardly seemed an auspicious start to a new career. He was cast as Lily Damita's naive husband, an Olympic javelin thrower whose frequent travels leave her time for a romance with her co-star, Roland Young. Essentially a feeble French bedroom farce, the piece called for

Grant to look foreign and faintly puzzled, while the action changed from Paris to Venice. But beside the blonde Miss Damita he was sufficiently striking to provoke *Variety*'s critic to note: 'He looks like a potential femme rave.'

Grant did not share the critic's good opinion. Early in April 1932, the morning after he had seen the first preview of the film, he called a friend in the Paramount publicity department.

'Good morning, I've called to say goodbye,' he told her. 'I'm leaving town.'

'What?'

'Yes, I'm checking out fast. I saw the preview last night. I've never seen anything so stinkeroo in my life, and I was worse.'

It took some considerable time for the publicity girl to persuade him not to pack his suits into the Packard and drive back across the continent to the comparative safety of the Shuberts and Broadway. It wouldn't be the first time that his insecurity would make him impossible to deal with when a film was being made and released. To many people who got to know him as they worked together at the studio, he seemed an actor 'virtually paralysed with fear'.

The *Daily Variety* critic had made matters worse by managing to call him Gary Grant in his review, thereby increasing the confusion with Gary Cooper. In the *New York Times* Mordaunt Hall called him 'efficient'. He certainly did not feel it. Nevertheless he was persuaded to go straight into making *Sinners in the Sun*, in which he acted in support of Carole Lombard and looked conventionally glamorous in a white tie and tails. But even Lombard, in the role of a hardworking fashion model, could not save the film. One critic said, summing up the views of the rest, it was 'A weak picture with an unimpressive future before it.' But by the time it was released Cary Grant had almost completed a third mediocre picture for Paramount, *Merrily We Go To Hell*. Starring Fredric March, this was another feeble story of unrequited love in luxurious surroundings, and Grant was not even to play a part in the film's principal story. Instead, he was to portray the leading man of the stage play that the drunken journalist played by March had written. Directed by the mannish Dorothy Arzner and co-starring Sylvia Sidney who was then having an affair with B. P. Schulberg, the film opened to less than enthusiastic reviews.

His first three films had done little more for Cary Grant than teach him the techniques of film making, but at least he had started to invest his money wisely. He had bought an interest in two haberdashery shops, one in New York and the other on the rapidly developing Wilshire Boulevard in Los Angeles – fruit of the interest in tailoring and cloth that he had acquired from his father. More important still, he had met two men who were to play a central part in his life for many years. One was Randolph Scott, who had become a featured player for Paramount shortly before Grant himself. The other was a tall shy man, reserved with girls and wary of talking about himself. His name was Howard Robard Hughes.

'We met at Paramount,' Randolph Scott told Hedda Hopper some years later. 'We were having lunch with some of the publicity girls, Cary had just come out from New York as Archie Leach, and he came over to our table and said he was looking for a place to live, so we got bachelor quarters together and lived there for five years.'

Tall, blond-haired and athletic, George Randolph Scott was only a year older than Cary Grant but he shared none of his insecurities. Born in January 1903 in Orange, Virginia, the son of a textile engineer, he was extrovert and relaxed, liked playing golf and riding and thoroughly disliked worrying. He had five sisters at home, by whom he was usually called Randy, and a nasty back injury, sustained in his junior year at college, which had ruined his chances of becoming an All-American football player. When he graduated from the University of North Carolina he persuaded his father to let him tour Europe for a year before starting work in Charlotte, North Carolina where the Scotts then lived. But after the tour he found he still could not settle down, and in 1928 he took a holiday in California. He knew no-one in Los Angeles, and had no particular interest in the movies, but he did have a letter of introduction from his father to Mrs Ella Hughes, the then wife of the strange young motion picture producer who had arrived in Hollywood in 1925. The tanned, easy-going Scott stayed as a guest with the Hughes's for a couple of weeks, playing golf with Howard Hughes whenever he could.

'Just about the time our stay was up,' Scott told Hopper, 'I asked if he could get us on a movie set so we could see how pictures were made. He said to me, "Why not work in a picture? That'll be better." '

Hughes called the casting director at United Artists and got Scott and a friend jobs as extras on one of the last silent films to be made, *Sharp Shooters*. They were to play Australian soldiers. Dressed in uniform, the tall handsome Scott caught the eye of the director, James Ryan, who persuaded him to do a screen test. But it was Cecil B. DeMille, just about to start making his first talking picture, *Dynamite*, who finally persuaded Scott that he might have a future as an actor. 'He advised me to stay here, said I had many things in my favour for becoming a movie actor, and suggested that, since talking pictures were coming in, I go to the Pasadena Playhouse and study for a while.'

Early on in his friendship with Grant, Scott introduced him to Howard Hughes. Hughes was confident, completely self-contained and utterly unconcerned about what Hollywood thought of him. One of his first ventures had been as the creator of *Hell's Angels*, which began as a silent film in 1928, switched to being a talkie, cost vastly more to make than any previous film in Hollywood, lost, in spite of denials, a cool one and a half million dollars, but ended up, after its opening on 30 June 1930, firmly establishing both the reputation of Jean Harlow and the legend of Hughes, who then went on to make *The Front Page* and *Scarface*.

Superficially it appeared that Howard Hughes, the maverick film-maker, and Cary Grant, the cautious contract player, were the antithesis of each other. Beneath the surface, however, they were remarkably alike. Both were Capricorns, as was Scott. Both were reticent, careful with their money, shy with women and given to outbursts of peevishness. For Hughes Cary Grant would become a friend who would help him to meet some of the most beautiful women in the world, a follower of his philosophy that women were there to make love to rather than to love. For Cary Grant the twenty-seven-year-old Texan millionaire would become an adviser and confidant whose opinion he would always listen to, a silent guide for his career. But Howard Hughes had another attraction for the young Cary Grant: he was unashamedly rich, even though he chose not to behave as some believed a rich young man should, and Grant had realized that he enjoyed the company of wealth. It was an appetite he never lost.

Not even Howard Hughes's wealth, however, could prevent Gary Cooper affecting Cary Grant's career. In the early summer of 1932 Cooper had made a regal return to Hollywood, stepping off the great Santa Fe Chief at Pasadena Railway Station – no star would have dreamt of getting off at Los Angeles-central – carrying a monkey he had brought back from Africa. The photograph of Gary and the monkey made every front page in town.

A relieved Adolph Zukor gave Cooper all he wanted, including the right to choose the films he made and to have a power of veto over cast and director. To celebrate Cooper's return he and Schulburg had decided to star him opposite Tallulah Bankhead in a picture to be directed by Marion Gering. They had also decided to use it as the American film debut for the British actor, Charles Laughton, and to add to the mixture, they decided to give their new young man, Cary Grant, a significant role. That would allow them to see how he compared with Cooper on the screen, and would serve to remind Cooper that no one was indispensable.

As *Photoplay* magazine pointed out a few months later, both men knew what was happening. 'They know that they're pitted against each other, and when the final gong sounds, one of them will be on the floor.' What Cary Grant feared was that it would probably be him.

Devil and the Deep was a triumphant return for Cooper. As *Variety* remarked after its opening in New York in August 1932, he was 'looking better than he has in a long time, and making a stunning figure in the uniform of a British naval officer'. A melodrama from start to finish, which had Laughton as the insanely jealous submarine commander who finally drowns himself in his cabin after he has rammed the submarine into a passing liner, it gave Grant little or no chance to prove whether or not he could act. Once again he was required only to look foreign and flashily handsome.

The experience was not entirely wasted, however, since it decided Schulberg to give Grant a chance to star beside Marlene Dietrich. She had just finished making *Shanghai Express* with Clive Brook, and her director, Josef von Sternberg, had a pronounced liking for 'Britishness' in the leading men in his films. The other leading man, who was to play Dietrich's husband, was the wistful-looking Herbert Marshall who had just arrived in Hollywood from success on the London stage.

Blonde Venus, as the film was to be called, did not start happily. Dietrich was extremely nervous. It was just after the kidnapping of Charles Lindbergh's infant son, whose body had now been found, and in Hollywood Dietrich received a series of letters threatening to abduct her own daughter, Maria. In addition, Josef von Sternberg was locked in argument with Schulberg. Paramount wanted one ending, von Sternberg wanted another – and refused to budge. Paramount replaced him as director, fined him $100,000, and in a rage he stormed out of Hollywood for a trip to Berlin. Dietrich announced that she would not work with any other director and refused to discuss the picture further. After weeks of trans-atlantic argument von Sternberg accepted a compromise. Filming began, and when *Blonde Venus* was released it won Cary Grant the best reviews of his career so far.

Mordaunt Hall in the *New York Times* said: 'Cary Grant is worthy of a much better role than that of Townsend.' On the first day of filming von Sternberg had grabbed a hairbrush and parted Grant's hair on the righthand side, the opposite side from his usual one, and it had changed his appearance dramatically. He now looked thinner, and a little frailer, on the screen, his natural uncertainty making him seem gallant rather than flashy. He never altered the parting of his hair again.

As the filming finished Grant and Scott found a house they could share on West Live Oak Drive. It was larger than the apartment they had been sharing and certainly larger than Grant could have afforded on his own, with its swimming pool and staff of maid and black cook. Carole Lombard, who knew them both, called it 'Bachelors' Hall', but maintained that when they told their friends they shared expenses it meant that 'Cary opened the bills, Randy wrote the checks, and if Cary could talk someone out of a stamp, he mailed them.'

The magazine *Silver Screen* noted after a few months: 'Cary is the gay impetuous one. Randy is serious, cautious. Cary is temperamental in the sense of being very intense. Randy is calm and quiet.'

Shortly after Scott had finished *Sky Bride*, the picture he was making for Howard Hughes, the studio agreed that he and Grant should star opposite each other and opposite the red-headed ingénue Nancy Carroll, in a film to be called *Hot Saturday*. Grant recreated the rich playboy he had played in *Blonde Venus* while Scott was asked to be the boyhood sweetheart who walked out on his marriage because he had heard rumours that Nancy had fallen for Grant. Grant now put to good use the lessons he had learnt from von Sternberg. He stopped acting too ostentatiously and allowed the camera itself to discover the inflection or movement he made. It worked. As *Variety* noted, he 'stands ahead of Miss Carroll and Scott in performance. He exercises extreme restraint towards his part.' Mordaunt Hall in the *New York Times* liked his 'nonchalant young libertine'.

Although Grant had made six films in Hollywood in less than a year, Zukor had no intention of allowing him to do nothing. As soon as *Hot Saturday* was finished he sent him straight back on to the set of another Marion Gering picture, once again starring Schulberg's friend, Sylvia Sidney. It was a film version of Puccini's opera *Madame Butterfly*, and Grant was to play Lieutenant Pinkerton. He had turned the part down; feeling that he didn't sing particularly well. *Variety* thought him 'rather cold' and said tersely: 'He sings one song and it isn't so hot.' Gary Cooper had also turned down the role, as he had turned down the one in *Sky Bride*: if Cary Grant's career was progressing, it seemed that it was doing so slowly.

All that was to change. By the time *Madame Butterfly* opened in New York, just before the New Year of 1933, Cary Grant had already been introduced to the woman who was to convince Hollywood that he had a talent for comedy – Mae West.

When Mae West had arrived from New York in June 1932 Hollywood's pre-eminent gossip columnist, Louella Parsons, had called her 'buxom, blonde, fat, fair and I don't know how near forty'. In fact she was thirty-nine and Broadway's biggest and most voluptuous star. Virtually single-handed she had made sex respectable on the stage by 'taking it out in the open and laughing at it'. Broadway in 1932, however, was hardly more stable financially than Hollywood. After getting an offer from Zukor to play a small role in a film he was planning for George Raft, who had become a star in Howard Hughes's *Scarface*, Mae West had decided to take Paramount's offer of ten weeks' work at a guaranteed $5,000 a week. 'Broadway was in real trouble,' she wrote in her autobiography. 'Maybe, I decided, I'd take a fling at Hollywood.'

But for her first eight weeks in Hollywood the tiny blonde had done nothing. Paramount had not been able to settle on a script for the Raft picture, and when they had finally managed to complete one Mae West refused to perform in it. After a protracted argument, during which she offered them her salary back if they would allow her to return to New

York, she re-wrote the part for herself. Almost her first words in the film, uttered to an awe-struck hat-check girl in Raft's speakeasy, who had exclaimed, 'Goodness, what beautiful diamonds!' were: 'Goodness had nothing to do with it, dearie.' They were to make her into a Hollywood star and to provoke Raft into remarking later, in his own autobiography: 'In this picture Mae West stole everything but the cameras.' They were also to encourage cinema owners throughout America to press Paramount to put her into a film of her own.

Cary Grant had first seen Mae West on a Friday night at the American Legion Stadium in Hollywood, where he and Randolph Scott went regularly to watch the boxing. Several movie stars made a habit of going: Chaplin was a regular attender and so was one of Gary Cooper's girlfriends, Lupe Velez, who liked to climb into the ring and encourage the boxers. Along with Sunday afternoons at the new Santa Monica Beach Club on the Pacific, and dinner on Saturday nights at the Trocadero, the boxing was one of the few relaxing occasions at which the Hollywood film community could meet each other socially. For the rest of the time they were working six days a week from 5.30 in the morning until at least 6.00 in the evening. All the same, Mae West's story, which she held to for years, was that she first caught sight of Cary on the lot at Paramount while she was talking to Al Kaufman and William LeBaron, who was to produce her new film.

'I saw a sensational looking young man walking along the studio street,' she wrote. 'He was the best thing I'd seen out there.

' "Who's that?"

'Kaufman recognized him. "Cary Grant."

' "He'll do for my leading man." '

Kaufman protested, but Mae West went on: 'If this one can talk I'll take him.' 'I could see he had poise, a great walk, everything women would like,' was her summing up.

Cary Grant came to resent this version. As he told *Screen Book* magazine: 'It seems that during her search for a suitable leading man she had seen me getting out of my studio car and decided I was the type to play opposite her. I suppose it was because she is blonde and I am dark and we make a suitable contrast.' He also pointed out that another reason for her choice was that Lowell Sherman, the director she had selected for the film, had liked his performance in *Blonde Venus*.

With costumes specially designed for her by Edith Head, Mae West started work on the film, now titled *She Done Him Wrong*, on 21 November 1932, immediately after Cary Grant had finished *Madame Butterfly*. It was completed in eighteen days of shooting without any overtime, as the actors had rehearsed together for a week before going in front of the cameras.

Grant was 'The Hawk', a Government agent who poses as a captain in the Salvation Army, and for the first time in Hollywood he was able to put to use his vaudeville training as a straight man. As well as being Mae's leading man, he also provided the best lines for her jokes.

'Haven't you ever met a man who can make you happy?' he asked at one point.

'Sure,' came the reply, 'lots of times.'

Parts of the dialogue passed into Hollywood legend. During the film Mae West referred to him as 'warm, dark and handsome', and she also explained:

'You know, I . . . I always did like a man in uniform, and that one fits grand. Why don't you come up sometime and see me? I'm home every evening.'

Then, pausing only for a moment: 'Come up. I'll tell your fortune. Aw, you can be had.'

His quizzical half-surprised reaction and faintly raised eyebrows proved that he was capable of far more than the flashy, wooden parts he had so far been given by Paramount. It showed he was one male star whom the greatest leading ladies could pursue without looking foolish.

Released in February 1933, *She Done Him Wrong* was an immediate success, taking more than two million dollars at the box office and pulling Paramount, temporarily, out of its dire financial straits. The studio had been contemplating an amalgamation with MGM and the sale of their seventeen hundred cinemas throughout America, but Mae West's success decided them to shelve that plan. Within three months Mae West was being paid $300,000 for her next picture, plus $100,000 for the screenplay; even Garbo could only command $75,00 a picture. Within a year Mae West was the highest paid performer in Hollywood, living in lonely luxury in her Ravenswood apartments with her pet monkey, Boogie. Grant, however, was put back into the straitjacket that Paramount had built for him. Brooding at his house near Griffith Park, he became convinced that the studio were intent on keeping him from playing any part which would allow him to establish his own personality on the screen, and the thought made him increasingly moody. He also felt angry that Gary Cooper could pick whatever parts he liked. On their side, the studio could claim that they were being generous. Had they not just raised his salary to $750 a week? Cary Grant determined from that moment never again to rely on the patronage of a single studio.

His suspicions were confirmed when he had completed *Woman Accused* with Nancy Carroll and was immediately put into a new John Monk Saunders flying story, to be called *The Eagle and the Hawk*, opposite Fredric March. The film was originally to have starred Gary Cooper and George Raft, but neither actor would do it. In desperation Paramount had added Carole Lombard to the cast, but even that bait failed. *Variety* called the film 'strictly a formula story'. Even in his next film, *Gambling Ship*, there was no sign that Paramount would allow Grant to do anything more than look handsome. This time he was to be the glamorous gangster who falls for Benita Hume in what *Variety* described as 'a fair flicker'.

Then Paramount put him back with Mae West in her next film *I'm No Angel*, casting him as the rich playboy who falls for her circus performer. It had few of the memorable exchanges that had enlivened *She Done Him Wrong*, but bad reviews did nothing to prevent its success at the box office. It earned Paramount two and a quarter million dollars, even more than their first film together.

In less than a year Cary Grant had appeared in the two films which had saved Paramount from bankruptcy and had earned them more than four million dollars; he felt he deserved recognition. But even as the fan mail began to flood into Paramount and the fan magazines took him up, Grant remained as canny as ever in not revealing anything about himself. He was charming to anyone whom the studio sent to interview him, but he carefully avoided saying anything about himself or his past life. The head of magazine publicity for Paramount, Julie Lang Hunt, was so irritated by his evasiveness that she complained bitterly about him after she had left the studio. 'Cary Grant will never know peace as long as his name spells news,' she wrote. 'His fixation, or complex, or mania (it is difficult to find the exact words for Cary's hyper-sensitivity) was planted during his childhood, and it was unwittingly nurtured during a strangely solitary youth.' She added that even Randolph Scott had told her: 'I can't tell you why but I've seen him actually lose sleep and weight after reading certain items that touched upon his personal life and thoughts.'

The insecure boy who had gratefully pulled on the debonair mask of a handsome leading man was still afraid that it might slip. As he had once admitted to Hunt, his poise on the stage did not translate to his ordinary life. 'When I go a-courting,' he had told her 'it's a very sad performance.'

'In spite of all his splendid training in poise and fluency for the stage, he becomes grotesquely tongue-tied, absurdly flustered, and unbelievably awkward when he plays the role of Romeo in real life,' the lady concluded.

Nevertheless Grant knew his responsibilities to Paramount. Every studio liked its young leading men to be seen out and about with the young actresses on their payroll. It was good for business, and it encouraged the audience to think that the romances they were seeing on the screen might be happening in real life. Although it was not actually written into their contracts, every dashing young leading man had to be accompanied by a suitably beautiful young lady. Cary Grant accepted the tradition happily enough. He and Randolph Scott would regularly be seen escorting new starlets around Hollywood, just as they would entertain them at home on Saturday evening or arrange to meet them at the Santa Monica Beach Club on Sunday.

But in addition to this, Grant cultivated an elegance that later became one of his trademarks. He made sure his suits were carefully chosen and tailored. He avoided hats because he felt he never looked good in them. He sunbathed whenever he had the opportunity, in order to preserve his tan. He kept his clothes neatly labelled in his wardrobe, always putting them back on their hangers as soon as he had finished wearing them, and he chose what to wear with obsessive precision. He wanted to create a reputation for elegance, just as he wanted to avoid being photographed smoking, even though he often consumed three packets of cigarettes a day. He had no wish to spoil the screen image he was required to adopt.

One of the young women he met regularly in public was Virginia Cherrill. She had been Charlie Chaplin's leading lady, the blind flower girl, in his silent film *City Lights*. Frail, with hazy, china-blue eyes and striking blonde hair, Miss Cherrill was another regular visitor to the American Legion fights on Friday evenings. It was there she had first met Chaplin and first saw Cary Grant. She had arrived in Hollywood from her native Chicago in 1928, at the age of twenty, after a disastrous first marriage to a lawyer named Irving Adler. As Chaplin recalled, she once met him at the Beach and asked, 'When am I going to work for you?'

'Her shapely form in a blue bathing suit did not inspire the thought of her playing such a spiritual part as the blind girl,' Chaplin wrote, 'but after making one or two tests with other actresses, in sheer desperation I called her up. To my surprise she had the faculty of looking blind.'

The seventy-second scene in which Chaplin as a tramp

avoids a traffic jam by getting into a limousine and out of it the other side, only to be mistaken for its owner by the blind flower girl, was one of the most famous debuts in Hollywood and the highlight of a short career.

By 1930 Virginia Cherrill had become a familiar figure at Hollywood's smartest parties. She had been engaged to the comedian and dancer Buster Webb, but had broken it off; and she had been described by Louella Parsons as 'Hollywood's greatest beauty'. In 1932 the town and the film industry had been convinced that she was about to marry the New York millionaire, William Rhinelander Stewart, who was regularly described as one of the most eligible bachelors in America. Amidst a barrage of publicity she had followed Stewart to Tahiti, where he was a guest on Vincent Astor's yacht, the *Nourmahal*, and Louella Parsons had reported breathlessly in Hollywood: 'The ceremony will be performed by Vincent Astor who, as captain of the boat, has the authority of performing the marriage at sea.' In spite of the speculation, however, Miss Cherrill was not married to 'Willie' Stewart on the *Nourmahal*, or even on Tahiti. Indeed, she never married him. Within a week she had returned to the Fox Studios to resume work under a contract she had signed a year earlier.

She soon found compensation. As Cary Grant began to tell his friends, 'I fell in love with her the moment I saw her.'

To a man normally so nervous in the presence of women, and apparently so settled in his bachelor life, Miss Cherrill proved a revelation. She was outgoing, cheerful, endlessly energetic, the embodiment of all the actor thought he should become. He began to pursue the petite blonde girl, contriving to meet her at other people's parties, inviting her to the parties he gave at West Live Oak Drive. Worldly, glamorous and yet still attractively frail, she seemed to him the ideal companion.

By the time *I'm No Angel* opened in New York in September 1933 and broke the Paramount Theatre's box-office record in its first seven days, Cary Grant was beginning to wonder whether Virginia Cherrill might not make him a wife. She could be infuriating, certainly, with her apparent desire to make him jealous and her habit of leaving California at a moment's notice for Honolulu, Palm Beach or Mexico City to 'forget the whole thing'. But she was also captivating. The more she ran the more he pursued. On one occasion he even chartered a tug to meet her cruise liner, the *Monterey*, as it steamed back to Los Angeles from Hawaii. The young man who had hardly had a girlfriend in his life before was infatuated. But he still had his responsibilities to Paramount. The studio had not had one of its best years, and Zukor had decided that they needed a major production ready for the Christmas rush at the box office. He wanted a family film, which everyone would regard as a classic, and had settled on *Alice in Wonderland*. A small talking version of the story had done quite well at Christmas two years before, and Zukor decided to put every available star into his new version.

To begin with, he had launched a nationwide search for the girl to play Alice. It persuaded nearly seven thousand young girls to apply, and then held a series of heavily publicized auditions. The studio's final choice had been Charlotte Henry, a seventeen-year-old from New York with no acting experience. Gary Cooper was to play the White Knight, Charlie Ruggles the March Hare, and Jack Oakie Tweedledum. The great silent comedian, Ford Sterling, was to be the White King, W. C. Fields Humpty Dumpty, and Edward Everett Horton the Mad Hatter. Originally the studio had also wanted Bing Crosby to play the Mock Turtle and sing Lewis Carroll's song about 'beautiful, beautiful soup' but he could not be persuaded to agree. In his place the studio drafted Cary Grant. The part must not threaten his reputation as a handsome leading man, so he was to play it in a large wooden mask and be dressed as a turtle. When the film opened in New York just before Christmas the *New York Times* admitted that it was a 'marvel of camera magic and staging' and thought 'the lachrymose Mock Turtle highly amusing'. But the production was only a minor success, not the major triumph Paramount had hoped for.

As the filming of Alice came to an end, Cary Grant decided to take a vacation from Hollywood. For a start he went on a trip to Phoenix, Arizona, at the suggestion of Howard Hughes, who had bought a slice of land there, but he and Virginia Cherrill, who had taken separate rooms at one of the hotels, were discovered by a group of reporters.

'We are not going to marry,' Grant told them angrily. Within a fortnight he had flown to New York to see her off on a trip to England, and less than ten days later he followed her there himself. But Virginia Cherrill was not the only woman Cary Grant had left America to see. He had also decided to find his mother.

5

Mr Hughes and Miss Hepburn

'In the real dark night of the soul it is always
three o'clock in the morning.'

F. Scott Fitzgerald, *The Crack Up*.

In the postwar England of Woolworths, cigarette coupons,
and the wireless and factory girls who looked like actresses,
Elias Leach felt uncertain and a little out of place. He was
sixty-one, a saddened, weary man with white hair, who kept
his memories at bay with whisky and the comfort of a pipe.
He had survived as a tailor's presser in Bristol, but it had
never been an easy life. His wife was still in the institution to
which he had committed her almost twenty years before,
and he had lived quietly for more than ten years with a
woman whom he could never legally marry but who had
nevertheless borne him a second son.

Although his eyes sparkled in the public bar when he
talked about the success of an actor called Cary Grant, even
he found it difficult to link that far-away figure with the
small, dark-eyed boy who used to sit opposite him at the
parlour table on a winter's evening playing Ludo. He had
barely seen him since, but now he was coming back.

In the past few years some members of the family had
taken to suggesting that perhaps it was time for Elsie Leach
to leave the mental institution but if anyone was going to
decide that, Elias believed it should be her son, Archie. He
had told him so when he had written to him in California.
They would decide between them what to do about the
fierce, wiry woman who had ordered both their lives.

In November 1933 Cary Grant swept into Bristol like a visiting Maharaja, arriving at Elias's door complete with chauffeur, suntan, immaculately cut dark suit, and an accent his father did not recognize. He was friendly and obviously delighted to see Elias again, but the elderly man felt shy and uncertain in the presence of someone so rich and so relaxed.

'You'll be going to see your mother?' he said finally.

It was the question Archie Leach had been waiting for, but Grant hesitated a full eight weeks before making up his mind. Then he decided. Elsie would be fifty-seven on 8 February 1934. They would celebrate her birthday together.

Cary Grant has never spoken publicly about his feelings as he walked into a small, bare room in the mental institution to be introduced to a woman who was called his mother, but whom he had not met for twenty years, choosing to let it remain a private grief. He never knew exactly how ill she had been, or even if she had ever been legally certified as insane; his father had hardly spoken about it.

At that meeting there was just his need for her to recognize him, and to be proud of him. The resentment he had felt all those years before when she had disappeared was pushed into the background. They were as hypnotized by each other as they had always been, the ferociously determined mother and the anxious-to-please son. But now there was irony, as the internationally known film actor confronted the one person whom he wanted above all to acknowledge his success, but who was also the one person who had hardly been aware of it. To Elsie Leach he was just her small son, and she would never forget it. Neither would he. His mother came back into his life as swiftly as she had left it, as though there had hardly been a moment's pause since they had seen each other last.

The other decision he had to make during those weeks in England was also vital to his life. Should he marry Virginia Cherrill? She was a beautiful companion, who had been there to meet him in England, and he thought they both wanted marriage. But there were so many things to take into account. Did he *really* want to be married? Would it mean he would have to live a different way?

For more than a month Grant dithered. He bought a marriage licence, but postponed the ceremony. He told his cousins that he would like to marry in London. He talked about going back to California, where he was due to start filming again in February, but decided against it. He fretted about what would be the right thing to do, but he could not quite bring himself to do anything. Instead, he contented himself with introducing Ginny, as he called her, to his uncles and aunts at a party for them all at the Grand Hotel, Bristol. Finally he decided he would get married in London, once he had visited his mother. But what would his mother say? The stiffness she had always had was still there, and so was the terror he had always felt that she would not approve of what he did. He told her, however, and the effort, once made, gave him an intense feeling of relief. Part of his life had returned.

Now there wasn't much time. Passages were booked on the French liner *Paris* from Plymouth the next day; indeed he and Virginia had even wondered whether it might not be more romantic to be married by the ship's captain once they were out in the Atlantic. But as they had already struggled with the regulations at London's most famous registry office, Caxton Hall in Westminster, they agreed it was probably best to go through with it there. The Registrar had insisted on seeing Virginia's divorce papers, which had been sent over specially from Chicago.

When he arrived at Caxton Hall, just before eleven o'clock the next morning, 9 February 1934, there was a mêlée of reporters, photographers and sightseers outside the ornate stone building, but there was no sign of his future wife. Desperate, he ran into the building and telephoned her.

'We're getting married, aren't we?'

Slightly stunned she said, 'When?'

'Right now.'

It took her barely a quarter of an hour to reach the office and even less time for the Superintendant Registrar to conduct the brief formal ceremony which married Archibald

Alec Leach to Virginia Cherrill, the former Mrs Irving Adler. But the day's confusion was not over. As Grant and his new wife pushed their way towards the two taxis that he had ordered to wait for them, and he shouted, 'We're so happy' to the struggling reporters, the new Mr and Mrs Cary Grant were separated. He had managed to push his bride into the first taxi and the cab had promptly set off, leaving him standing in the middle of the jostling, heaving crowd. As he pulled himself gratefully into the second taxi he heard the cab driver say, 'Better follow the other one, hadn't I?'

Reunited at the hotel, where they collected their luggage before rushing off to Paddington Station to catch the boat train, Grant vowed not to submit himself to such public scrutiny again. As he and his wife stepped off the train in Plymouth he told the waiting reporters: 'We are both due back in California for work on pictures, and so our honeymoon will be short.'

Cary Grant was not altogether pleased to be back in Hollywood. He felt misunderstood and misused by Paramount, yet unable to escape; and he felt crushed by Gary Cooper. Nevertheless, within twenty-four hours of stepping off the Santa Fe Chief at Pasadena, he was back on the Paramount lot to start shooting his third film with Marion Gering as director, and his second opposite Sylvia Sidney, another light comedy called *The Thirty-Day Princess*. Once again he was dressed up in white tie and tails, this time as a newspaper publisher. When he asked if there might ever be a chance of his being cast as other than a matinée idol in parts which asked him to do something more than change into evening clothes, the studio retaliated by loaning him out to Joe Schenk, who had been appointed president of United Artists a year before. A loan-out by one studio to another was usually designed as a punishment to bring recalcitrant performers into line, and this instance was no exception.

Born to be Bad, scripted by the actor Ralph Graves and directed by Lowell Sherman, suffered from the attentions of the film industry's new Production Code which Mae West's ribald dialogue had helped to create. Nine minutes were cut out of the film at the last minute, and only Grant's co-star, Loretta Young, survived unscathed in what the *New York Times* called a 'hopelessly unintelligent hodge podge'.

Still determined to keep him playing mindless leading men, Paramount immediately put Grant into another light romantic comedy, *Kiss and Make Up*, also destined to sink without a trace. There was just one small variation from the formula. Instead of white tie and tails he was now dressed in a cravat and black jacket as the manager of a Paris beauty salon.

Again without a pause Paramount cast Grant in another equally lightweight comedy, *Ladies Should Listen*, based on a play which had not even survived a provincial try-out, let alone the ordeal of Broadway. In three months he had made four films, all of them disastrous. In despair he asked to be loaned out by Paramount to appear in the film MGM were planning of a new book about Fletcher Christian's mutiny on the *Bounty* in 1789.

Louis B. Mayer's brilliant protégé, Irving Thalbert, had approached Grant about the possibility of his playing a good supporting role in the picture. He had already reached agreement with Clark Gable to play Christian and with Charles Laughton to play Captain Bligh, although he had to spend a great deal of time persuading Gable that his slightly bandy legs would not look ridiculous in naval knicker-bockers. The thirty-four-year-old Thalberg, who had just recovered from an illness, was determined to mark his return to production with a major success and Cary Grant knew he could do what was required of him.

Adolph Zukor, however, refused to release him. 'Grant stays at Paramount,' he replied. Reluctantly Thalberg announced that Franchot Tone would be given the part he had had in mind for Grant, and Zukor arranged for his leading man to appear opposite Elissa Landi in a film with an operatic background, *Enter Madam*. All Grant had to do was to look right, Zukor argued, and he could play opposite all the beautiful young women in Hollywood. What had he got to complain about?

As the heat of that 1934 summer began to die away Cary Grant's private depression began to deepen. The insomnia he had always suffered grew worse, and he started to spend evenings morosely searching through his press cuttings. There had been depressions before, but even Randolph Scott had never seen him in one as bad. 'No-one seems to care about me,' he would mutter bitterly to a mystified Virginia Cherrill. The unfortunate girl found herself no longer married to one of the most publicly charming young actors in Hollywood but sharing a house with a man possessed by private fears and obsessed with imagined slights, a husband who refused to let her out of his sight but would not go anywhere with her, a depressive who could not bear to hear how well Clark Gable seemed or Gary Cooper had performed.

Virginia Cherrill became a prisoner of her husband's moods. When they did go out it was often only to see Howard Hughes or Randolph Scott. If they were invited to one of the huge parties at the beach house that William Randolph Hearst had built for Marion Davies, Cary would insist that she talked to no-one except him. If she refused, he would accuse her of preferring other people's company to his. He would shout at her, but before the shouting began he would start to whistle. She came to dread that whistle. 'I don't know how much longer I can go on,' she told her mother.

There was no doubt in the mind of Mrs Blanche Cherrill Wilcox about what her daughter had to do: she had to leave her husband. If there was one more outburst she was simply to walk out of the house. Within a fortnight she had done so. In the middle of September 1934 Virginia Cherrill told her mother that the apparently debonair Cary Grant was not only given to murderous rages, but he had even threatened to kill her if she did anything he did not approve of.

Three days later an apologetic but cheerful Cary Grant arrived to visit his wife at her mother's house. It had all been a terrible mistake, he told her, he would never behave so abominably again, he could not live without her, she was the most important person in his life. Wouldn't she come back to him? The slight, twenty-six-year-old blonde looked at her dashing handsome husband, kissed him on the cheek and walked out to the Packard with him. The reconciliation did not last. Just two weeks later, on Saturday, 20 September 1934, less than seven months after their marriage, Grant sat through a dinner party he had already told his wife he did not want to attend, looking sullen and drinking steadily. When they got home he accused her of ignoring him. 'I won't stand for it,' he told her, moving across the room towards her. Just after midnight Virginia Cherrill ran out of the house and went back again to stay with her mother.

As she told Louella Parsons the next morning, 'Whether it is permanent or not is up to Cary. I will not discuss the reason for our trouble, but things have been going from bad to worse. I left Cary two weeks ago and consulted a lawyer, but we later patched things up and I hoped we might make a go of our marriage because I am in love with my husband.'

To the habitually secretive Cary Grant the telephone calls from the news agencies and the newspaper gossip columnists were an ordeal. Finally he told Louella Parsons, 'It's silly to say that Virginia and I have separated. We have just had a quarrel, such as any married pair in Hollywood might have . . . I hope when I get home tonight that Virginia will be waiting for me.'

She wasn't. She never went back to him. Gradually the realization that he had once again been abandoned by a woman he had been prepared to trust swept over Grant, followed by the feelings of guilt he had never lost since his mother had first disappeared. On the night of Wednesday, 4 October, less than a week after their final argument, he started drinking alone and then began telephoning his friends. As the evening wore on he became less and less coherent. Shortly after two o'clock in the morning he telephoned Virginia Cherrill and asked her to come back to him.

'You've never understood, everything will be different. Let's try again.'

His young wife tried to explain that they had already tried again.

'This will ruin me,' she heard him telling her, before he hung up.

Greatly worried she called back, to be answered by the houseboy. She asked him to go into the bedroom and see if her husband was all right. When the manservant got inside the room he discovered Grant lying unconscious across the bed, wearing only his underpants and with a bottle of pills marked poison on the bedside table. In a Hollywood only too familiar with suicide, the manservant immediately assumed that his master had killed himself. At 2.28 a.m. on 5 October he telephoned for an ambulance.

Within an hour the police surgeon, Dr C. E. Cornell, was using a stomach pump on the unconscious actor in the Hollywood Hospital. Because of the pills he had seen beside the bed, he was convinced he was fighting for Cary Grant's life, yet no trace of poison was found in the actor's stomach, and when he had woken up in hospital a desperate Grant had persuaded Paramount's publicity department to put out a story that the whole thing had been a prank. 'I had been at a party with friends, and when I got home they tried to play a joke on me,' he explained. 'They called the police. It was all a colossal gag.' In a town where gossip was still the second most important industry, he had no wish to see his reputation for carefree charm threatened by reports of a miserable suicide attempt. He was badly frightened.

Later – but not till some considerable time later – he came nearer to admitting the true story. 'I had been drinking,' he said finally. 'Most of the day before and all that day. I just passed out. The servant found me, became alarmed, and called the cops. You know what whisky does when you drink it all by yourself,' he added. 'It makes you very sad. I began calling people. I know I called Virginia. I don't know what I said to her, but things got hazier and hazier. The next thing I knew they were carting me off to the hospital.'

*

While the Hollywood gossip columns speculated about a reconciliation, Cary Grant moved back to West Live Oak Drive and the friendship of Randolph Scott. He returned to work, first in the well-worn white tie and tails as Elissa Landi's long-suffering but devoted husband in *Enter Madam*, then – at last – to a change in style as an aviator intent on breaking world speed records in James Hood's *Wings in the Dark*, where his co-star was Myrna Loy, straight from *The Thin Man*. In the age of Lindbergh and air races, the film's flying sequences were designed to attract the audience. But it was Grant's performance as the flyer blinded in an explosion and forced to rely on a guide dog which attracted the best reviews. The *Hollywood Reporter* called him 'splendid' and *Variety* added that he 'tops all his past work' when the film opened at the beginning of February 1935.

In spite of this breakthrough he could not shake off the suspicion that Paramount saw him only as a pale imitation of Cooper. When, hard on the heels of *The Lives of a Bengal Lancer*, the studio announced that they intended to use him in yet another film about the North-West Frontier, he was more than ever convinced he would never succeed in escaping his rival's shadow. Bitterly, he concluded that he was unlikely to succeed at Paramount, and Zukor, for his part, was coming round to the same opinion. For him, Cary Grant was an ungrateful actor who could not recognize his own luck.

Another blow was the impression created by the proceedings at his acrimonious and extremely public divorce. On 11 December 1934, Virginia Cherrill told a Los Angeles Superior Court judge that she had been forced to pawn her jewellery just to live in the two months since she had separated from her husband. Looking nervous and drawn she told Judge William Valentine: 'I was obliged to pawn my engagement ring and wristwatch and borrow on my automobile,' and went on: 'I have been unable to work because of ill health and needed the money with which to live.'

Asking the court to order her husband to pay her $1,000 a month, she explained that he had only given her $125 in the ten weeks since their separation at the end of September. 'I must look presentable if I work,' she said.

When his own lawyer cross-examined him on the witness stand, and asked why he believed his wife could get along on just $150 a month rather than the $1,000 she was claiming from him, Grant replied tersely: 'She managed to before we were married, she could do so again.' Hardly the remark his public would have expected of Grant, the screen hero, especially as he had already explained to the court that Paramount had in fact agreed to extend his contract by one further year from 1 January 1935, at a salary of $1,250 a week.

Judge Valentine was not impressed by the actor's testimony nor by his apparent charm. He awarded Virginia Cherrill maintenance of $167.50 a week, or $725 a month, pending the full hearing of their divorce, and he ordered that the actor should put up a $20,000 bond to guarantee that he would pay both her and her lawyers, and that he should be prevented from disposing of any property until the divorce hearing was settled. Even that was not the end of it. A few days later Virginia Cherrill's lawyers returned to court again to amend their original complaint still further. The new complaint – extensively reported in the Los Angeles newspapers – included the assertion that Grant 'drank excessively, choked and beat her, and threatened to kill her'. A nervous Paramount knew the time had now come to act: the charge that the charming actor might have beaten up his wife and threatened to kill her must never come to court. On Christmas Eve lawyers for both sides agreed on a settlement, but the damage had been done.

As soon as the filming of *Wings in the Dark* was completed at the end of January 1935, a shamefaced and reticent Cary Grant left Hollywood for a trip to England. Once more he intended to visit his mother on her birthday and, though he could not know it, his decision was well timed, for this would be his last chance of seeing his father alive.

Dressed in a blue suit and wearing dark glasses, Virginia Cherrill arrived at Judge Charles Haas's courtroom in Los

Angeles shortly before ten o'clock on the morning of 26 March 1935, and not long afterwards began what one newspaper was to describe as 'a long list of the asserted shortcomings of her actor-husband'. When she slipped off her glasses and tucked them into her bag, she looked even more the sad waif than she had done as Chaplin's blind flower girl.

She began by telling the court that she had been ill. Then her lawyer Milton Cohen asked her to describe her life with Grant.

'He was very sullen and disagreeable,' she said softly, causing the judge to bend forward towards her. 'He refused to pay my bills. He told me to go out and work myself and then discouraged me every time I had a real opportunity. He was like this almost from the first.'

The newspaper reporters crowded together in the back of the courtroom could hardly believe their ears as Virginia, taking out a lace handkerchief, continued in her soft voice: 'He told me he didn't care to live with me any more, a number of times.'

'Please speak a little more loudly, Mrs Grant,' the judge interrupted. The frail blonde nodded and smiled at him.

'He was sullen, morose and quarrelsome in front of guests. He falsely accused me of not appreciating him or his efforts.'

The courtroom was silent when Judge Haas asked if her husband drank.

'Yes, he was inclined to drink quite a bit all during our marriage.'

Virginia was allowed to step down from the witness stand. Her mother took her place, testifying that she had indeed seen her son-in-law insult his wife, just as Virginia had described. In less than an hour her daughter had been awarded a divorce.

There were no claims for maintenance to settle, so Virginia Cherrill walked gratefully into the spring sunshine to talk to a small crowd of reporters and photographers. She was twenty-seven and had been married just over thirteen months. In a little under two years' time she would become, by her next marriage, Countess of Jersey. For the moment, however, she just kept on looking frail.

In the year of his divorce from Virginia Cherrill Grant made one more picture for Paramount, *The Last Outpost*, in which he played a rather foolish British officer on the North-West Frontier rescued by Claude Rains as another British officer working behind the Indian lines. As *Variety* tartly noted when the film was released in October 1935: 'Due to the Italo-Ethiopian squabble, the general run of picture-goer may not relish watching hordes of archaically equipped blacks being mowed down by machine guns.'

Grant's rescue from Paramount came through Howard Hughes, who, since his own divorce from his wife Ella in December 1929, had become another of the most public bachelors in Hollywood. The gossip columns speculated about his relationships with the actresses Billie Dove, Ida Lupino and Marian March, but in 1935 he had met an angular, independent and uncompromising actress who was to put all these in the shade.

Tall, bony, and unconventional, Katharine Hepburn had been involved with her agent Leland Hayward until he had suddenly married the highly-strung actress Margaret Sullavan and she became fascinated by Hughes, a millionaire since the age of nineteen. Both neurotically shy of publicity, the couple had a great deal in common, including a liking for swimming, golf, tennis and aeroplanes. As Hughes said in a rare interview later: 'She was brilliant, kind, devoid of sham and pretence and a woman who couldn't give a damn for convention.' It was inevitable he would talk to her about his friend Cary Grant.

Several years later Grant also would recall his own fascination on meeting her. 'She was this slip of a woman, skinny, and I never liked skinny women. But she had this thing, this air, you might call it, the most totally magnetic woman I'd ever seen, and probably have ever seen since. You had to look at her, you had to listen to her, there was no escaping her.

'But it wasn't just the beauty it was the style. She's incredibly down to earth. She can see right through the nonsense in life. She cares, but about things that really matter.'

Hepburn, who had been tempted to go to Hollywood from the New York stage when David O. Selznick, then in charge of production at RKO, had offered her a contract worth $1,500 a week, had achieved remarkable success in her first four films under his guidance. *A Bill of Divorcement, Christopher Strong, Morning Glory* and *Little Women* had all been box-office hits and *Morning Glory* had won her an Oscar in 1933, when she was still only twenty-six. Since Selznick's departure for MGM to join his father-in-law Louis B. Mayer, her career had faltered. She had made three terrible films at RKO, and had only stopped a disastrous run with the help of a new director, George Stevens, and the film *Alice Adams*. Her choice of this story, about an awkward girl who wants to make her way in the world but feels she lacks the poise to do it, encouraged RKO to let her pick her own films in future. Her next choice was an adaptation of Compton Mackenzie's 1918 novel, *The Early Life and Adventures of Sylvia Scarlett*, and Cary Grant was to play opposite her.

Loosely based on part of the Crippen murder case, the story concerned the escape of an embezzler from France to England, accompanied by his daughter who wears men's clothes to escape detection. George Cukor, a former Broadway director who had also been taken up by Selznick at RKO, had wanted to make the film for several years. At least one major studio had already turned it down but Hepburn, who was Cukor's close friend, was enthusiastic and so, therefore, was RKO. Hopes ran so high that Cukor even suggested the young Evelyn Waugh should be hired to write the script and he paid the great English actress Mrs Patrick Campbell a fee of $2,500 for playing a small part. But Waugh was not hired and Mrs Campbell never appeared.

Cary Grant was introduced to Pandro S. Berman, who was due to produce the film, in June 1935. Both Berman and

Hepburn liked him, and told Cukor they thought he might be able to play the part of Jimmy Monkley, the English confidence trickster. Berman had already borrowed Randolph Scott from Paramount, and he didn't believe he would encounter much opposition when he asked to borrow Grant. As Berman explained later: 'He had no chance at Paramount. He was a failure there. I gave him a part because I'd seen him do things which were excellent, and Hepburn wanted him too.' Grant was to be paid $15,000 for the six weeks of filming, considerably more than his regular Paramount contract but much less than Hepburn's $50,000.

When filming got under way in the late summer of 1935 on the coast north of Malibu, Howard Hughes flew to the location in his private plane. He arrived for lunch and left shortly afterwards, and according to Brian Aherne everyone thought the sudden appearance of the remote, awkward and slightly deaf Hughes something of a joke. The effect of Cukor's direction on Grant was remarkable. He seemed to blossom. His public cockiness deepened into true confidence in front of the camera. With Cukor's help he began, for the first time, to use his natural intelligence to create a character. Instead of constantly fussing, as he had so often before, he began to relax.

'For once they didn't see me as a pleasant young man with black hair, white teeth and a heart of gold,' Grant said later. And, as Cukor was to remember: 'It was the first time he began to feel that an audience could like him. He had an awfully good part (he'd had a lot of experience but he'd never arrived) and he suddenly felt on firm ground with his knowledge of the whole milieu. I think he gave a remarkable performance and that started him.' Hepburn herself maintained that 'George brought the Archie Leach out in Cary Grant.'

He was virtually the only success in *Sylvia Scarlett*. Berman calls it now, 'Probably the worst picture ever made.' After the first preview in front of an audience he rushed round to Cukor's Hollywood home to attack him for making the film in the first place. 'The audience didn't know what it was about,' he told the director, 'and not one person understood a word of those English accents.'

'Now don't you worry,' Hepburn burst in, 'because we're going to make it up to you for this. We're going to make another picture for you, for free!'

'Oh my God, no,' Berman replied. 'Anything but that. I don't want either of you ever to work for me again.'

Cukor never made another film for RKO, but when *Sylvia Scarlett* opened at the vast 6,200-seat Radio City Music Hall in New York on 9 January 1936, Cary Grant received his first really enthusiastic notices. A good director, and a part which captured something of his wry arrogance as well as utilizing his strutting sharpness, encouraged André Sennwald to say in the *New York Times*: 'Cary Grant, whose previous work has too often been that of a charm merchant, turns actor in the role of the unpleasant Cockney and is surprisingly good at it.' *Time* magazine added: '*Sylvia Scarlett* is made memorable by a role that almost steals the show from Miss Hepburn's androgyne: Cary Grant's superb depiction of the Cockney.'

Ironically, Grant was not in America to savour his first critical success as an actor. In the middle of November he had sailed for England on the Cunard Liner *Aquitania* to film *The Amazing Quest of Ernest Bliss* at Elstree Studios. He wanted to be near his father, whose health had been failing steadily since his last visit, and Alfred Zeisler's decision to direct a new version of E. Phillips Oppenheim's famous light comedy about a rich young man who takes a number of lowly jobs for a bet, provided the opportunity. He was only just in time.

On 2 December 1935, a week after shooting on the film had begun, Elias Leach died in his Bristol home of what the death certificate described as 'acute septicaemia' and 'gangrene of the bowel'. Perhaps the strain of suppressing the memory of his wife's illness, and then of living a separate life in her shadow with another woman and another child, had eventually taken its toll. He was just sixty-three.

Cary Grant had not seen his father again, but he was there

to mourn the man he called 'my first hero', and to bury him in the local churchyard. 'He was a wise and kindly man and I loved him very much,' was his son's epitaph – for once, straight from the heart.

6

The Awful Truth

'Yet, despite his appearance, he was really a
very complicated young man with a whole set
of personalities, one inside the other like a
nest of Chinese boxes.'

Nathaniel West, *The Day of the Locust*

Elsie Leach still turned her head away when he bent down to
kiss her. Only her cheek was left for his lips to brush against.
Stiff-backed, with her shawl drawn around her shoulders,
and her fingers turning the small gold locket at her throat,
she looked exactly as he remembered her.

After his father's funeral Grant had brought her to London with him while he went back to filming at Elstree. In the
evenings he would try to get to know the tiny woman who sat
opposite him, an upright fifty-eight-year-old, with her hands
clasped in her lap, looking straight ahead of her. It was not
easy. He would ask her if she would like to come to California, and hear her reply:

'Never lived anywhere but Bristol. Don't want to: only
place I know! I'm too old to go gallivanting off thousands of
miles.'

Although he would never admit it, even to himself, her
answer was a relief. The personality he had so gratefully
accepted in Hollywood had to be preserved. The tall carefree
Cary Grant would never have had a tiny elderly woman
sharing his house. His mother was a part of his life that had
to remain isolated in the past, sealed away from the public
world of parties on the beach or crowds swarming round

outside Grauman's Chinese Theater before a première. The two halves of his life could never be allowed to mix. Elsie was the mother of the insecure Archie Leach. But the only progenitors of the dazzling Cary Grant were the cinema screen and the audience in their darkened seats. They had truly created him, and could with equal ease consign him to dust.

When he wasn't trying to talk to his mother, Grant consoled himself in the company of his co-star on *Ernest Bliss*, Mary Brian. Unusually for one of his girls, she was brown-haired and almost as small as his mother. A former beauty contest winner who had acted in small parts in Hollywood over the years, and had even appeared briefly in Howard Hughes's 1931 version of *The Front Page*, she was in regular work at the studios, but few executives thought she would ever break into the Claudette Colbert class. Grant had suggested her for the part in *Ernest Bliss* as she was already filming in England. She on her side was captivated by his gallant manners. Inevitably it was only a matter of weeks before one London evening paper was reporting that they had fallen in love. When any journalist asked him about this, he took to answering: 'Well, don't you think Mary is an awfully nice girl?' It was just the sort of pleasantly flip turn-aside that Cary Grant might have made on the screen.

By the time filming was finished at the end of January it was clear that *The Amazing Quest* was not going to be a success. The script was written by John Balderston, who had worked on *Lives of a Bengal Lancer*, but Alfred Zeisler's direction had not suited the comedy. When it finally opened the verdict of most critics was that the silent version of the story, made fifteen years before with Henry Edwards, was greatly to be preferred.

Grant settled his mother back into a house in Bristol near enough to her brothers for them to be able to look after her. He also made a sensible arrangement with the local paper whereby, in return for their agreement not to bother her, he promised to give them an exclusive interview every time he visited her. If his mother seemed now simply a statue from his past, an embodiment of a life he wanted to forget, so did she regard him. Sometimes a messenger boy would knock at Elsie's door and, more often than not getting no reply, would shout through the letter-box: 'Got another cable from Hollywood for you, Mrs Leach!' But Elsie would sit unmoving in her kitchen and only after the messenger had gone would she walk down the hall and pick up the message, folded in its brown envelope, from the mat. As the evening wore on she would walk round the house bolting every outside door, and then locking each of the doors inside until she finally felt it was safe to go upstairs. Once in the bedroom of her sturdy stone-terraced house she would lock herself in and push the dressing table across the door, as a barricade. In the silence of her room she would read the message from this man who called himself her son. But she took to telling anyone who asked about him: 'I am a virgin.'

On the surface life in Hollywood had hardly changed for Cary Grant. He and Randolph Scott still lived together in West Live Oak Drive, and worked for Paramount. But an upheaval was pending.

Randolph Scott had decided to marry a girl he had known since they were both children. She was Mariana du Pont, a member of the millionaire du Pont family. Married once before, she had left her first husband in 1925 and returned to Virginia. She now made it clear that she would not move to California. Randolph made it equally clear that he would not move back to the South. It was a strange match for an actor who was making his name playing buckskinned cowboys, and he waited five months after signing the marriage certificate – in Charlotte, Virginia, in March 1936 – before announcing the news in Hollywood.

As Louella Parsons remarked some years later: 'Scott's marriage to the du Pont heiress was always a mystery. She was years older than Scott and completely uninterested in the theatre. From the beginning the disparity in their tastes and years was so marked that Randy's closest friends never understood why he, a successful movie star, had married this very rich woman, who had been his neighbour in Virginia.

As Parsons, however, did not point out, it made no difference to the actor's life in Hollywood. He and Cary Grant continued to share their house. When the new Mrs Scott came to Hollywood she stayed with them, but that happened so infrequently that their routine of life was hardly affected.

In fact they were even considering moving to a new home on the beach. Built by producer Joseph Schenk and his actress wife Norma Talmadge, the house they had in mind had seven bedrooms, a swimming pool and an uninterrupted view of the Pacific. It had another advantage. The beach at Santa Monica was becoming one of the most fashionable and relaxed areas of Los Angeles. Hearst had built a substantial beach house there; so had Irving Thalberg. It was becoming increasingly popular with actors anxious to escape the fierce summer heat of Hollywood. Norma Talmadge had told them that she was prepared to sell the house, and they had already agreed between themselves that 'the first to marry should have the right to buy out the other'. Randolph Scott had no intention of exercising his right. Within two years he announced that he and his wife had separated on friendly terms, adding: 'It's a case of being separated too much, which did not prove compatible with marriage.' In the meantime Cary Grant had been perfectly content to sit in the soft sunshine on the beach, deepening his suntan.

The closeness of the two men's relationship led to some unkind gossip, but they remained unaffected. Scott had inherited his friend's role as Mae West's foil in her latest film *Go West, Young Man*, and the studio were talking about using the two men together again in a new film about the Arctic, to be called *Spawn of the North*; they were to co-star with Carole Lombard. Before the project got under way, however, the studio changed its mind and gave their parts to Henry Fonda and George Raft.

The suggestion that both men were what was politely

known as born bachelors was scotched by the belated announcement of Randolph's marriage, and by speculation that Cary Grant might be marrying Mary Brian. Cary, however, pooh-poohed this idea. Mary was 'a lovely person', he told *Photoplay*. 'We get along together and I'm terribly fond of her, but there's no engagement. There hasn't been any talk of marriage at all. It'll be five years before I'm ready for that.'

Meanwhile both men's relationship with Paramount was beginning to break down. Scott would depart soon. The studio were prepared to co-operate with Cary Grant to the extent of letting him play a detective in *Big Brown Eyes*, his first film for them in 1936, but the experiment was not a success. He seemed uncertain in the role of a wisecracking private detective who was occasionally forced into fist fights. Nor did relations improve when the eighth Academy Awards ceremony was held at the Biltmore Hotel in Hollywood, in March 1936. *Mutiny on the Bounty*, the film for which Zukor had refused to release him to MGM, not only won the Oscar as Best Picture, but also saw its three male stars, Gable, Laughton and Franchot Tone (in the part Grant would have had) nominated for the Best Actor Award, though none of them actually won it. Few Paramount films had been nominated at all, and only the scriptwriters Ben Hecht and Charles MacArthur won an Oscar for the studio with their original story for *The Scoundrel*.

As it happened, at the moment when the Oscars were being announced Grant was making his first film for MGM, but the fact that Paramount had chosen this sensitive moment to lend him to Louis B. Mayer only increased his bad humour. The film was *Suzy*, to be directed by George Fitzmaurice. Grant was a French flying ace in love with Jean Harlow, Howard Hughes's discovery and now one of MGM's biggest stars, who was to play an American showgirl. He had not been anxious to appear in the film anyway. He knew the script had been worked on by Horace Jackson, Alan Campbell and Dorothy Parker, and he now discovered that it had been given to Leonore Coffee to rescue. Indeed he was only persuaded to make it after Coffee and MGM's Eddie Mannix had told him that they were confident it could be tailored to fit his image. In the end the flying sequences (re-used, to save money, from Hughes's *Hell's Angels*) and a memorable song, 'Did I Remember?', which Grant sang and which was later released as a record with considerable success, were the film's only redeeming features. Harlow's sexuality was wasted in an innocent role and in spite of the endless amendments to the script, Grant did not look or feel at ease.

Back at Paramount, he was once again cast opposite his co-star from *Big Brown Eyes*, Joan Bennett, in Paul Gallico's newspaper story, *Wedding Present*. Once again his unease at the studio was reflected in his performance on the screen, and the *New York Herald Tribune* called his playing 'lackadaisical'.

Grant's depression deepened. So did the studio's, some of whose executives were beginning to say privately that they doubted whether he would ever find a part that satisfied him – 'He's such a perfectionist, how could he?' – while others doubted whether he could tell a good script in the first place – 'He's never had any judgement.' – criticisms that would be repeated many times in the future.

In the autumn of 1936 Grant decided that *Wedding Present* would be his last film for the studio. Now that *Spawn of the North* had been scrapped, he would not walk on to their lot again; any offers from elsewhere would be preferable. So, as *Wedding Present* opened in New York, coinciding with Roosevelt's 'present' from the American electorate in the form of a landslide victory and a second term in the White House, Cary Grant started to plan what to do next.

In five years at Paramount he had made twenty-one films, yet he had never felt appreciated. As he told his friends privately: 'I seemed to be getting all the roles Gary Cooper didn't want. I saw no reason why Gary and Cary should be confused.' Publicly he contented himself with remarking that, 'They had a lot of leading men with dark hair and a set of teeth like mine, and they couldn't be buying stories for all of us' – but that only concealed the anger he felt at the studio's assumption that he could never be more than a matinée idol. In future he would try to make sure that there were always at least two studios interested in him, and he would see to it that any contract he signed would give him everything he wanted, including a choice of scripts and the correct billing. Plus, of course, the sort of salary he felt he deserved.

Paramount no longer cared whether he stayed or not. They had already offered to increase his salary to $2,500 a week, which in their view was extremely generous, but they had refused his demand to choose his own films. They knew that only Mae West and Marlene Dietrich had this right, and it was not a privilege they saw any reason to extend to an actor who in their view had not proved himself.

While the negotiations were going on they agreed to his suggestion to be lent out to Harry Cohn's Columbia to star in a musical called originally *Interlude*, with the opera singer Grace Moore. The new film later re-titled *When You're in Love*, promised well. It was based on a script by Robert Riskin, who had written Frank Capra's two award-winning comedies, *It Happened One Night* and *Mr Deeds Goes to Town*. But if Grant had hopes that the new film would do for him what those two had done for Clark Gable and Gary Cooper he was due for a disappointment. Cohn had agreed that Riskin could direct the film himself and Riskin, alas, was no Capra. The film flopped – and once again Cary Grant had failed to prove that he could choose himself a box-office hit. Next, RKO asked to borrow him for a film biography of the Wall Street pioneer Jim Fisk, and the studio accepted gratefully. Edward Arnold, borrowed from B. P. Schulberg's own production company, was to play Fisk, while Grant and Frances Farmer were to have two roles for which RKO had toyed with the idea of getting William Powell and Ginger Rogers. With a script that amalgamated two different books and had been worked on by six different writers, *The Toast of New York* turned out to be the biggest financial disaster of the year for RKO, losing more than $500,000. But, by the time it opened in 1937, Grant had already signed his first contract after leaving Paramount.

At this point in his career Cary Grant was far from certain precisely what sort of actor he intended to become. In private he would admit: 'I suddenly became aware that I wasn't sure what or who I was on the screen. As an actor I had a thin veneer of sophistication, carefully copied from Noël Coward, I'd casually put my hand in my pocket and it would get stuck there with perspiration.' Yet he was anxious to protect the only role he felt comfortable playing, his conception of Cary Grant, the star. That role had a vital part in his life, for it reassured him that he did know who he was. He clung to it like the wreckage of a sinking ship – to keep him afloat – and it made his reaction to any change of role distinctly ambivalent. He wanted to prove he could act, and he had enjoyed playing in *Sylvia Scarlett*, but he was also afraid to let go of the only existence he felt he had, as the slightly flashy, voluptuous-looking young man of *Blonde Venus*.

'I don't think any non-actor can ever know how horrifying it is to hear your voice, see yourself, see how you walk,' was how he put it. The well-dressed young player, whose suits were tailored at Howes and Curtis in London, who whistled when he was nervous and who was edgy in the company of strangers, liked to cultivate the appearance of confidence and the certainty of a star even if it concealed an almost paralysing insecurity and awkwardness. As Frances Farmer, his co-star in *The Toast of New York*, eventually wrote: 'He was an aloof, remote person, intent on being Cary Grant, playing Cary Grant . . . He remained polite but impersonal.' If anyone he did not know and trust penetrated the image he wanted to present to the world then his existence was in danger.

That was one good reason why he had been so keen to move to the Talmadge house on the beach at Santa Monica. 'I like the ocean because no-one can build a house in front of me or plant a high hedge or put up a billboard,' he said. When he and Randolph Scott had moved in, he had col-

lected all the photographs of himself taken in the previous
five years in Hollywood and had put them in his own
bathroom. He thought that was an appropriately private
place for them.

As 1936 drew to a close, Grant's luck turned. In the past two
years talking pictures had come out of their own depression.
In the United States an estimated eighty-one million people
each week went to one of 18,200 cinemas. Audiences were
growing rapidly again throughout the world and in the next
year Hollywood produced 778 feature films, more than it
had done since its golden year of 1928.

The New Deal had begun to revive America's spirits, and
as it did so the kind of films made in Hollywood began to
change. In the new Hollywood disasters could always be
overcome, no-one need be downhearted all the time, and
even a fool could marry the daughter of a millionaire if he
had a mind to do so. All that was needed for survival was to
laugh. The film critic, Pauline Kael, later described the
change by saying: 'Comedy became the new romance, and
trading wisecracks was the new courtship rite. The cheerful
whacked-out heroes and heroines had abandoned sanity;
they were a little crazy, and that's what they liked in each
other.'

Heroines were no longer the aimless, lovelorn girls, yearn-
ing after unattainable men. They were independent, good
arguers, and looked on members of the opposite sex not so
much as their protectors as their prey. Marriage for them
could be a cheerful sparring-match, on the pattern of *The
Thin Man* with William Powell and Myrna Loy, and
courtship the saucy affair that Clark Gable and Claudette
Colbert had made it in *It Happened One Night*. Fast and
feminine were the words for Hollywood comedy by the end
of 1936, with the verbal wit of Broadway increasingly
leavened with farce and slapstick. When farce was mixed
with drawing-room comedy it was no longer vulgar; it was
'screwball'. All the emphasis was on speed, and the directors
who emerged to capture the new style came from the

traditions of the old two-reel comedies. Improvisation became the name of the game. As Kael put it: 'No longer so script-bound, movies regained some of the creative energy and exuberance – and the joy in horseplay too – that had been lost in the early years of talkies.'

For Cary Grant that strain of comedy was to provide the perfect expression of the personality he needed to sustain. He became the man every woman wanted to pursue – but was never quite able to catch. Elusive and attractive at the same moment, the eternal bachelor who always seemed to be divorcing his wife, he was charming, witty and alluring, an image which perfectly suited both Cary Grant and his audience.

As he looked out across the sand towards the Pacific from the patio of the new house in Santa Monica in the first weeks of 1937, Cary Grant felt relaxed. His new agent, Frank Vincent, had agreed to pay Zukor $11,800 for the residue of his contract with Paramount, and he had negotiated a four-picture deal with Harry Cohn at Columbia which would guarantee $50,000 each for the first two films and $75,000 each for the next two. Thus, so long as he made films at the rate of two a year or better – and in 1936 he had made five – he would be certain to earn at least $100,000 in the year. This was not quite in the Claudette Colbert bracket of $300,000 a year, but it was still not a bad sum for an actor who had started in Hollywood at $450 a week, and who had not appeared in any list of top box-office attractions. By careful steering he had turned his own financial corner. Within a few weeks his contract with Columbia was signed. It would start on 1 May 1937 and would last for two years. It would also make him a star at last.

Beside their new pool Grant and Scott entertained. One regular visitor was the small blonde girl who had become one of RKO's biggest stars, Ginger Rogers. She had been friendly with Howard Hughes, who called her 'a delight to be with', but Grant had become keen on her himself. Another persistent caller was the comedy producer Hal

Roach, who lived next door, and who had taken to dropping in most lunchtimes for a swim. Sometimes pompous, perhaps from knowing himself a contributor to the success of Harold Lloyd, Our Gang, and Laurel and Hardy, Roach had just bought the rights to Thorne Smith's ghost story *Topper* with the idea of turning it into a film. Hollywood had recently developed a taste for ghost stories, particularly ones which had a comic element, after the acclaim heaped on Alexander Korda and Robert Donat for *The Ghost Goes West* and Noël Coward's success in *The Scoundrel*.

Lying beside the swimming pool one lunchtime Roach discussed the idea with Grant. They played a game of casting the leading roles. Roach suggested W. C. Fields should be Topper, while Grant suggested Jean Harlow as the ideal Mrs Kerby.

'And I wish you'd play the husband,' Roach told him.

'You can't afford me. I know I can get $50,000 for a picture at Columbia.'

But Roach did not give up. For days he badgered Grant, until finally he persuaded him to make the film.

'Oh what the hell. I'll do it. If it makes dough, you can pay me my price,' Grant told him.

It was a risk, but a small one. Columbia did not want him to start filming until 1 May, and in the meantime he thought he could finish *Topper* quickly. It was only a few weeks' work and if a major studio picked up Roach's production he was certain to get paid.

Finally Roland Young was signed to play Topper, and Constance Bennett to play Grant's ghostly wife, Marion Kerby. Roach persuaded Grant to allow Bennett top billing, which he did with reluctance. He also raised a string of objections, in his best fussy manner, when the film's director, Norman Z. McLeod, with whom he had worked on *Alice in Wonderland*, suggested to him a change in the way he should play his part.

'I had had another idea,' Roach said later. 'When the Kerbys go off together to do their good deed Grant tells Bennett to watch her step, and she asks why. He tells her:

"After all, you're my wife." But she protests. "Oh no, the contract says 'till death us do part'." The vision I had was that Grant would be trying to make love to and court his own wife. Out of the clear blue sky Grant refused and said: "I'm not going to run after Constance Bennett."

'I talked to him but he was adamant. He was not too keen on Bennett and, I think, the real story was that at that particular time he was in love with Ginger Rogers, and he didn't feel like making love to anyone else.' Nothing Roach could do would persuade Grant to change his mind.

When the film was released by MGM in July 1937 the *New York Times* called it 'rather a heavy consignment of whimsy to be shipping from the printed page to the screen'. But Cary Grant did not care. He had lost interest. He had been paid his fee, and had started work on his first film at Columbia with the gifted but decidedly eccentric director, Leo McCarey.

Amiable, shrewd and unrepentantly individualist, McCarey looked remarkably like the man he was now to direct. He was just a little shorter and slightly fuller in the face, but like Grant he had brown eyes and a slightly wistful expression which could turn to a smile. Born and bred in Los Angeles, the son of one of California's best-known boxing promoters, he had started in movies as soon as he had finished law school, beginning as a third assistant director to Tod Browning and going on to direct himself. It was McCarey who had put a thin, worried-looking comedian called Stanley Jefferson and a chubby cheerful extra whom he nicknamed 'Babe' together in 1924, and had seen them triumph as Laurel and Hardy; and by the beginning of the 1930s his reputation was established. In 1933 he joined Paramount, where his many films included *Duck Soup* with the Marx Brothers, but the studio was never happy with him. He liked directing without a fixed script, improvising scenes as he went along, and playing the piano on the side of the set whenever he needed inspiration. It was not a style to which Zukor and Paramount warmed.

Late in 1936 McCarey and Grant met on the corner of Vine Street and Melrose Avenue, not far from the newly opened Hollywood branch of the Brown Derby Restaurant. 'Paramount let me go, I'm on the streets,' was Grant's opening remark, to which McCarey replied: 'And what do you think I'm doing? Paramount kicked me out too.' Unknown to each other they were both negotiating with Harry Cohn's Columbia, but neither let on about this. It would have spoiled the dramatic effect.

Columbia's Frank Capra had admired McCarey's work, particularly with the silent comedian Harry Langdon (who failed to recapture any of his phenomenal success once McCarey had left him). McCarey knew Capra's genius but did not know that Harry Cohn was trying to prove to himself that he could do without Capra.

When Columbia Studio finally hired McCarey, early in 1937, they gave him an uninspiring project to start with, a script by Dwight Taylor based on Arthur Richman's 1922 play, *The Awful Truth*, which had been filmed twice before. Undismayed, McCarey tore up the script and started writing another with Vina Delmar. The two of them would sit in McCarey's car outside Columbia's studios on Hollywood Boulevard working out ideas. Neither Cohn nor McCarey knew exactly who to cast in the film, but as Cary Grant had just joined the studio and Irene Dunne, who already belonged to them, had just been nominated for an Academy Award as Best Actress for her comic role in *Theodora Goes Wild* and was waiting for her next film, they decided to put the two stars together.

When filming started in early June 1937 Cary Grant was as neurotic as he had been at the start of *Topper*, and McCarey's habit of arriving on the set in the morning bearing bits of script written on scraps of brown wrapping paper, and then improvising as he went along, did not prove exactly soothing. Within a day he was asking Harry Cohn if he could change his part to the smaller one being played by Ralph Bellamy, and finally, in desperation, he offered Cohn $5,000 to let him out of the picture entirely.

Shortly before his death in 1969 McCarey was asked why Grant wanted to get out of the picture.

'He had no sound judgement.'

How then was he convinced to stay in?

'The studio had to convince him. I was so mad at him I wouldn't talk to him.'

Indeed McCarey was so angry when he heard about the five thousand dollars that he said to Cohn: 'Well, if that isn't enough I'll put in five myself and make it up to ten.'

Cohn told them both to get on with the picture, but McCarey's view of his star actor did not change; even thirty year laters he still described him as nervous, uncertain and insecure:

'Cary Grant was impossible.'

Irene Dunne also remembered: 'Cary used to be very apprehensive about nearly everything in those days. So apprehensive in fact he would get almost physically sick. If the script, the director, an actor or a particular scene displeased him, he would be greatly upset.'

Despite all this, McCarey's methods transformed Grant's career; they seemed to create a nervous tension in the actor that inspired him to comic improvisation. McCarey's technique was simple. In one scene he simply told Dunne to open the door of her apartment, discover Grant standing there and say with surprise, 'Well, if it isn't my ex.' He didn't tell Grant what to reply, but the latter was spurred into making one of the film's best remembered lines: 'The judge says this is my day to see the dog.'

The story of a man who divorces his wife but then wants her back again bore echoes of his own marriage to Virginia Cherrill, and another of his improvisations in the film came even closer: 'Trouble is with most marriage, people act as if they were in prison. They exaggerate every little trifle – and the first thing you know they're in the divorce court.' At another point he put in: 'You can't have a happy married life if you're always suspicious. There can't be any doubts in marriage . . . marriage is based on faith, and when you've lost that you've lost everything.' Just as Cukor had discovered the sly cockiness of Archie Leach in Cary Grant, so McCarey now revealed the uncertain reach for understanding behind his aloof arrogance.

With the wire-haired fox terrier Skippy from *The Thin Man* series now playing the Warriners' dog, Mr Smith, and Ralph Bellamy splendidly cast as Dunne's hapless suitor, the comedy was acclaimed when it was released in October 1937. Divorce had never before been considered a subject for film comedy. Now Otis Ferguson, critic of the *New Republic*, echoed every other when he described *The Awful Truth* as 'a foolishness that doesn't go wrong or strained'. The *New York Times* said that 'Its unapologetic return to the fundamentals of comedy seems original and daring,' and *Variety* called the film 'Cary Grant's best fast light comedy performance to date.' It perfectly captured the sentiment of the time that marriage could be fun and unreasonable all at once.

The success immediately sent Harry Cohn searching for a new script for Grant and Dunne, but it was almost two years before they played together again. Soon after *The Awful Truth* had finished shooting, Cary Grant had agreed to make three films for RKO, to be spread over the next two years. He was to be guaranteed an initial fee of $50,000 plus a percentage of the profits of each picture he made, which was to amount to at least another $50,000.

In April 1937, as its first film made under the new contract, RKO decided to adapt a short story from *Collier's* magazine, to be written by a studio scriptwriter, Hagar Wilde, and directed by Howard Hawks. A slightly mysterious figure in Hollywood, Hawks had started in comedy, but had gone on to make dramas, including *Scarface* for Howard Hughes. Articulate, with sharp features and a precise determination, he preferred, as a film-maker, to tell good stories rather than make intellectual points. Impeccably dressed, and 'a-purr with melodrama' as his friend Ben Hecht said of him, he had joined RKO in 1936 as a producer and director at the request of the production head, Sam Briskin.

When the *Collier's* story of a shy palaeontologist whose life is turned upside down by a fey New England heiress was first mooted, RKO and Hawks knew they wanted to use Katharine Hepburn, who was still under contract to the studio but whose career had hardly recovered since *Sylvia Scarlett*. After it she had made three more films for RKO, which turned out to be flops, and some executives had begun to ask why she was still under contract. Gregory La Cava's *Stage Door*, in which she had played opposite a sarcastic Ginger Rogers, had restored some of their confidence, but commercially the film had not been a success. Depressed, Hepburn still relied on the encouragement of Howard Hughes, who had followed her recent tour in a stage version of *Jane Eyre* in his private plane.

RKO wanted her to play the scatty New England heiress, Susan Vance, but were uncertain who to cast opposite her as the palaeontologist. Sam Briskin had talked about Ray Milland, but a loan could not be arranged. Fredric March had been mentioned and so had Leslie Howard, and Robert Montgomery. But with the success of *The Awful Truth*, Briskin and Berman decided to use Hughes's other friend, Cary Grant.

However, when Hawks went to talk to him about the role of the palaeontologist, Grant replied: 'I won't know how to do a thing like that. I wouldn't know how to tackle it. I'm not an intellectual type.'

'You've seen Harold Lloyd, haven't you?' riposted Hawks.

'That gave him a clue – the innocent abroad,' Hawks later recalled. Hepburn, by contrast, was fascinated with her part. 'She had not been trained in comedy at all, but she wanted to play comedy.'

Playing the heiress with a pet leopard called Baby – which can only be subdued by the song, 'I can't give you anything but love, Baby' – Hepburn dragged Grant through the film at a frantic pace. RKO were worried about its unromantic tone. The script called for Grant to wear glasses and they didn't like that. They were aware that his fan mail had increased from two to fourteen hundred letters a week since *The Awful Truth*, and they wanted to see it continue growing. They were also anxious for Hepburn's hair not to look too unruly. They wanted the comedy to be gentle and glamorous, rather than just slapstick.

Bringing Up Baby cost more than a million dollars to make and Grant was finally paid more than $120,000 for his work. When the picture opened it was greeted warmly, but not rapturously. Frank Nugent in the *New York Times* said: 'Miss Hepburn has a role which calls for her to be breathless, senseless and terribly terribly fatiguing. She succeeds, and we can be callous enough to hint it is not entirely a matter of performance.' *Time* magazine added that its slapstick was 'irrational, rough and tumble, undignified, obviously devised with the idea that the cinema audience will enjoy (as it does) seeing actress Hepburn get a proper mussing up'.

Before it opened, however, Howard Hughes had come to the financial rescue. He had bought it in a job lot of ten films from the studio and sold it on to the Loew's chain, but this shrewd act did nothing to alleviate the resentment that was brewing up towards Hepburn. As the filming of *Baby* finished, shortly before Christmas 1937, the Independent Theatre Owners Association were compiling a list of the ten performers who were 'box-office poison'. Katharine Hepburn was the first name on their list, followed by Joan Crawford, Garbo and Dietrich. When the film, destined to become a cult two decades later, failed to win the hearts of the audience and lost the studio $365,000, RKO began to give up their last hopes that Hepburn would succeed.

In contrast *The Awful Truth* had established itself as a box-office success, and a favourite in the movie business. When the 1937 Oscar nominations were announced in February 1938, it appeared in no fewer than five categories, including that of Best Picture. Irene Dunne and Ralph Bellamy were both nominated for individual awards, and Leo McCarey was nominated as Best Director. Significantly the only one of its stars not nominated was Cary Grant – an omission which some observers put down to his unselfish playing but which others felt should more properly be attributed to his aloof disregard for his fellow performers. Unfair perhaps; yet his reputation in the industry for being a moody, financially demanding perfectionist was gathering force.

Nevertheless the film made his name, and Columbia were anxious to follow up its success with another Dunne and Grant comedy. They wanted to remake Philip Barry's Broadway hit of 1928, *Holiday*, which had first been filmed in 1930 with Ann Harding, Richard Ames and Mary Astor, and they had asked George Cukor, who had just left MGM after making *Camille* for Irving Thalberg, to direct it. Cukor, however, had his own ideas. Katharine Hepburn had understudied Hope Williams in the original Broadway run, and she had even used the part for her first Hollywood screen test. Cukor urged the studio to give Hepburn the part of Linda Seaton. When Harry Cohn asked RKO if they could borrow her the studio agreed. It was the first time they had ever loaned Hepburn. As a result the aristocratic, gentle Irene Dunne, who had won Oscar nominations in each of the past two years, lost the part she had wanted desperately. As she recalled later: 'When I heard about it I cried the entire weekend.'

With a script by Donald Ogden Stewart, a friend of Barry's who at one time had even appeared in the play himself, and Sidney Buchman, *Holiday* was an examination of the wealthy Seton family of New York, through the eyes of Johnny Case, a young man who finds himself engaged to their spoilt daughter, Julia, but who finds himself more attracted to their other daughter, Linda. When it had first appeared in 1928, Case's message in the play that 'I don't want to make any more money, I want to enjoy life' had seemed startlingly impudent. A decade later, after a depression which had seen thousands ruined, it seemed curiously irrelevant. Unlike McCarey or Hawks, Cukor asked Grant to play his part as the idealistic and romantic Case almost straight, capitalizing on his training as a straight man in vaudeville. As he had in *Sylvia Scarlett*, Cukor encouraged Grant to relax on the screen.

As the *New York Times* remarked when the film opened at the Radio City Music Hall in June 1938: 'Mr Grant's Mr Case is really the best role, although it is quite possible that neither Mr Barry nor Columbia saw it that way.' But Hepburn's performance as his foil did not endear itself to everyone. The *Times* commented, 'We cannot get over our feeling that her intensity is apt to grate on a man, even on so sanguine a temperament as Cary Grant's Johnny Case.'

Holiday did not turn out to be the triumph Columbia had hoped for. It was overshadowed by some of the year's other films; notably *Alexander's Ragtime Band* with Tyrone Power; Walt Disney's unforgettable cartoon *Snow White*; *The Adventures of Robin Hood* with Errol Flynn; and *Boys' Town* with Spencer Tracy. Indeed neither of the first two pictures Cary Grant had made in 1938 had particularly endeared him to his two new studios, nor had they proved financially very successful to them. Nevertheless after making $175,000 in 1937, and on the way to making more than that in 1938, Grant felt himself established. He had always measured his success by the financial returns on his films, rather than the critical reaction to them, and he always would. Despite his nerves in the early stages of filming and previewing, when the reviews were printed and the experience of filming was over, he would remember only the grosses. To some actors it seemed an alarming, impersonal trait, but to Grant it made its own sense. It also, on this occasion, alerted him to the fact that his next film needed to be a big box-office hit.

Pandro S. Berman at RKO had nursed the idea of making a film from Kipling's poem 'Gunga Din' ever since his mother had first read it to him. It had been in the pipeline at the studio since 1936 when Ben Hecht and Charles Mac-Arthur had prepared a script and Howard Hawks had been brought in to produce and direct. Hawks felt it would be ideal for Ronald Colman or Robert Donat, with Spencer Tracy as the second male lead, but when the production head, Sam Briskin, approached Colman he was turned down. Early in 1937 Ray Milland and Franchot Tone had been talked about, but again nothing had been settled, and the project had been put off as Hawks had started on *Bringing Up Baby*. But Berman, as he himself explained, 'took Hawks off *Gunga Din* after he spent too much money on *Bringing Up Baby*, and put in George Stevens as producer and director in his place.' Stevens had made a series of films for RKO, including *Alice Adams* with Hepburn and *Swing Time* with Astaire and Rogers. A former cameraman with Roach, he had worked with McCarey on Laurel and Hardy and had a reputation for being sensible, and easy to get on with.

Grant was now to play the lead as Ballantine, the sergeant determined to give up the army and marry; Douglas Fairbanks was to play his friend, Cutter; and Victor McLaglen, who had won an Oscar in 1935 for his role as Gypo Nolan in John Ford's elegant film *The Informer* at RKO, was to play MacChesney, the third member of the trio. But once again no sooner had the film begun than Grant became twitchy. He went to Berman and asked if he could play Cutter instead of Ballantine. 'I think it's going to make a wonderful part and I want the part Doug is supposed to have,' he explained.

Slightly mystified that Grant should want the second lead, Berman nevertheless agreed that his principal star could change roles, and he also agreed that he could call the character 'Archibald Cutter'. As he had agreed to pay Grant $125,000 for his original part compared with $117,000 for the Fairbanks role and $62,000 for McLaglen's, Berman felt no compunction in making the switch that Grant desired. It was a switch which proved justified for Grant, unlike the decision to replace Hawks by Stevens: far from going through quickly, the film took a hundred and four days to complete, seventy-five of them on location; it became the most expensive film RKO had ever made, at a cost of more than $1.9m.

In spite of this, *Gunga Din* became one of RKO's biggest box-office successes, earning the studio more than $3.1m even though a foreign release was severely hampered by the impending war in Europe (indeed it did not reach England until after the Second World War). Only *Jesse James*, starring Tyrone Power, Henry Fonda and Randolph Scott, earned more money in the United States in 1939. The simple flag-waving story of three friendly sergeants caught in the midst of a Thuggee rebellion in India, which Stevens later said was so simplistic that 'If I'd experienced another year I'd have been too smart to make it,' took more money than Judy Garland's *The Wizard of Oz*, Greta Garbo's *Ninotchka*, or even Robert Donat's magnificent *Goodbye Mr Chips*.

With *Gunga Din*, which he would later call one of his two favourite films, Cary Grant confirmed his reputation in Hollywood as an actor who could draw an audience into the cinema. In just under two years he had been transformed from a promising young leading man into a star.

Star or not, in the silence of his house on the beach at Santa Monica Cary Grant took to sitting alone in the evenings, looking through his press cuttings, with no sound to listen to except the distant rumble of the Pacific breakers. It made an incongruous scene – Hollywood's Grant sitting alone on the enormous eight-foot-wide bed Howard Hughes had given him, studying reports on his life and career. When dusk fell, and the cicadas started croaking on the hillside behind him, he felt proud but a little frightened. The Cary Grant that Archie Leach had gratefully become just six years earlier was now a star recognized by millions of cinema-goers throughout the world, earning a quarter of a million dollars a year at a time when the average weekly wage was less than $100, and with a status that enabled him to choose his studios, directors and co-stars.

He was also a man who found difficulty in sleeping and was often off his food. The stiffness and uncertainty he had always felt with strangers had not vanished with his success; neither had his shyness with women. On the screen he had developed confidence, even daring, but off it he was still the superficially charming but privately rather morose man who had left Paramount in a huff. *Once Upon a Honeymoon*, the film he was to make with Ginger Rogers, had to be postponed when both she and the director, Leo McCarey, fell ill; by now Grant's feelings for Fred Astaire's enchanting dancing partner had gradually evaporated but the break with her had in no way affected his public image. He was as popular with Hollywood's many beautiful young actresses as he had always been; indeed, he seemed constantly pursued by them, even if he still preferred to retire to the solitude of 1018 Ocean Front Avenue and the companionship of Randolph Scott.

There were only one or two women whom he was prepared to see regularly. One was Phyllis Brooks, a five-foot-five-inch blonde from Boise, Idaho, with something of the waif-like look of Virginia Cherrill; she had been under contract to both Fox and Universal but her career had never quite taken off. She had been on location at Lone Pine with Grant while he had been working on *Gunga Din*, and he had treated her as he had once treated Virginia – at one moment showering her with presents, flowers and telegrams, at another virtually ignoring her.

In short, he was as cagey as ever. He was a member of the large British community in Hollywood, but even then he would tend to remain the distant outsider rather than an active participant. As Joan Fontaine, who was then still married to Brian Aherne, recalled later: 'The Beverly Hills British Colony was a tight little island,' whose 'self-appointed king' was, in her view, Ronald Colman, 'while the self-appointed queen was Basil Rathbone's wife'. Among the other members were Sir Cedric Harwicke, David Niven, Merle Oberon, Christopher Isherwood, Ray Milland, C. Aubrey Smith, Boris Karloff and Cary Grant. In fact Hollywood was about to go through a distinctly British phase, with plans to film a string of British novels including *Mrs Miniver*, *Pride and Prejudice*, and *Wuthering Heights*.

Most British visitors ended up seeing Grant. As Hedda Hopper reported in the middle of 1938, 'Noël Coward and Cary Grant took up where they left off about a month ago – I mean Noël as Cary's houseguest.'

Like many other Hollywood reporters, Hopper was suspicious of Grant. *Photoplay* had already called him 'zany, like a fox', and had reported that the RKO press office had taken to warning anyone against ever enquiring about his personal life. His reticence in the face of Hollywood's curiosity meant that most of what was printed about his private life was speculation. The columnist Ruth Waterbury pointed out: 'The moment you touch on heavy things, the moment you query him about his faith or his life or his ambitions, he turns the subject aside with a deft insinuation that another cocktail would help and that the weather of Southern California is really tremendous.'

Still, he seemed to like Phyllis Brooks. After his trip to England at the end of 1938 he telephoned her from the liner *Normandie* to tell her he hoped she would come and meet him in New York. He was going to stay with Bert Taylor, whose sister Dorothy had become one of Hollywood's most famous hostesses, the Countess Di Frasso, and when Phyllis arrived he was openly pleased to see her. 'I think we'll probably get married but I'm not sure,' he told one reporter. 'We may get married tomorrow or we may have a quarrel and never speak to one another again. I will not live my life for a lot of journalists. I'm not going to marry a girl to make some newspaper a good headline.' And he stalked off to a waiting car. As he did so another woman with whom he had had dinner on the voyage quietly disembarked. She was Barbara Hutton, heiress to the Woolworth fortune.

Even though he was paying income tax at the rate of eighty-one cents in the dollar, Cary Grant had not lost the appetite for work. Before *Gunga Din* had opened to long queues in New York in January 1935, he had already returned to Columbia to make another film with Howard Hawks, but this time he insisted that he was going to play a truly serious role. 'You've got to show 'em you're versatile in this business or you're licked,' he declared; and he chose a role which showed him primarily in the company of men. In so far as women featured in 'Plane Number Four', as the project was first called, they were there to observe the masculine world.

In Hawks's story of a small South American town where Grant was in charge of a tiny airline running mail across the Andes, he seemed happier than ever before. The film, later to be retitled *Only Angels Have Wings*, allowed Hawks to experiment with the tough, wisecracking female character that was to appear in so many of his later films. Jean Arthur, playing the showgirl who ends up falling for Grant, was the prototype of Bacall in *To Have and Have Not* and *The Big Sleep*. And the atmosphere of male camaraderie which Hawks created in the film was to emerge again a decade later in his film *Red River*. Men in Hawks's world were professionals who played down the dangers of their lives. Grant caught the mood, and gave one of his finest performances. Of the film itself *Newsweek* was to say that it 'outranked most of its plane-crashing, sky spectacular predecessors' at the 'tail end of an overworked screen cycle'.

The film was not released until May 1939, but in the interval Grant had resisted all suggestions that he should appear in another comedy. Instead he had gone back to RKO to make a love story. To be directed by John Cromwell, who had made his reputation in 1934 with a brilliant version of Somerset Maugham's *Of Human Bondage*, the new film, *In Name Only*, based on Bessie Brewer's novel about a loveless marriage in which the husband is driven into the arms of a neighbouring widow, was melodrama, but good melodrama. But still Grant started fretting before shooting had even begun and was miserable during the making. He was so unhappy that after the film was finished and he had gone on a visit to England, George Schaeffer, president of RKO, was provoked to send him a telegram. 'Dear Cary,' it ran, 'you sure paid a terrible price with all your worries and fears. You can come home now. The picture is really a hit.'

The critics agreed. *Time*, more guarded than most, said: '*In Name Only* will puzzle cinemagoers who thought they knew just what high jinks to expect when screwball Cary Grant falls in love with screwball Carole Lombard.' But the novelist Graham Greene, then writing on films in the English weekly *The Spectator*, added: 'This is a well made depressing little picture of unhappy marriage. It is often sentimental, but the general picture which remains is quite an authentic one – a glossy photographic likeness of gloom.'

Grant himself had begun to feel gloomy about his own prospects of marriage. He had agreed with Phyllis Brooks that they should announce their engagement but then told her that he did not feel he could go through with it. She was very distressed; he relented; the news of their disagreement leaked out. Within two months their engagement was officially broken off. Afterwards she told Louella Parsons: 'We talked it over. He has his career, in which he is deeply interested, and I have just now had a contract offered to me.' The contract was in England. RKO had not been sorry to see her leave their star alone, and Cary Grant did not allow the loss to worry him unduly. He was too busy working on his third film with Howard Hawks, yet another remake of Ben Hecht and Charles MacArthur's 1928 stage hit *The Front Page*. It had first been filmed in 1931 by Howard Hughes, from whom Columbia had now bought the rights. Hawks had got the idea for remaking the film at a dinner party. He had asked a woman guest to read the part of Hildy Johnson, the reporter who wants to leave the paper, while he himself had read the part of Walter Burns, the editor who doesn't want her to go.

Hawks had tried to get a series of actresses to take on the part of Johnson. He had approached Ginger Rogers, Irene Dunne and Jean Arthur, but all three had turned him down. (Indeed Dunne had also turned down his offer of Jean Arthur's part in *Only Angels have Wings*.) Finally Harry Cohn suggested that he should consider Rosalind Russell, then under contract to MGM, and fresh from her success in George Cukor's film *The Women*. A trial lawyer's daughter from Connecticut and a devout Catholic, Rosalind Russell was to become one of Cary Grant's few very close women friends. Articulate and engaging, she was also determined, and as soon as she saw the script of *His Girl Friday*, as the film was to be retitled, and realized that it gave all the funniest lines to her co-star, she hired herself an advertising copy-writer to improve her part in the script.

Grant, who was already being encouraged by Hawks to ad lib whenever he wanted to, suddenly found himself in competition with Russell. As she put it later: 'He'd be standing there, leaning over, practically parallel to the ground, eyes flashing, extemporizing as he went, but he was in with another ad libber. I enjoyed working that way too.' At one point Grant was so taken aback by one of her replies that he looked across at Hawks behind the camera to ask: 'Is she going to do that?' The director so enjoyed his pained expression that he left the remark in the film, just as he left in some of Russell's best additions to the script, including her magnificent response when Grant, playing Burns, says: 'Some day that guy's going to marry that girl and make her happy.' 'Sure,' she replies. 'Slap happy.' Russell said later, 'Cary was terrific to work with because he's a true comic, in the sense that comedy is in the mind, the brain, the cortex.' She knew he was also lonely. 'He was between girls then . . . During the making he used to call up and ask if I would like to go jigging.' There was never any suggestion of romance between them, but Grant felt comfortable in her company.

Just before Christmas 1939 the London agent Freddie Brisson, who had become one of Grant's friends in England, came to stay with him in Santa Monica. Brisson was anxious to be introduced to Rosalind Russell, but although Grant invited her for Christmas and the New Year she never turned up, leaving the two men to celebrate the holiday on their own. Every time Grant asked Russell, 'Do you know Freddie Brisson?' she had taken to answering: 'No. What is it – a sandwich?' until one evening, when she arrived at the house to collect her co-star to go dancing, he introduced them. Within two years he was best man at their wedding.

The chemistry between Grant and Russell in *His Girl Friday*, and Hawks's use of rapid dialogue in which the words were allowed to overlap with one another, helped to make it his most memorable performance. If he had seemed a little too anxious opposite Dunne, and a little too frenzied opposite Hepburn, with Russell he relaxed. His natural arrogance provided the perfect film version of the Walter Burns character, who seemed to capture some of his own secret desire to manipulate women. When the film was released in January 1940 Frank Nugent commented in the *New York Times*: 'Cary Grant's Walter Burns is splendid, except when he is being consciously cute.' And *Variety* described him as doing his role 'to a turn'.

In the course of *His Girl Friday* Grant had ad libbed angrily: 'The last person who said that to me was Archie Leach, just a week before he cut his throat.' It was hardly a joke. Cary Grant had begun to wonder whether he should not cut Archie Leach's throat. It was becoming increasingly difficult for him to get back to England: war had been declared between Great Britain and Germany in September 1939, and he was considering the possibility of becoming an American citizen.

7

Poor Little Rich Girl

'That's the way films got made in Hollywood:
back the hot crapshooter who had rolled four
sevens in a row.'

Frank Capra

On the ocean front at Santa Monica today the distant
thunder of the waves is almost drowned by the roar of
engines as a tidal flow of cars pours up and down the Pacific
Coast Highway. The beach itself looks tired, like a dishcloth
washed once too often; the sand is grey rather than yellow.
But in December 1939, when *Gone With the Wind* had its
world premiere in Atlanta, Georgia, and the reputation of
Hollywood echoed round the world, Santa Monica was an
altogether quieter place, with a more temperate climate than
Hollywood itself, or even the newer inland suburb of Beverly
Hills. It had become as fashionable a place for successful members of the Hollywood community as Malibu did
twenty-five years later. It suited Cary Grant perfectly.

He had organized his career in the past four years as
meticulously as he emptied the ashtrays in his house. The
details of the financial arrangements for each picture had
occupied his attention every bit as much as the quality of the
script; the size and position of his billing were as important
to him as the choice of his co-stars. For Cary Grant still did
not see himself primarily as an actor, but as a 'star' whom
audiences could recognize.

In many ways he was as elusive and enigmatic as Howard
Hughes. He spent money carefully, and relatively unostenta-

tiously. He had no chauffeur, no string of secretaries, not even a personal masseur. He ate in restaurants, but not as regularly as some, and he favoured Dave Chasen's shack on Beverly Boulevard, which had opened in 1936, over the more expensive Beverly Hills Hotel, The Brown Derby or The Vendôme. He would go to the Trocadero on Saturday evening, as many other actors liked to do after the week's work, but it would be a brief uncomfortable appearance, conducted with the remote charm of a man who seems a little surprised to find himself in the public eye. 'If people want to find out about me they can look at me on the screen,' he would say. One reason he liked Chasen's Restaurant was that the proprietor kept out autograph hunters. The whole idea of being beseiged by people asking him to autograph a book or a piece of paper had come to appal him.

As he told Louella Parsons: 'This autograph evil – and I do think it is an evil – has got entirely out of hand. Originally it was charming. Every player is grateful for admiration. To scrawl your name on a piece of paper, by way of expressing thanks, doesn't seem a thing. I can think of nothing more inconsequential than any actor's autograph.' But 'to be torn apart, and insulted, while you're writing it, several hundred times wherever you go – then it becomes intolerable. It's got so that no movie star can move outside Los Angeles and Beverly Hills where people are used to us.' He preferred, in fact, to remain an image on celluloid. Indeed he had taken to introducing himself to strangers, on the few occasions when he had to meet them, as though he were another person. 'Hello, I'm Cary Grant,' he would say, even though everyone knew. His name, like his career, was something he had created. But he did not feel confident enough to expose his creation to the pressures of ordinary life.

In the late spring of 1940, as the 'phoney war' in Europe was coming to an end and the British Expeditionary Force was retreating towards Dunkirk, the release of *His Girl Friday* confirmed his position as one of Hollywood's new stars, but his life did not change. He ventured out comparatively rarely, and usually only to the houses of his friends.

In private he saw no reason to keep up the conventional Hollywood star façade. The house on the beach, which he still shared with Randolph Scott, was large, certainly, with seven bedrooms and a games room, but it was nothing like as opulent as the vast estates of John Barrymore or W. C. Fields. It did not boast a library that could be transformed into a screening room like those of Marion Davies and Cecil B. DeMille, and although he and Scott employed a valet and a Negro cook, they kept nowhere near the number of servants that Louis B. Mayer's household seemed to require only a few hundred yards away. Neither did Grant need expensive motor cars to underline his success. He did not own a Duesenberg like Clark Gable, nor a Kissel convertible like Clara Bow – who had it painted the same colour as her hair. He bought himself a new Ford convertible, and then sold it. Randolph Scott said later: 'It drew too much attention to him, and he didn't like that.'

McCarey had conceived his new film, *My Favorite Wife*, as a sequel to *The Awful Truth* and he had signed Grant to appear again with Irene Dunne. As ever McCarey had no intention of following the script, this time written by Bella and Samuel Spewack, the authors of the successful play and film *Boy Meets Girl*: it was based on an idea from Tennyson about a character who comes back to his family after being long presumed dead. The plot, only too familiar in Hollywood, had Grant, a supposed widower, on the verge of remarrying when the wife he believed drowned at sea reappears, having spent seven years on a desert island with a handsome scientist. Grant and McCarey had decided that Randolph Scott would be the ideal candidate to play the scientist and Irene Dunne was to be the wife. Just before shooting started McCarey was badly hurt in a car accident.

With McCarey now in hospital, RKO decided to appoint a replacement director. Dunne was costing them $150,000 for the ten weeks of shooting, while Grant was guaranteed $112,500, plus two and a half per cent of the producer's revenue. They could not afford to wait and in desperation picked the young Garson Kanin, who had just finished making a film with Ginger Rogers. Kanin, then twenty-eight years old, was not at all worried to be taking over a McCarey film but McCarey was definitely worried. As soon as he was able to escape from hospital – after two or three weeks – he started visiting the set to see what was happening, and what he saw did not please him. He held what he later called 'lots of conferences'. He shot a section of the film again. As he put it later: 'We shot about a reel that replaced two or three.'

In spite of his personal reservations about Grant, whom he had taken to calling 'The Happy Worrier' since his behaviour in *The Awful Truth*, McCarey recognized that his star's ability to seem surprised and yet fascinated on the screen had been honed to a fine art. As *Time* pointed out when the film opened in May: 'At times *My Favorite Wife* tends to get bedroomatic and limp, but it pulls itself together in scenes like those in which Cary Grant scampers between his wives' hotel rooms pursued by the distrustful but admiring clerk; or gets caught in his wife's hat and dress by a suspicious psychologist; or tears around in Gail Patrick's leopardskin dressing gown.'

The *New York Times* critic Bosley Crowther described the film finally as 'A frankly fanciful farce, a rondo of refined ribaldries and altogether delightful picture with Cary Grant and Irene Dunne chasing each other around most charmingly in it.' It was a view shared by audiences. In spite of McCarey's private concern, it was one of RKO's greatest successes in 1940, earning the studio more than half a million dollars in profits, and extending the run of success at the box office that Cary Grant had begun with *Gunga Din*.

Even in McCarey's semi-absence the film captured something of his instincts about Grant. At one point in the script Dunne said of her co-star, 'He was the sweetest boy you ever saw. But faithless!' In view of the speculation about the star's private life, it was a delicate joke.

My Favorite Wife failed to lift Grant on to the *Motion Picture Herald*'s list of the top ten box-office attactions for the year, which was dominated by Mickey Rooney, Spencer Tracy,

Clark Gable and Gene Autry, but it confirmed his place as one of Hollywood's 'new aristocracy', a group now attracting the attention of another elite, America's older aristocracy of wealth. Till then, to some people's surprise, actors were not acceptable escorts for Huttons, Vanderbilts and Du Ponts. For heiresses, as one American newspaper put it, this development marked the end of America's 'quaint old social custom that forbade them to choose their boy friends from the theatrical profession'.

Grant set off after the shooting of *My Favorite Wife* on a visit to New York. Katharine Hepburn and Howard Hughes had helped to finance a Broadway production of Philip Barry's play *The Philadelphia Story*, which the author had written specially for Hepburn. Now Hughes was trying to sell the film rights in Hollywood, but so far without success. Hepburn's reputation as bad news at the box office continued to dog her. The hope was that Grant would play the role of C. K. Dexter Haven, Hepburn's divorced husband, when the film was finally made (Joseph Cotten was playing it on Broadway). But first Grant had another film to make for Columbia.

The Howards of Virginia, as it came to be called, was based on Elizabeth Page's 1939 bestseller *The Tree of Liberty* and concerned a Virginia backwoodsman who marries the daughter of an aristocratic family. Cohn thought it might extend Grant's appeal by showing that he could be more than just an elegant, witty, comedian, but it did not prove a success. It merely served, in fact, to put Grant off his stroke. For a start, he felt uncomfortable in the blue and buff uniform which the plot of this historical drama required him to wear, and neither did he fancy his long, pony-tailed hairpiece. In the end, he found it impossible to obliterate the character he had spent so much time and trouble creating. Frank Lloyd, the Scottish-born former actor, who had succeeded so triumphantly with the Laughton-Gable version of *Mutiny on the Bounty*, was unable to save the day; *Newsweek* said that the film came to life 'all too infrequently' and that

Cary Grant was 'obviously miscast'. Bosley Crowther pointed out in the *New York Times*: 'There is a familiar comic archness about his style which is disquieting in his present serious role, and he never quite overcomes a bumptiousness which is distinctly annoying.'

The experience convinced Grant that he should leave aside character parts and concentrate on refining the personality he had already created. In the future he was to refuse several attempts to get him to play in costume drama again, only accepting once and bitterly regretting even that decision after he had taken it. Now he gratefully went back to work with Hepburn and Cukor, this time at MGM. Hepburn and Hughes had succeeded at last in selling the film rights of *The Philadelphia Story* to Louis B. Mayer, who paid $175,000. Cukor, now back at the studio, was to direct it and RKO and Columbia had agreed that Grant could be released.

James Stewart was selected as the film's other star. The immensely tall, Indiana-born actor had started in the theatre in New York, sharing an apartment with Henry Fonda and Joshua Logan; he had just made two excellent films, *Mr Smith Goes to Washington* with Jean Arthur and *Destry Rides Again* with Marlene Dietrich. Another Hollywood bachelor, Stewart had established a uniquely American presence on the screen. He made it seem that he was never acting anything but himself, an honest, down-to-earth American, and he had taken great pains to prevent his considerable intelligence and technique from showing through in his performances.

Philip Barry's friend Donald Ogden Stewart was commissioned to write the script, and was provided with a tape-recording of the Broadway performance to assist the process. 'So as the writer' he was later to say, 'I had to hear that goddamned recorder and then make sure those laughs were in the film play, too, whether or not they belonged there.'

Filming began in July 1940. Cukor liked a quiet set, and the whole process took nearly three months. Grant's performance as the slyly confident Haven, opposite Hepburn's tough but sensitive Tracie Lord, saw him very much in character. His Dexter Haven resembled his Walter Burns, who had in turn resembled his Jerry Warriner, all three of them clever, witty men of the world who knew what they wanted but were not always quite able to get it. Romantic and elusive, commanding the affections of every woman except the one they really wanted, they seemed both victor and victim.

Many years later I interviewed James Stewart in the elegant, dark study of his Beverly Hills home. Grant, he recalled, 'seemed very relaxed and he was very good . . . George Cukor had told us we could pretty much do what we wanted, and I'd kind of worked out what I was going to do.' In the scene towards the end of the film when Stewart and Grant meet in the library, Stewart had decided that if he was called on to be drunk, as the script required, he 'wasn't going to be too drunk – not slobbering – just a little. I'd decided I would have the hiccoughs, but I wouldn't tell anyone about it, just sort of try it out, so we could always do a retake.

'Well, we did it, I hiccoughed, and Cary said: "Excuse me" all of a sudden, and I said, "I have the hiccoughs" and it made the scene.' Grant's ad lib of 'Excuse me', delivered with his eyebrow cocked and his head slightly on one side, was the perfect expression of his new confidence. As Stewart put it: 'He had such humour. Kind of like a legitimate actor doing comedy rather than a comedian.'

Billed first for the first time ever above Hepburn, and guaranteed more than $100,000 for his services, Grant did not feel he need concern himself over much with the film's critical success. All the same, when it finally opened in New York on Boxing Day 1940, the response was overwhelming. Bosley Crowther of the *New York Times* described it as 'having just about everything that a blue-chip comedy should have – a witty romantic script derived by Donald Ogden Stewart out of Philip Barry's successful play; the flavour of high society elegance, in which the patrons inevitably luxuriate, and a splendid cast of performers.' The *Hollywood Reporter* added: 'It's the type of entertainment which will set a box office on fire. It has youth, and beauty, romance and SEX and oh what sex!' *Variety* said: 'The picture is highly sophisticated and gets a champagne sparkle, jewel polish job of direction by George Cukor.'

By the middle of January 1941, when it had played at the Radio City Music Hall in New York for an unprecedented six weeks, breaking the theatre's attendance record set by Walt Disney's *Snow White and the Seven Dwarfs* in 1937, the film had taken nearly $600,000 in that one cinema alone – more than half the revenue from Hepburn's entire Broadway run in a year. It went on to become one of the year's biggest box-office hits, surpassed only by *Sergeant York*, the First World War story starring Gary Cooper, which Howard Hawks had gone on to make after he had been squeezed out of making *Gunga Din*; and it re-established Hepburn as an actress Hollywood was prepared to work with.

Yet it was the last film Grant and Hepburn made together. Although neither realized it at the time, *The Philadelphia Story* marked the end of the period of high romantic comedy that had helped create Cary Grant. The 'screwball' comedies of the late 1930s were overtaken by events. A world at war seemed to have less and less appetite for the giggling high jinks and the clever, brittle dialogue that marked them. As the critic Pauline Kael put it later: 'After 1940 [Grant] didn't seem to have any place to go – there were no longer Cary Grant pictures.'

Grant himself had been wondering what to do next – not in connection with his films but with the war. He had already initiated the procedures necessary for becoming an American citizen, but in the meantime he was anxious to know what he could do to help the war effort, especially since the English press had dubbed him and others who stayed away 'The Gone with the Wind-Ups'.

Just before *The Philadelphia Story* had started filming, Grant and Sir Cedric Hardwicke, another stalwart of the Hollywood British colony, had flown to Washington to see the British ambassador, Lord Lothian. Before he left Hollywood the thirty-six-year-old Grant told one reporter: 'You

157

feel so damn helpless here,' and both were anxious to hear what Lord Lothian thought they should do. 'Stay put and carry on doing what you do best,' was the intelligent reply. Naturally it did not prove acceptable to the jingoistic British press, which continued its attacks on shirkers, but it did something to assuage Grant's conscience. Lothian helped a little more by adding, 'It is quite unfair to condemn older actors who are obeying this ruling as "deserters".' Grant went back to work. By the end of 1940 he had proved the genuineness of his concern by donating his $125,000 fee for *The Philadelphia Story* to the British war effort.

He returned to Columbia to make his next film for them due under the contract first signed nearly four years before and since then regularly amended and renewed. The producer and director was to be George Stevens, who had left RKO in spite of the success of *Gunga Din*. Grant was again to star opposite Irene Dunne, who was billed above him for the third time; but *Penny Serenade* was not to be a comedy, which is what he might have liked, but an old-fashioned, melo-dramatic tear-jerker. Morrie Ryskind, whose successes had included *My Man Godfrey* for Carole Lombard and William Powell, and *A Night at the Opera* for the Marx Brothers, had written the script. The plot, adapted from a *McCall's* magazine short story by Martha Cheavers, concerned a childless couple who look back over their marriage to the strains of old phonograph records, remembering their efforts to adopt a child, and the tragic consequences. As Dunne said later: 'Cary thought it was much too serious.'

Once again he tried to persuade Harry Cohn to let him out of the picture, and once again Cohn refused. Unhappy and peeved, Grant returned to the filming, certain it would turn out badly. Dunne told him: 'If you really stick with this and give it everything you have, I think you'll get an Academy Award nomination.' In one thing she was right: Grant's performance was admirable, and Harry Cohn was delighted with him. He wired after seeing a preview: 'This is your finest picture, and a newer and greater Grant. Let's continue to disagree and make more just like it.' The ten weeks of

Movie star: his performance opposite Irene Dunne in Leo McCarey's The Awful Truth *in 1937 confirmed Cary Grant as one of Hollywood's new stars.*

The inimitable Katharine Hepburn: her effect on Cary Grant was rarely less than dramatic in four films together, and seldom more so than in Howard Hawk's Bringing Up Baby *in 1938.*

*The happy worrier:
Leo McCarey was the first
director to unearth the full
range of Grant's comic
ability which he
exploited in four films,
here with Ginger Rogers
in* Once Upon a
Honeymoon, *in 1942.*

*Poor little rich girl?
Barbara Hutton described
Grant as 'The one
husband I really loved,'
even though their marriage
in 1942 was destined to
last barely three years.*

Notorious: *Alfred Hitchcock discovered the threatening manner which could lie beneath the smooth charm of Cary Grant and revealed it brilliantly here in his 1946 film with Ingrid Bergman.*

The third Mrs Grant: the actress
Betsy Drake, who met her husband on
board the Queen Elizabeth, and
subsequently travelled the world with
him after his first retirement; she
remained his wife longer than any of
her predecessors.

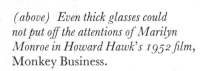

(above) Even thick glasses could
not put off the attentions of Marilyn
Monroe in Howard Hawk's 1952 film,
Monkey Business.

(left) Four films together: Alfred
Hitchcock helped to sustain Cary
Grant's enormous success at the box
office, and here they celebrate Hitch's
eightieth birthday together.

filming had also earned the actor $100,000. Artistically, though, a galling disappointment was in store for him. He had hardly finished filming *Penny Serenade* when the nominations for the Academy Awards for 1940 were announced. To his utter despair, every member of *The Philadelphia Story* seemed to have been nominated for an Oscar except himself. The film was nominated as Best Picture of the Year, Cukor as Best Director, James Stewart as Best Actor, Hepburn as Best Actress, and Donald Ogden Stewart as author of the Best Screenplay. At the annual banquet at the Biltmore Hotel on 27 February 1941, addressed by President Roosevelt on a radio link, James Stewart was awarded the Oscar as Best Actor of the Year for his performance as the uncomfortable gossip writer Macaulay Connor, beating Chaplin in *The Great Dictator*, Henry Fonda in *The Grapes of Wrath*, and Laurence Olivier in *Rebecca*. The irony was not lost on Cary Grant; he had originally thought about playing Connor himself but had chosen Dexter Haven instead.

Try as he might Grant found it impossible to overlook the fact that for the second time in four years his peers in Hollywood had deliberately overlooked him. The nominations were made by his own profession, and so were the awards, yet his work seemed to be ignored. Although he still presented the confident smiling face of Cary Grant to anyone who met him, the omission deepened his inveterate sense of being an outsider. It forced him further back into himself, confirming his suspicions about the film community, convincing him that he was right to remain slightly apart and aloof from it.

One person who shared his sense of isolation from the community, and indeed from most of the rest of the world, was the small woman who, over the past few months, had come to play an increasingly important part in his life, Barbara Hutton.

To anyone who met her for the first time, Barbara Hutton seemed as if she might break. With clear blue eyes set in pale cheeks fringed with wisps of blonde hair, she looked like a tiny Dresden doll – wistful, vulnerable and sad. At the age of five she had inherited more than $20m from her grandfather Frank W. Woolworth. It seemed as though the weight of all these riches threatened to crush her. Yet slender though she looked (she weighed only a little over six stone, and stood less than five feet two inches in height), she was more than capable of defending herself and of making up her own mind. Married for the first time at the age of twenty to Prince Alexis Mdivani, who came from Georgia in Russia, she had divorced him after three years in May 1935 and within twenty-four hours had walked to the altar again, this time with a German who had become a Danish citizen, Count Haugwitz Hardenberg Reventlow. She bore him a son, Lance, in London in February 1936, but before the child reached the age of two she had legally separated from his father and had left Europe for the United States.

Those who did not know her tended to describe her as spoiled but that was less than fair. She had simply known no other life than the one she led, surrounded by servants and advisers, protected by well-meaning friends and body-guards, swamped in affluence. Delicate and often lonely, she would tell her friends in America: 'You know my money has never brought me happiness. You can't buy love with money.'

When Barbara Hutton had first arrived in California from her native New York, she had been on the way to Honolulu for a holiday with Dorothy Di Frasso, one of Hollywood's more flamboyant personalities, who had had a long love-affair with Gary Cooper but had more recently taken up with the mobster, Bugsey Siegel. Just before they left, Di Frasso reintroduced her to Cary Grant, whom she had last encountered on the *Normandie* in 1938; when they got back she arranged a series of dinner parties at which both Hutton and Grant were guests.

Appropriately enough, *The Philadelphia Story* itself concerned the romantic whims of an heiress. As filming continued at MGM's studios in Culver City, the timid, real-life heiress and the sometimes frightened film star began to cling

together for comfort. In spite of their widely different up-
bringings, Hutton, at twenty-eight and Grant, at thirty-
six, were instinctively drawn together. Both were uncomfortable in the presence of strangers, nervous of committing
themselves, and yet given to sudden, childish impulses.
Steadily, almost without noticing it, Cary Grant fell in love
with Barbara Hutton, and for her part she thought she felt
love for him. But, nervous about the publicity that any
relationship with him might attract, she took care to conceal
her feelings for several months. She and her four-year-old
son Lance moved into Buster Keaton's former house in
Beverly Hills, and she surrounded it with security guards.
There had been a series of threats to kidnap the boy, and
memories of Lindbergh were still strong in Hollywood.

When she went out with Grant they avoided restaurants
or nightclubs, went only to dinner parties with friends whom
they knew well, and were never photographed together. But,
in spite of their efforts, by November 1940 the news of their
friendship had begun to leak out. *Photoplay* magazine was
calling it 'the most hushed up love story in Hollywood' and
speculating that they would be married within a year. But
neither Grant nor Hutton had any intention of admitting
anything. Their friends were equally discreet. Douglas Fairbanks Jr and his wife Mary Lee, Ricardo Cortez, Noël
Coward when he was in Los Angeles, even Elsa Maxwell,
who regularly wrote about Hollywood society, remained
studiously silent. Hutton regularly went home to bed by
eleven o'clock, and she refused to visit Cary on the set.
Instead she would go to the Santa Monica house after lunch
for a swim. In the evenings he would sometimes take her
north along the Pacific Coast Highway towards Malibu in
his convertible and buy the girl who could afford everything
hot dogs from a roadside stand.

The relationship did not make him more popular in
Hollywood. Before long the town's less generous commen-
tators were calling Hutton and Grant, 'Cash and Cary', a
sobriquet that was to rankle with them both for years, and
justifiably so. For this was not simply the case of an ambi-

tious careerist actor trying to better himself. Hard though it was for Hollywood critics to accept, Cary Grant had fallen in love. He never described to anyone, not even to his closest friends, how he felt that summer. Some would say later that his happiness seemed to come through in the filming of *The Philadelphia Story*, so close was the parallel with his own life. Certainly he took to disappearing from the set as soon as Cukor would release him and returning to Santa Monica to prepare for their evening rendezvous. This man, who had determined never to let his defences slip or his image either, for that matter, had succumbed to a simple romantic emotion. For him Barbara Hutton was a woman he could protect; not a small fierce mother to argue with, but someone who relied on him. He had never experienced these protective feelings before, even when he had first met Virginia Cherrill. This time he really did seem to be the most important person in somebody else's life, and the thought delighted him.

While he fretted over *Penny Serenade* the relationship between them deepened. The distinction between the two halves of his life, the public one played out in front of the camera and the private one confined to the seclusion of his home, had never been more marked, but he saw no problem in that. By the time George Stevens had finished shooting the film, Irene Dunne had worked on it for seventy-four days with hardly a rest and had lost eight pounds in weight. As a result, her doctor ordered her to leave Hollywood to recuperate. Grant, by contrast, felt in no need of a rest. He was determined to go straight on and had agreed to return to RKO for his next film under their contract.

This time he was to be directed by the English-born Alfred Hitchcock, whose first film in Hollywood, *Rebecca*, had just been nominated for the Academy Award as Best Film of the Year. Hitchcock, under contract to the independent producer David O. Selznick, had been loaned to RKO and had started work on a story the studio had bought six years earlier. Based on a novel called *Before The Fact*, by the English thriller-writer Frances Iles, it was about a woman who comes to believe that her husband is planning to kill her.

There was, however, a considerable snag. Neither RKO nor Grant himself were prepared to accept that he could play a murderer. The weepy melodrama of *Penny Serenade* was one thing, but Grant as a cold-hearted villain was quite another. Finally Hitchcock agreed to shoot the film as though Joan Fontaine, who was to play the frightened wife, was only imagining her husband to be a murderer. He wanted to call the film 'Fright' but after a survey conducted for the studio by George Gallup, RKO settled for the title *Suspicion*. In the first weeks of 1941 the film began shooting, with its star receiving $112,500 and Fontaine nearly $70,000.

Hitchcock said later: 'The real ending I had for the film was that Grant brings his wife the fatal glass of milk to kill her. She knows she is going to be killed so she writes a letter to her mother saying, "I'm in love with him, I don't want to live any more, he's going to kill me, society should be protected." Folding up the letter she leaves it by the bed and says to him, "Would you mind mailing it for me?" She drinks the milk, he watches her die. The last shot of the picture, Cary Grant whistling very cheerfully, goes to the mailbox and pops in the letter.' But, as he drily admitted: 'It was heresy to do that to Cary Grant in those days.'

The confusion over this central premise of the film remained throughout the shooting. Fontaine, already somewhat intimidated by Hitchcock after her experiences with him in *Rebecca*, and with her marriage to Brian Aherne about to break up, found her co-star pleasant but exceptionally distant. She found his aloofness slightly distressing, and his niggling worries about tiny details irritating.

But was Grant or was he not going to be shown as a murderer? While Hitchcock was away in New York, RKO deleted those sections of the film which pointed to the fact that he was actually going to murder his wife, but they relented on Hitchcock's return and allowed him to reinstate them. That did not prevent a bitter debate between director and studio about whether the film should end with Grant's suspicious actions explained away, or with the audience left to make up its own mind about whether he was guilty or innocent. The argument went so far that two alternative endings were shot and then tested in front of audiences. The reactions were invariably in favour of a happy ending, and it was this version that was finally used.

The professional relationship between Hitchcock and Grant would continue for the rest of that spellbinding director's life. Different though they appeared, the elegant actor with the deceptively smiling façade and the restrained director with the conventional suit and tie were in fact instinctively similar. Neither was naturally relaxed, both were deeply suspicious of strangers, cautious about their careers, capable of being frightened by women, unhappy in crowds, and on occasion distressingly aloof.

What Hitchcock intuitively realized was that Grant's sleek charm disguised a darker and more brooding side to his character, that a chilly, potentially manipulative quality lay behind the comic timing and the dark, heavy handsomeness. He extended the image the audience had become used to by revealing what it might conceal, but he and he alone was permitted by Grant to do so. With other directors he restricted himself to his familiar image of the man in the smiling mask.

The mischievous alchemy worked on his screen image by the portly and crafty Hitchcock transformed Cary Grant's reputation as an actor. As the *New Yorker*'s critic John Mosher put it when *Suspicion* opened in New York on the Thanksgiving weekend of 1941: 'Cary Grant finds a new field for himself, the field of crime, the smiling villain, without heart or conscience. Crime lends colour to his amiability.' *Variety* agreed. 'Grant puts compelling conviction into his unsympathetic but arresting role,' it declared, and went on to compliment Hitchcock: 'The story has the same dark glitter and portentous drama as *Rebecca*, which Hitchcock also directed and in which Joan Fontaine came to her high estate as an actress.'

Yet the difficulty Hitchcock had encountered in coping

with Grant and the studio's conception of what sort of role he should play had weakened the picture. The ending ruined what might have been a truly memorable film. The *Hollywood Reporter* commented: 'If this sop of a happy ending was dragged in by the heels, as it appears, it serves only to spoil a great picture.' Whatever the critics' reservations about the ending, *Suspicion* made RKO more than $400,000 and became the studio's most profitable picture of the year, although when the national list of box-office hits was published it turned out not to have been as successful as either *The Philadelphia Story* or *Penny Serenade*.

By the time the filming of *Suspicion* was finished in May 1941, Grant had made five films in fifteen months, working almost without a break. As soon as it was over he decided that the time had come to take a rest and to consider what sort of films he should make in the future. The reviews of *Penny Serenade*, which had just appeared, convinced him that he could handle melodrama without frightening away his audience. *Variety* had called it 'sound human comedy drama' and the *New York Daily Mirror* had rated it 'even better than *The Awful Truth*'. He may not have been among the top ticket-selling stars – that list was still headed by Mickey Rooney and Clark Gable – but he had earned more than $200,000 in the year and had also donated more than $125,000 to the British war effort.

In the next year Cary Grant made only two more films, but he still dithered over two highly significant decisions: whether to become an American citizen, and whether to marry Barbara Hutton.

After spending the summer quietly with her Grant felt the time had come to look round for his next film. The producer Hal Wallis had just bought for Warner Brothers the rights to the Broadway hit comedy by Joseph Kesselring, *Arsenic and Old Lace*, and Frank Capra wanted to direct it. But there was not much time for that: Capra had decided to join the American Army, in the Signal Corps as a major, even though he was forty-four, and the terms of Wallis's deal were that the film could not be released until after the Broadway run had come to an end.

Jack Warner had considered offering the part of Mortimer Brewster, the only sane member of the eccentric Brewster family, to Bob Hope, but Capra was anxious that Cary Grant should have the part. When Capra approached him, Grant told him he might be interested, even though he hadn't seen the play on Broadway, but that his fee would be high. Frank Vincent, as Grant's agent, began negotiations with Warner Brothers on the basis that he would accept $50,000 for the picture, on condition that Warners were prepared to donate a further $100,000 to three charities that Grant would specify. Vincent explained that Grant wanted $25,000 to be given to the United Service Organization, $25,000 to the American Red Cross, and $50,000 to the British War Relief Association, whose chairman in Hollywood was Ronald Colman. Warner Brothers were familiar with the suggestion: not long before, Edward G. Robinson, another of Vincent's clients, had donated a fee of $100,000 to the United Services Organization.

While the negotiations dragged on Grant spent more and more time with Barbara Hutton. She would come over in the afternoon to swim, and he would go back to her house for dinner, although sometimes the large gatherings of guests she collected there on most evenings, and her passion for the company of European aristocrats, overwhelmed him. He wanted to spend quiet evenings with her alone, but 'The Princess', as her staff called her, liked to entertain regally.

Early in September 1941 Grant asked Warners if they would send him to New York so that he could see *Arsenic*, but the ever-wary Jack Warner warned Capra in a cable that 'He should sign contracts before coming here or he may want to stall after seeing the show.' Grant signed, and did not stall, but he did request that the part of Mortimer Brewster, played on the stage by Allyn Joslyn, should be expanded, for both he and Capra agreed that as originally written it was too insignificant to warrant his playing it.

His co-stars included three of the principals from the

Broadway production, Josephine Hull and Jean Adair as the Brewster aunts who killed elderly gentleman callers, and John Alexander as their likeable brother convinced that he was President Teddy Roosevelt. Warners could not agree a deal with Boris Karloff to play their evil brother Jonathan, so in his place they cast Raymond Massey and made him up to look like Karloff. Grant's new wife was to be played by Priscilla Lane, a young actress the studio had under contract and were trying to launch. A chirpy blonde, she had once written to Grant asking him for an autographed photograph. 'But I never got one,' she told the disheartened publicity man as the film started.

After building a huge set on Warners's vast No. 7 sound stage, thirty-five feet higher than any other stage in Hollywood, the company started work on 20 October 1941, with the ebullient, confident Capra well aware that, because of Columbia's terms, he had only six weeks of Grant's time. The set, which consisted of a reconstruction of the Brewster family home, and included a scale replica of the Brooklyn Bridge, featured a graveyard. A prop man had carved on one of the tombstones the name Archibald Leach.

Things, as usual, did not go according to plan. After the first few days Capra and Grant were struggling and the director decided to shoot the film in sequence, as though it were a stage play, which terrified the unit manager, Eric Stacey. Grant was fussing as usual, obsessed by detail and discussing every scene; the director's fiery Sicilian temperament was only just under control but his general enthusiasm was having a bad effect on Grant. Instead of playing his part with the restraint that a McCarey or a Hitchcock knew how to draw from him, he found himself overacting, forcing the role for its comic qualities rather than simply playing it along.

Then, on Sunday, 7 December 1941, the Japanese bombed the American fleet at Pearl Harbour and America was drawn into the war. Capra was given special leave to finish the picture in six weeks before joining the army, and five days later Grant left Warners, his role complete. It was not until after the liberation of Paris in September 1944 that Americans saw the final version of the film: the play stayed on Broadway for three and a half years, taking more than $4m at the box office in the process.

Grant went back to Columbia to make his third film with George Stevens, the success of *Penny Serenade* having convinced Harry Cohn that Stevens and Grant could make another profitable picture for him. That film had been the thirty-six-year-old director's first for Columbia after leaving RKO, and the new project, under the working title of 'Mr Twilight' would be the second. Before long the title was changed to the 'The Gentleman Misbehaves', then 'Three's a Crowd' before finally becoming *The Talk of the Town*.

For this story of a small town schoolteacher who has to choose between marrying a law professor who hopes to be appointed to the Supreme Court of the United States, and a mill hand whom she hides after he has been falsely charged with arson and murder, Columbia had wanted Irene Dunne to star opposite Grant again, but finally settled for Jean Arthur. They had also considered Melvyn Douglas for the part of Professor Lightcap, but in the end invited Ronald Colman to take it. The courteous, careful Colman, who had been a star since the 1920s, naturally expected to be given first male billing, but he had calculated without Grant's sensitivity to his own position. After some delicate negotiation Columbia agreed to give Grant first male billing over Colman, just as MGM had given him billing over Hepburn in *The Philadelphia Story*. It may have been surprising to those outside Hollywood, but the picture business was now well aware that Grant was a star who could deliver an audience. They also knew that he could be difficult to deal with if he did not get precisely what he felt he deserved.

Stevens, who had just finished directing Hepburn and Spencer Tracy in *Woman of the Year*, their first film together, recalled later that in the event there was comparatively little rivalry between the stars. He recalls: 'The only time I saw any sensitivity between the three of them about who was doing what was at the very end. Cary became very uneasy about walking down that long Supreme Court corridor with Jean following him. I don't know whatever got into his head, but he figured she was upstaging him, doing all kinds of witty things that must be fantastically interesting because people were laughing around the set . . . but there never was a moment that Cary worked with Ronnie when that happened.'

In February 1942, for the second year running, Grant was overlooked at the Academy Awards dinner, and this time it was even more wounding a neglect than it had been the year before. He was nominated as Best Actor for his performance in *Penny Serenade*, while Joan Fontaine was nominated for her performance in *Suspicion*, in which, of course, she had played as his co-star. When the awards were announced at the annual banquet at the Biltmore Hotel not only did he watch Fontaine win the award as Best Actress, but he also had to smile graciously as he lost as Best Actor to his old rival at Paramount, Gary Cooper, honoured for his performance in Howard Hawks's film *Sergeant York*.

One person who did appear to appreciate him, however, was Barbara Hutton. They were closer than ever and had talked more and more about marriage, but she was still troubled by the publicity which would ensue, while he did not wish to be cast in the role of a gold-digging Lothario. In fact, on this occasion, the cynical gossip was wrong. Certainly Grant was careful with his own money, and his reputation for driving a hard bargain was well deserved, but he also had his pride, just as his mother had hers. If he married Barbara Hutton, one of the richest women in the world, he would not touch a cent of her money to support them, and he would also specifically waive any rights he might have to a share of it should they divorce. He had no intention of accepting the $1.5m that she had given her last husband when they married. He just wanted to make her his wife.

There was also the delicate question of his citizenship. Barbara had considerable resources in dollar reserves in a London bank vault. Were she to marry an Englishman those dollars would be frozen there. If she were to marry an

American citizen, however, they would be allowed to move across the Atlantic, and she would be able to donate some of them to one of the charities nearest to her heart, the American Red Cross. So the question of his citizenship became additionally important to both of them, and they agreed not to go ahead with their wedding until it had been settled.

It was a difficult decision for Grant. He had told his friends that he wanted to become an American: 'I've lived in this country for more than twenty years. It gave me a chance.' But he could not forget some of the hostile comments in the English press; even the normally affectionate magazine *Picturegoer* had felt called upon to remark: 'To most of us the voluntary renunciation of our nationality is an unbelievable thing. Patriotism, despite the modern fashion of decrying it, is still a warm blood emotion to you and me, we cannot understand the renegade, we can only detest him.' Counterbalancing these extremely harsh remarks, it had added: 'Grant is sincere in believing that he ought to become an American.'

In the event, he applied for his final papers soon after Pearl Harbour, but it was not until June 1942 that they were finally processed. On 26 June, together with more than three hundred others, Archibald Alec Leach took the oath of allegiance from Senior Federal Judge Paul J. McCormick in Los Angeles, and on the same day he officially changed his name to Cary Grant. Ten days later he arranged to have lunch with the head of publicity for RKO and told him that he and Barbara Hutton intended to get married.

'Barbara wants to invite her friends, and she doesn't want to elope,' he told him. 'We thought the best time to do it would be in two days' time. I have a day off.' He was shooting his third film with Leo McCarey, this time co-starring his old friend, Ginger Rogers. McCarey had told him he could be spared for one day and that he could be an hour late the next morning. 'But that's all.'

The following day Barbara Hutton, her friend Madeleine Hazeltine, and some from among the eleven members of her personal staff, drove from her home in Beverly Hills to Frank

Vincent's house in the beautiful countryside near Lake Arrowhead. On that same evening of 7 July they were followed to the house by the studio's head of publicity, a press agent, a cameraman and a laboratory expert to send the resulting photograph back to Los Angeles.

On the sunny morning of 8 July 1942 Cary Grant and his secretary, Frank Horn, drove out of the Santa Monica house and started on the two-hour drive east to Lake Arrowhead. Soon after they had started they stopped at a Beverly Hills florist. No-one had been prepared to give the newspapers even a hint of the impending marriage by ordering flowers. As the best man, Vincent had arranged the marriage licence but had left the names blank, and even now Horn told the florist that he was buying the orchids, carnations and bridal bouquet for his sister's wedding in Long Beach. The girl behind the counter was not convinced, especially when she saw Grant sitting outside in the car, waiting for Horn to come back.

At 12.30 that afternoon Barbara Hutton, wearing a simple blue suit and a cyclamen-coloured blouse, and Cary Grant, dressed in a blue-grey suit and a dark tie, were married in the shade under an oak tree in Frank Vincent's garden. The ceremony, conducted by the Reverend H. Paul Romeis, pastor of the San Bernadino English Lutheran Church, took just six minutes. The marriage licence gave the groom's age as thirty-eight and the bride's as thirty.

Randolph Scott was not there, and neither was Dorothy Di Frasso; only Madeleine Hazeltine, Genevieve Tocquet, Hutton's companion, and Frank Horn. Grant had not forgotten the mad scenes outside Caxton Hall eight years before; and Hutton never wanted to repeat the vast ceremony of her first marriage to Prince Mdivani. The most famous newly-weds in the world since Fairbanks and Pickford did not feel their marriage was of any concern to anyone but themselves. That night, as they drove back to Hutton's house in Beverly Hills, where he had arranged to take over the lease, Cary Grant murmured to his new wife: 'I can't understand why someone like you would marry me.'

He had said it to her before, and she had always just squeezed his hand. This time was no different. The following morning at ten o'clock Cary Grant went back to RKO to continue shooting the film he was making with Leo McCarey. It was called *Once Upon A Honeymoon*, but there was no time for him to take one.

8

Mr Lucky?

'Life was pretending to be someone else.
Otherwise it was rather dull.'

Daphne Du Maurier, *The Matinée Idol*

The quiet dinners together, the late night telephone calls, the
flowers and the soft searching glances as they drove up the
beautiful Pacific Coast Highway in the moonlight were what
Cary Grant and Barbara Hutton remembered. But the
reality of their life together was quite different.

The household Grant had taken over was nothing like the
one that he and Randolph Scott had shared. Barbara Hutton not only lived with her son Lance. There was also her
own companion, Germaine Tocquet, who had been with her
for almost twenty years; a secretary; a valet; a chauffeur; and
half a dozen other servants, including a cook. She needed
them all, she would tell her husband to entertain her many
guests. He may have insisted to his friends: 'If she wants to
buy diamond overshoes that's her privilege, but all routine
items, such as rent and groceries, will be strictly on me,' but
he could never have conceived exactly what that would
mean. He had planned that they would move into his house
on the beach, and for that purpose had bought Randolph
Scott's share in it when they married, but his wife said she
thought it would be 'rather too small for the staff we will
need'. Reluctantly he sold it back to his friend.

She had been accustomed to entertaining friends at home
since she was a girl. Though timid with strangers, and
hating to be photographed or asked for her autograph, she

had always survived by surrounding herself with people she believed to be her friends, particularly minor members of the European aristocracies; and Hollywood had become a popular refuge for such exiles, many of them chased out of their native lands by the invading German armies. Hutton was fascinated by them.

They moved into a house a little further north, at Pacific Palisades, which had once belonged to one of his leading ladies Elissa Landi, and more recently to Douglas Fairbanks Jr. Called Westridge, it boasted a vast terrace looking out towards the Pacific, a large swimming pool and a tennis court, and would have quite enough room for guests and the servants. Husband and wife would have separate bedrooms. Hers would have an open fire, overstuffed sofa pillows and some of her paintings. His would have a view of the Pacific, its own fireplace, and room for the Boudin seascape she had given him as a present. She hoped he might collect more works by this painter over the next few years, to hang beside his three Canalettos.

In the late summer of 1942 life at Pacific Palisades got under way. Grant took to staying at home with his wife almost every evening. When they were not entertaining they would play gin rummy together, and he would usually win, but he avoided playing bridge, which many of her friends preferred. As Hutton told Hedda Hopper: 'When Lance is home we go to the beach to swim or ride in the afternoon and in the evening I like nothing better than to curl up with a good book. I play tennis every morning.' Grant would play tennis with his stepson whenever he got the opportunity, for as he put it to Louella Parsons: 'I just don't want Lance to be lonely. As a child I was terribly lonely and I don't want him to have that kind of childhood. Children should not be alone.'

By the autumn, however, the endless string of visitors and the formal dinner parties were beginning to take their toll. 'It's bedlam,' Grant would mutter. 'The servants have so many shifts to feed at meal times that my wife and I are lucky to get a hamburger.' He preferred, as he had always done, the courtship of a woman to her company every day. No matter how hard he tried to suppress it, he could never escape a desire to disappear on his own. A vast house filled with people left him feeling trapped. So although he treated his wife, whom he always called Barbara, never Babs, with the kindness, courtesy and charm she had come to expect of him, he frequently longed to retire into himself. Grant remarked later: 'I liked Sunday evenings when that army of servants was away and just Barbara and I were there. She is an excellent cook and she would go into the kitchen and cook for the two of us.' Those private moments, harking back to their courtship, were now all too rare. Barbara Hutton had never been used to living that way. She saw no reason to start now. If her husband looked upset she would call him 'grouchy' and he would stalk into his bedroom and firmly shut the door.

Meanwhile Selznick had invited him to appear in a film he was planning of the play *Claudia*. The deal had fallen through, because Grant refused to budge from his fee of $100,000 and a percentage of the profits, though Selznick said the film would be good for his reputation. But *Once Upon A Honeymoon* was progressing satisfactorily. Leo McCarey seemed a little abstracted, and the plot was hardly the full-blooded comedy that Grant had expected, but he knew his director had discarded all the other stories he had been working on to do this one because the State Department wanted Hollywood to make an anti-Nazi film.

There was one cloud on the horizon. The ever-determined Ginger Rogers, who was being paid $175,000 for her performance, would not agree to give Grant billing above her as both Hepburn and Ronald Colman had done in the past two years. For his part, he was not prepared to forego top billing again, even though he was being paid only $112,500 plus a share of the profits. Finally, after a lengthy negotiation, RKO agreed that for half the film's advertising the top billing would be his, and for the other half hers.

Cinema audiences were growing rapidly and studio profits were rising in their wake. *Yankee Doodle Dandy* and *Mrs*

Miniver were doing spectacularly well at the box office, as were *Casablanca* and Orson Welles's new film *The Magnificent Ambersons*. But when *The Talk of the Town* was released in August 1942, it disappointed Columbia's hopes. *Variety* called it 'one of the season's more important entries', but it never quite caught the audience's imagination. Neither did *Once Upon A Honeymoon* when it was released late in October of the same year. The *New York Times* noted sadly that McCarey had made the mistake of 'trying to mix romantic comedy with tragedy too stark and real', so that 'The two are completely repellent when brought together so glibly in one film.' And was Cary Grant's appeal at the box office beginning to wane? Some people began wondering.

To his friends in the autumn of 1942 Cary Grant seemed even more isolated than when he and Randolph Scott had lived together at Santa Monica. He was famous certainly, married to one of the richest women in the world, a prince in the Hollywood aristocracy. But he seemed diffident and unsettled to those who knew him well, uncomfortable with the fame that he had so obviously wanted to achieve.

At the Beverly Hills Tennis Club he would appear from time to time, as carefully charming as ever to anyone who spoke to him, but all the same a little uncertain. The tennis professional there was Milton Holmes, who one day caught him as he was climbing into his convertible, and told him an idea he had had for a film. Holmes had never written a screenplay or indeed a story before, but in the best traditions of Hollywood Grant told him 'it sounded a swell idea' for RKO. Besides he had thought up a good commercial title. The picture would be called *Mr Lucky*, a nice twist – for that was how many people saw Cary Grant.

So in November 1942 Grant started work on the film at RKO, starring opposite the beautiful Laraine Day, whom the studio had borrowed from MGM. In the daily rushes he looked more handsome than ever: the fleshiness of his face had thinned so that his jaw was sharper, and he looked younger than his thirty-eight years. There was none of the exaggerated comedy in his part that had marred some of his earlier roles. He was expected to look like a scoundrel, and he did. He even seemed to relish the thought of breaking away a little from his image. His part as the handsome gambler with a neat line in slick dialogue who decides to fleece the American War Relief Society was the centrepiece of the film. Since his marriage to Barbara he appeared willing to take more risks.

Laraine Day remembers him as 'constantly telling jokes' on the set. 'He was a professional. He always knew where the camera was, what he needed to do, and he worked very hard. He had managed to teach himself a lot of tricks, like the double take, and he used them and taught them to other people. It was a treat to work with him.' Yet Day remembers that in the evenings he was utterly transformed. 'We used to go to Hank Potter, the director's house for dinner, and he would come with Barbara Hutton. Then he wasn't the bright cheerful person he had been on the set all day, he was subdued, a completely different person. It was astonishing.' On evenings at home he took to retiring to his own room to eat alone and study the next day's script, so uncomfortable did he feel in the presence of most of his wife's friends.

Barbara's dislike of the film business was already becoming clear, and the strain of trying to keep her happy in the company of his professional colleagues began to show through. 'He used to look after everyone on the set, and then in the evenings he seemed to be looking after her as well, although in a different way.' Indeed the fierce contradictions between his professional life and his position as the heiress's husband were beginning to tell. Early in 1943, even *Photoplay* noticed that 'He gets sudden periods of depression.' As Hedda Hopper remarked: 'Cary was upstairs cramming twelve solid pages of script into his head. Up at six for a studio call, home late dead tired, and was not amused by the upper crust goings on around his place.'

No matter how difficult life had so quickly become, Grant was still in love with Barbara. Both he and his wife would have liked to have children, and in the first months of their married life there were persistent reports of miscarriages.

Certainly two years after they were married Hutton was telling Hopper: 'If only Cary and I could have a baby some day. We'd like to have at least three. We're praying, both of us. Maybe our dreams will come true.' Perhaps had they managed to have a child the isolation they felt from each other might gradually have disappeared; but their dreams were not to be fulfilled. Barbara never had another child after Lance, and it would be twenty-four years before Cary Grant became a father.

After the shooting for *Mr Lucky* had been completed in the first week of 1943, Grant decided that he would stop making films for a time: he owed it to his wife, and to their life together to take a rest. He would do some War Bond tours, and entertain the troops when the opportunity presented itself, but most of all he would try to create a life they could live together rather than apart. He felt it was the least he could do to try and understand her life and her attitudes, even while realizing that she was so used to a life in which a dozen places were habitually laid for dinner that she would never be able to free herself of the habit. Taking a break from filming would also give him more time for himself: he wanted to know as much about art and music as his wife did, to rid himself of the feeling that he was the only ignorant guest in his own house.

As he sat beside the pool in the mornings he comforted himself with the thought that the risk he had run in playing in *Mr Lucky* had paid off at the box office. When it opened in May 1943 *Newsweek* described it as having 'its bright moments, the overall theme of redemption is as realistic as Hans Christian Anderson and occasionally several times as arch', but in spite of this cautious note it became one of RKO's biggest hits of the year, making the studio a profit of more than $1.6m. Grant's canny attention to his career had once more paid dividends.

Mr Lucky remained one of his favourite films, not just because the character he played had rather more depth than some of his earlier roles had shown but because: 'The character I played was more like the real Cary Grant than any before. Mr Lucky was seemingly a happy-go-lucky guy, but that was a cover for a sensitive soul.'

When the Academy Awards were announced in March none of Grant's work was honoured, indeed none of the films he had appeared in in 1942 was nominated in any category. *Mrs Miniver*, the box-office sensation of 1942, took most of the principal Oscars, with only James Cagney triumphing as Best Actor for his performance as the irrespressible George M. Cohan in *Yankee Doodle Dandy*.

At home Grant tried to understand more about his wife, and she tried to settle into the routine he seemed to want, a quieter life with fewer visitors. It was a transformation that neither could manage. Gradually the envious tittle-tattle surfaced. They were 'million dollar recluses' who 'never go anywhere to see any Hollywood people' and who 'dine formally every night on silver plate for family and gold plate for company.' In the next few months Grant started touring army camps while Barbara remained in Hollywood. He had begun to give up the effort to change himself. He thought it could never work, and the realization depressed him. It seemed to him that he could never find peace with anyone, that he was destined to do nothing but suffer. In despair he went back to making films. He did not know what else to do.

The battle in the Pacific was absorbing the American public, and at Warner Brothers, Delmer Daves, who had started as a prop man, worked up a story based on an article in *Liberty* magazine about a United States submarine's trip to Tokyo Bay and back. While Grant was away on a War Bond tour in May 1943 Jack Warner suggested that he should make his first war film. Grant was willing but said Warner would have to be quick, because he had just signed a new agreement with Columbia – Harry Cohn wanted him at the studio at the start of August to begin work on a film with Janet Blair.

Jack Warner wanted to film the first 'realistic portrait' of American submarines in action. Part propaganda, part melodrama, the film would allow Grant to capitalize on his

serious role in *Mr Lucky* by playing the submarine's commander. Warners had enjoyed some success with *Air Force*, a
dramatization of the life of the Flying Fortress air crews
which Howard Hawks had directed for them, and in this
new picture they intended to use John Garfield and Faye
Emerson, who had both appeared in that earlier film.
Delmer Daves was asked if he would like to direct it himself.
The studio had given untried directors a chance in the past
two years – they had allowed John Huston his first opportunity with *The Maltese Falcon* – and they saw no reason why
Daves should not do equally well. The thirty-nine-year-old
writer said later, 'I didn't know what the hell I was letting
myself in for.'

With Grant's approval Daves began work on *Destination
Tokyo*, as the film was to be called. Jack Warner sent the
script to Washington for clearance, and after getting special
approval from the Navy Department, and agreeing to a
request from President Roosevelt that there should be no
reference to radar or to military electronics, the shooting
began in June 1943.

Grant, as usual, fretted about details – his uniform and the
correct way of saluting – but he seemed content to be
breaking out of his stereotype again. There would be none of
the frenzied comedy of *Gunga Din* in Daves's film. Grant was
to be a commander who did not joke with his men. Strong,
silent, handsome and perhaps a little sad, he was to epitomize the stoic strength of the armed forces.

On the set Grant told the young Robert Hutton, whose
first film this was, that stardom did not guarantee happiness.
'Does it bring you happiness? Yeah, for a couple of days,
And then what happens. You begin to find out that your life
is not your own any more, and that you're on show every
time you step out on the street.' The misery and contradictions of his own success came pouring out. 'Your eyes are
weak and you wear dark glasses to protect them from the
sun. "Look at that show-off trying to disguise himself,"
you'll hear people say. You buy a new suit, because you need
it. "Look at that guy, spending all his money on clothes,

trying to be another Adolphe Menjou," you'll hear them say. You dodge some autograph hunters because you're shy, you hate to make a spectacle of yourself. "Huh, big shot, hasn't got time for the common people now," they go on.' To the young actor's astonishment Grant suggested that he might be better off with a job in the Lockheed aircraft factory.

In the six weeks that Daves had at his disposal he did all he could with the cast and with the specially constructed submarine that had been built on the Warners sound stage on Sunset Boulevard. But for all his efforts the shooting was not quite complete by the time Grant was due to start work at Columbia in the first week of August. To get the film finished, he had to work with Daves at night after he had left the Columbia studio. Cary Grant was quite important enough to justify the expense of paying extra money to an entire cast and crew, especially if he could deliver them a hit at the box office for Christmas.

Needless to say, Barbara was not pleased that her husband was now spending both day and night in film studios, but he could not help that. He had decided that his work came first. At Columbia, Louis B. Edelman was producing a film which had started as a radio sketch. With echoes of *Bringing Up Baby*, it called for Grant to play a Broadway producer who discovers a nine-year-old boy who has trained his pet caterpillar to dance to the song, 'Yes, sir, That's My Baby' when he plays it on his mouth organ. Grant, as the producer, was to start out as a villainous type, but to be shown as having redeeming features, a role that suited him well. Filming finished just before Christmas 1943. Barbara was preparing to entertain forty guests over the holiday at Pacific Palisades, and Grant's resentment began to show. He knew he didn't want to live like this but he also knew that he loved his wife. The more he thought about it the less there seemed to be any solution to their marriage. Inexorably he slipped into deep depression, convinced that he could never sustain a relationship with any woman.

Yet there were still things that kept him at home. He and

Barbara shared a sense of the ridiculous. She would use the word 'ig' to describe something she felt lacked taste: once, when they had once visited a house in California which sported a huge apricot-coloured bar in one corner of its main living room, the owner had said to Grant, 'Don't you just love the bar?', and Grant had told him, 'Yes, it's so wonderfully ig.' His wife burst into such a fit of hysterical laughter that they were forced to leave. But such moments were not enough. By the time the New Year celebrations for 1944 were over it had become clear to Grant that their marriage was on the brink of collapse. She was distant and withdrawn, and their only real contact was through Lance, who had taken to calling him General whenever he saw him. It was Lance, not quite eight years old, who kept them, temporarily, together over the few months. The boy seemed to miss Grant whenever he was out of the house, and Grant was determined that he would not abandon Barbara's son as his own mother had abandoned him.

Destination Tokyo opened to enthusiastic reviews in New York just after Christmas. The *New York Times* called it 'a pippin of a picture'. *Newsweek* gave its verdict that Grant had turned in 'one of the soundest performances of his career'. But the queues forming outside the cinemas for the film did nothing to alleviate his feeling of emptiness. He was aware of his own vanity, of his obsessive perfectionism, his irritability and depressions, yet he felt that his wife should have done more to understand him and accept his weaknesses. When he made an effort, as he was obliged to do on most occasions, to seem the relaxed charming man that his public expected, the experience terrified him, leaving him desperate to shrink away into a cocoon. He had dreamed of a life with a woman who was as timid and reserved as he was; yet instead he was surrounded by people who seemed only to take pleasure in belittling his achievements.

The film about the caterpillar had not much amused Grant, and he did not particularly want to go back to Columbia if that was all they could think up for him. He wanted to continue to extend his range as an actor, to capitalize on the success of *Mr Lucky* and *Destination Tokyo*.

Charles Koerner, RKO's general manager, had been looking for the right project for him and had heard about a new novel by Captain Richard Llewellyn Lloyd, author of the best-selling *How Green Was My Valley*, which had won the Oscar as Best Picture for Darryl F. Zanuck in 1941. Llewellyn Lloyd, who wrote under the pen name of Richard Llewellyn, had published another novel in September 1943, this time about life in London rather than in the mining valleys of Wales, called *None But The Lonely Heart*. With Cary Grant in mind, RKO had bought the film rights for $60,000.

Although Koerner did not realize it, Llewellyn's story bore some similarities to Grant's own upbringing. The central character, Ernie Mott, lived with his mother, a secondhand furniture dealer, who was dying of cancer. Grant was enthusiastic and, Koerner, delighted but slightly surprised, instructed one of the studio's producers, David Hempstead, to make the film. Hempstead had the idea of asking the left-wing playwright, Clifford Odets, to write the screenplay. Odets had moved back to Hollywood in the middle of 1943, shortly after his marriage to Bette Grayson. Intellectual, ferocious and happier in New York than Hollywood, the thirty-seven-year-old Odets had reservations about the project and even more apprehensive when, after a few evasions, Hempstead told him that the studio were casting Grant for the role of Mott.

'Cary Grant?' he exclaimed in astonishment. 'Do you realize that Ernie Mott is nineteen years old?'

'Of course,' Hempstead had told him. 'It'll be just fine.'

So the author of *Rocket to the Moon* and *Clash By Night* found himself rewriting Llewellyn's novel with Cary Grant's clearly established screen persona firmly in his mind rather than the novel's original central character. It was the sharp, shrewd slyness which Cary Grant had refined over the years that finally emerged in his screen version, and Odets was not displeased. He knew RKO were anxious to win an Oscar for their star, and for themselves; and they wanted a script good

183

enough to do it. He thought he had managed to write one.

The next difficulty was to find an actress to play Grant's mother. The obvious choice was Ethel Barrymore, sister of Lionel and John, and a member of what was always described as the Royal Family of Hollywood, even though she had not set foot on a sound stage since making *Rasputin and the Empress* with her two brothers for Irving Thalberg at MGM in 1932. RKO approached her about returning to Hollywood but she turned the idea down flat, on the grounds that she was too busy with the touring version of *The Corn is Green*, in which she was the star. Undeterred, RKO sent her the script, and offered to pay the $66,000 salaries of the whole touring company for the six weeks she would be needed on the set, in addition to the $50,000 they were prepared to offer her. After reading Odets's script she agreed, but with hesitation. Her elder brother Jack had died of alcoholism and despair in Hollywood just eighteen months before, and the story of Mott and his dying mother brought painful memories.

Grant, who had the right of approving the director, suggested that Odets might be given the chance of directing the new film himself, since that idea had worked so well with Daves. Once again Odets was astonished, but flattered. He had considerable experience on Broadway, but his rebellious attitudes and opinions had made some studios suspicious of him. Grant saw him, however, as someone who would listen, and keep to the style of the part that he had in his mind. The two men seemed utterly different but they became friends as a result of the film, indeed Odets quickly realized that Grant was not what he appeared. 'His simplicity covers up one of the most complex men I've ever met,' he said years later. 'I sometimes feel I really don't know him at all.' It was a view Leo McCarey shared: 'I still don't know what makes him tick. Of the sixteen hours a day when he's awake I don't think there are twenty minutes when he's not complaining. I've never seen a man more constantly in turmoil.'

Directing *None But The Lonely Heart* was an experience Odets was not to forget. Like many other directors before him, the playwright realized that his star's compulsive perfectionism made him endlessly question everything on the set, every piece of furniture, every accent, every line of dialogue. On more than one occasion Grant stopped the filming and told Odets that the dialogue as it was written was 'not the way a Cockney would say it'. Then his co-star, June Duprez, who had also been born in England and had started her film career there, would interrupt to say that she didn't think her co-star was right either. A weary but fascinated Odets struggled to keep the film going.

Part of Grant's concern stemmed from his realization that *None But The Lonely Heart* was important to his career. After the reviews of Columbia's caterpillar film, now titled *Once Upon A Time*, had appeared in May 1944, he knew that his performance with Odets had to be good enough to convince the critics that he deserved to be taken seriously.

The influential James Agee had noted in the *Nation*: 'The story of a dancing caterpillar which becomes an international personality, a political and religious symbol, and a baby Armageddon for science and commercialism, and what is popularly thought of as innocence and idealism, might, with great skill, imagination and avoidance of whimsy, become wonderful. But *Once Upon A Time* is not wonderful.' Even worse, as far as Grant was concerned, at the Academy Award ceremony in March he had yet again to watch Gary Cooper nominated for an Oscar as Best Actor for his performance in the successful film version of Ernest Hemingway's novel *For Whom The Bell Tolls*, which had outgrossed both his own *Mr Lucky* and *Destination Tokyo* at the box office. He himself had not been nominated for any award at all, and once again he felt that his achievements in the industry were ignored. As the filming of *None But The Lonely Heart* went on in the early summer, he became more and more determined to try and win an Oscar himself.

The impending return of his stepson, Lance, to the house on Pacific Palisades cheered him up. 'Strange how the little

185

chap has gotten under my skin,' Grant had told his friend Elsa Maxwell. 'When he's away from us I can never get him out of my mind.'

Lance had spent almost six months with his father, Kurt Haugwitz Reventlow, who had recently married the New York socialite, Margaret Astor Drayton, and he was due to return to his mother on 1 July 1944, while shooting on *None But The Lonely Heart* was winding up. But on the day before his expected arrival Reventlow's attorney telephoned to tell Barbara that his client had no intention of sending back her son. Before the shock had fully sunk in, Reventlow instituted a suit alleging that she had 'used coarse and vulgar language in the boy's presence' and had 'sought to undermine his affection for his father'. He also demanded that the boy should not be allowed to speak to Cary Grant and, as a final blow, said that he was taking his son away.

Devastated, Barbara and Grant decided to fight the action. They went to meetings with lawyers and with California district attorneys in an effort to reclaim the boy, and at every turn Grant was forced to tell reporters: 'Yes, I am happily married to Miss Hutton.' Yet nothing really had changed. The household was every bit as large as it had been before; Madamoiselle Germaine Tocquet, his wife's companion, was still fearsomely in evidence; and Grant was still inclined to stay in his room in the evenings, worrying about the next day's shooting. The custody action brought them closer but its effect did not last. As it became clear that the legal battle over custody of Lance might well take months, their unity began to break down; in its place came realization that the separation they had talked about was now inevitable.

In the first week of August 1944 Grant disconsolately packed a few of his own belongings and moved out of the house on Pacific Palisades, and he set out to move into an apartment in Beverly Hills. The woman he had loved seemed lost to him.

Within four days he was back, trying to persuade his wife that they could begin their marriage again. But Barbara was not convinced. 'I think it's better for both of us if we part now. You aren't happy and you've only stayed here because of the difficulties with Lance.'

With that she left the house and went for a drive with her favourite cousin, Jimmy Donahue. When they returned they discovered that Grant had moved his clothes back into the house.

'We've got to try again,' he told her. 'There's no reason why we can't.'

In tears she packed her own clothes and moved out.

The following day Barbara told Louella Parsons: 'There is no chance of reconciliation, and I think it's unfair and dishonest to take advantage of the name of my husband and to seek his protection because I am fighting to hold my child.'

Parsons herself added: 'The last time they were together was at a party, at which time Cary told me that Barbara was so sweet and gentle that she didn't deserve all the trouble she had had. He said he was going to aid her in her fight for the child.'

The separation could not have come at a more difficult time for Grant. Jack Warner had negotiated with Harry Cohn to take over the last of the eight films Grant was obliged to make for Columbia under the terms of his original 1937 contract. He wanted to make a film biography of Cole Porter, who was a close friend of Grant's and the composer was insisting that Grant should portray him. Michael Curtiz, whose *Casablanca*, also produced by Warners, had just won the Oscar for Best Picture, was to direct, and Warner had even offered to allow Humphrey Bogart to make a film for Columbia if they would release Grant to play Porter.

But Warner had calculated without Barbara Hutton. Grant did not want to think about making any more films. His life, he said, was in ruins. In Pacific Palisades he moped about, refusing even to pick up the telephone, unless it was to plead to speak to his wife. Warner was in a difficulty. He assured Grant that he did not want to press him into working too soon; but he could not halt the work that had already started, so he told Steve Trilling to talk to Frank Vincent, Grant's agent, and see when they could go ahead.

Their discussion was not encouraging. In a memo on 26 September Trilling told Warner: 'In Vincent's opinion, because of Grant's mental condition he possibly would not be ready to make a picture for an indefinite time – certainly not by November 1 or 15. Might be a few months from now, or might be six months from now.' Trilling added gloomily, 'Vincent suggests we might look in other directions to cast Porter.'

Two days later, after talking to Frank Vincent again, he reported that Grant believed 'In his present frame of mind he could not give a good performance – it is something much more important than making a picture, with his whole life's happiness at stake.' Vincent, in fact, had sensibly been advising his client to keep active rather than sit miserably at home, but as Trilling put it: 'Grant seems to be so low that he cannot get straightened out.'

That weekend, six weeks after their initial separation, Cary Grant decided to make one final effort to get his wife back. He knew she was staying in San Francisco with her friend, Mrs Oleg Cassini, the actress Gene Tierney, and so he set off to drive the four hundred miles north along the California coast to see her. To his surprise she agreed. She went out with him that weekend and admitted that, perhaps, there was some way they could live together again. He told her how the servants upset him, and how he felt that they were never alone, and smiling she replied, as they swept around the dance floor together, that she wanted him to be happy with her.

When the weekend was over he drove back to Los Angeles, and by the middle of the week she too was on her way back, to a house she had bought in the exclusive Bel Air estate in Beverly Hills. An English-looking house in what the real estate agent called 'Cotswold style', it looked out across the fourth tee of the Bel Air golf course. Large though it was, however, it could not accommodate all the staff; they would remain in Pacific Palisades.

A delighted Cary Grant told the RKO publicity department to issue a brief statement to the press. It said simply: 'Yes, it is true we have effected a reconciliation. The truth of our misunderstanding and eventual reunion, despite all gossip and conjecture, is known only to us and we feel sure that the press and public will respect it as being our affair.' But before the statement was issued, husband and wife had left Hollywood. They had no wish to discuss their marriage with the newspapers. In fact the only gossip to circulate recently had concerned Grant's relationship with another young blonde, an actress called Betty Hensel. Some of the industry's gossips believed she had been the cause of their estrangement, but Miss Hensel herself tried to scotch the idea by announcing her engagement to Lieutenant Henry William Dodge Jr, of the Army Medical Corps.

The reconciliation was of no help to Warner Brothers. Frank Vincent told Steve Trilling only a few days later that Cary Grant was not prepared to start work on the Cole Porter picture until at least April 1945, and probably not until 1 May 1945. But for what it was worth he was prepared to assure them that Grant would not make any other picture before working on it.

In their new house in Bellagio Road Grant spent most of his time with his wife. He looked after her, stayed with her, amused her as well as he could. There was no need to go to a film studio, he was not making a movie, all he had to do was to make his wife happy. For a time things seemed to work. Barbara could still be flattered by the attentions of one of the most handsome men in the world, who was so clearly in love with her. But the woman who had been raised an heiress, educated in Europe, married to a prince and then to a count, knew in her heart that her third marriage could not last. She knew her husband missed the picture business, knew how much he hated the dinners that she loved to organize when her guests would speak only French, just as she knew that she hated the American Legion prize fights he loved. She watched as, gradually, her husband's dark moods returned, creeping back into their lives like an unwanted guest, until she realized that there was nothing she could do to help him.

Even the reviews of *None But The Lonely Heart*, which had opened in September 1944, failed to cheer him up. *Time* magazine reported: 'However the film makes out financially, it is one of the pictures of the year, a feather in the cap of all concerned in its making. In the US, major productions have rarely dared to tackle so wholeheartedly so harshly human a subject.' Bosley Crowther in the *New York Times* called Grant's performance 'an exceptional characterisation of bewilderment and arrogance'; the *Hollywood Reporter* described it as 'the finest thing he has ever done'; and *Variety* declared that it was a 'class picture apparently aimed at critical approval rather than levelled for popular consumption'.

It had hardly opened when *Arsenic and Old Lace* was finally released to almost equally enthusiastic reviews, although Howard Barnes in the *New York Herald Tribune* remarked: 'For some reason or other, a fine actor merely mugs through the part of the sane member of the Brewster clan. Since he is a star his part has been built up out of all proportion to the plot. That is not to his advantage.' Still, the crowds for Capra's films seemed almost as enthusiastic as those for the Broadway play, and Grant's ability to attract a film audience was affirmed again.

Meanwhile, the legal battle for Lance was still going on; Reventlow was now claiming that his former wife's intention was to take her son to Europe as soon as the war was over. Throughout the winter Cary Grant kept Barbara's spirits up as best he could, but that did not prevent arguments. On one occasion his friends Ros Russell and Freddie Brisson the agent had to intervene to get them back together again. As Russell recalled later: 'They wound up sleeping in Freddie's room at our house, and Freddie moved in with me. Next morning Freddie went back to his own room to get a pair of socks and saw Barbara alone in bed. Then he went into his bathroom and there was Cary asleep on the floor. Stepping over him Freddie picked up a toothbrush and came back to me. "I think we've got trouble again," he said.'

They had. By the middle of February 1945 Cary Grant and Barbara Hutton agreed that their reconciliation had not worked out. On 26 February she moved out of the new house on Bellagio Road and back to Pacific Palisades.

This time there was no talk of getting together again. A terse statement announced: 'After much thought and with great consideration we have decided we can be happier living apart. As yet no formal plans have been formed regarding a divorce.' As Louella Parsons put it in her column the next day: 'In my opinion, the Hutton heiress will seek a divorce and I believe she'll leave Hollywood, for since her reconciliation with Cary not one of her friends has seen her. Neither she nor Cary has gone to any parties. They have been in complete seclusion.'

Hardly a fortnight after Barbara's departure the results of the seventeenth Academy Awards were announced. Grant had been nominated for an Oscar as Best Actor for his performance in *None But The Lonely Heart*, as had Ethel Barrymore as Best Supporting Actress. But at Grauman's Chinese Theater on the night of 15 March he lost to Bing Crosby in his role as Father O'Malley in *Going My Way*, directed by Leo McCarey. Even Ethel Barrymore's success did not alleviate Grant's despair. He could not play the role of husband; it seemed he could not play any role well enough.

In the next few months Grant hardly set foot outside his house. He even started sleeping downstairs on the couch instead of going upstairs to bed; and he refused to make any more films. At Warner Brothers the biography of Cole Porter was still waiting for him, but he refused even to consider it. For the moment he didn't care if he never made another movie in his life.

9

Notorious – But Never to Alfred Hitchcock

'A man may be a fool and not know it; but
not if he is married.'

H. L. Mencken

It was almost a year since Cary Grant had set foot on a
studio sound stage, and in the bright June sunlight he
blinked hard as he pushed open the soundproof door and
walked on to the dark set at Warner Brothers to start work on
Night and Day. He did not want to be there. He did not want
to be making films. But he knew he could not just sit around
the house all day moping. He had to work, and he had
promised Jack Warner he would make this film before he did
anything else.

Smiling at the film crew, some of whom had worked with
him on *Destination Tokyo*, he could not quite get Barbara out
of his mind. There was no hope of a reconciliation, he knew
that, but he could not bear the knowing looks and the side-
long glances that everyone seemed to give him. They made
him shrink back within himself, grateful for the blacked-
out limousine the studio had provided to bring him to the
set each day. If anyone wanted to see him they could pay at
the box office. That was where he could be judged; that was
where he truly existed. He did not intend to become an
exhibit in the public freak show of Hollywood. When he was
not actually shooting he would stay at home in Bel Air.

Jack Warner had decided to promote the film biography
of Cole Porter to mark the twentieth anniversary of the first
talking picture, *The Jazz Singer*, and he intended to put the

full weight of the studio's publicity machine behind it to make it a hit. This was essential – Warner had agreed to pay Cole Porter $300,000 over ten years for the right to use thirty-five of his songs, and had also accepted Grant's usual fee of $100,000 as an advance against a percentage of the profits. If the film did well Cary Grant would do well, exceptionally well. That, at least, was a consolation for him.

This was Michael Curtiz's seventieth film in a career which stretched back to 1926. While he had been waiting to start on it, he had directed Joan Crawford in *Mildred Pearce*, and now he was impatient to get to grips at last with a project which he and Jack Warner had first discussed back in 1943. He did not think it would be too difficult. Warners had some experience with musical biographies – they had already filmed the life of George Gershwin as *Rhapsody in Blue* – but Curtiz reckoned without his star.

Eric Stacey was again the unit manager, and his daily reports on the film's progress showed just how badly Curtiz had miscalculated. On the third day of shooting he wrote: 'Cary Grant complained all day long yesterday about the dialogue – how bad it was, how poorly written – and what lousy characterization it gave him.' A fortnight later things had not improved. 'Cary Grant is apparently very upset at the way he looks in the picture and claims he is being photographed too light.' By Day 22 Stacey was adding: 'This is another example, as mentioned several times before, of Mr Grant not particularly liking to do things the way the stand-ins are rehearsed.'

An anguished Stacey went on to report that Curtiz and Grant were constantly locked in negotiation about the changes necessary to the script, partly occasioned by the problems of portraying the occasionally homosexual Porter as a romantic lover of women. After two months of shooting, with the picture behind schedule, Stacey explained: 'Mike is just about frantic with all this rewriting (for your information it comes mostly from Cary Grant picking at and criticizing the script). The writers are out there two or three times a day changing things round.' On Day 69 he wrote: 'They do

193

not know how the end of the picture is going to be done. They have been writing this story for two years and still it is not on paper.'

Finally, after three months' shooting, Curtiz threatened to walk off the set because Grant wanted to direct the picture himself. Then Grant refused to meet Jack Warner to talk about how the film might be finished. The crew started to joke that Truman would have done better to drop the atomic bomb on Warners rather than Hiroshima – that way the war between the director and the star would have come to an end. Finally, on 15 October 1945, Cary Grant left the studio and walked on to the set of his next picture at RKO; but he returned for three days in November to finish his part. He had never worked with Michael Curtiz before and the day after those extra inserts were finished he said to the tiny Hungarian: 'Mike, now that the last foot of this film is shot I want you to know that if I'm chump enough ever to be caught working for you again, you'll know that I'm either broke or I've lost my mind. You may shanghai crews and cameramen to work with you, but not me, not again.'

Curtiz replied: 'Yes, Cary, yes, Cary,' but the following morning he rang the doorbell at Grant's Bel Air house. 'Cary, last night I read the most perfect script for us to do. No story could be as good for you as this one – I'll wait until 1948 or 1949. Together we can . . .'

Grant interrupted him. 'Didn't you understand me yesterday? Let me repeat, I'll never be lunatic enough to play in another of your pictures. Now do you understand me?'

'Yes, Cary, fine, Cary. But I'll leave the script.'

It was not until after the trade showing of *Night and Day*, nearly eight months later in July 1946, that Grant sent Curtiz a telegram of appreciation for his work. As he told *Photoplay*'s Ruth Waterbury: 'That's me, I raised hell all the way through the picture – I knew it was going to be a flop – so it turns out to be a top success. As for that Curtiz, there's a feverish man to work with, but I'm no dish of weak tea either.' But Cary Grant had had a great deal more on his mind than Michael Curtiz during the shooting of *Night and Day*. Three weeks after he had started on the picture, Barbara had decided to go ahead with her plan to divorce him.

In the middle of July 1945 Barbara's lawyer filed her suit in the Los Angeles Superior Court on the grounds of mental cruelty. At the end of the month Grant legally renounced any claims that he might have had to any of his wife's $50m fortune, and both he and Hutton agreed that neither would make any financial claims against the other.

On 30 August 1945, just as the shooting of *Night and Day* was becoming particularly troublesome, Barbara appeared in the Los Angeles court before Superior Judge Thurmond Clarke for the divorce hearing. Grant could not bring himself to witness the proceedings. Frank Vincent went in his place.

Standing quite still, with her hands clasped calmly in front of her, Barbara told the court that her husband had caused her 'great mental anguish'.

'Kindly explain that to the court,' said her lawyer, Jerry Geisler.

'Well, Mr Grant and myself did not have the same friends. On more than one occasion when I gave dinner parties he would not come downstairs but would have dinner in bed. When he did come down he obviously was not amused.'

'How did this affect you?' the judge asked her.

'It made me rather nervous.'

'Did you require the services of a doctor?'

'Yes, I did.'

Geisler did not pursue this line of questioning. Instead he produced the agreement signed by Hutton and Grant releasing each other from any financial claims. Then he called on Germaine Tocquet to corroborate her mistress's evidence.

As *Time* reported afterwards: 'In Hollywood, where marriages wither even faster than reputations, a spoiled little rich girl named Barbara Hutton dropped husband number three last week. The whole thing took four minutes. She would have made it in three if she had not taken time out to pose for the photographers.'

Despite the divorce Grant remained her only real love. The man of whom she had complained: 'He never took me out at night when we were married. I hardly saw him. At night he was always busy with his clippings or the radio,' became one of her few close friends. She admitted as much many times during the rest of her life, adding: 'He's really very sweet and kind.' For his part Cary Grant contented himself with remarking: 'The trouble wasn't with her. People just can't dissociate her from her money, and they act like idiots around her. She seldom gets to know people as they really are.'

Within six months of the divorce, Barbara had left America for Europe and was considering buying a house in Tangier because, she said, she had always wanted to live like an Arab. She added: 'My money has never brought me happiness. You can't buy love with money.' From now on Grant would be her constant support when she felt lonely, the unofficial guardian of her son Lance, who had been reunited with her just before the divorce proceedings started. She was dependent on him until the sad end of her immensely rich life, hardly a mile from his house in Beverly Hills.

It was some time before Grant would look back on the filming of *Night and Day* with any great pleasure. Jack Warner was so grateful to him for having played the part that he promised to give him a projection room for his house in recognition of his exceptional services to the film; but even so it took more than three years for the studio to honour this pledge and then only after a strong letter from Grant's lawyers.

On the set of his new film at RKO, however, Grant felt happier. For a start the director was Alfred Hitchcock. He did not believe in looking through the lens of the camera and acting out every move for his actors; instead he told them what he wanted and let them get on with it – so long as what they did worked. He also took more interest in his leading ladies than his leading men.

For more than a year, Hitchcock had wanted to make a film about a man in love with a girl who, in the course of her official duties, had to go to bed with another man and eventually marry him. Grant was to play Devlin, a United States government agent; the girl he was in love with but who had to do her duty and marry someone else for the sake of her country was to be played by Ingrid Bergman. Hitchcock had originally prepared the project for David Selznick, but Selznick had grown dubious about it, and had sold the whole thing early in 1945 to RKO for $800,000 and a share in the profits. Hitchcock, Bergman and Grant retained their involvement, however, as did the scriptwriter, Ben Hecht. The film was called *Notorious*.

Bergman accepted that Cary Grant's name could precede hers above the title, though her fee was $175,000 while he was still working for a percentage of the profits and his familiar advance of $112,500. She and Grant had met before, and he had introduced her to his friend Howard Hughes. Established as one of Hollywood's most beautiful actresses, she had just won an Oscar for her performance in *Gaslight*. She was cool, dark-haired and with a luminous, unforgettable beauty that audiences loved; she also had a gift which Hitchcock greatly admired – she could seem sexually attractive and distant at the same time.

The filming turned out to be the exact opposite of the torture of *Night and Day*. Grant liked Bergman and admired Hitchcock, prepared to accept that the portly director knew as much about film-making as he did. Accordingly he reduced to a minimum his customary fussing about costumes, setting and script. His resultant concentration on acting helped to transform the film, for while he had struggled consciously to give a strong performance in *None But The Lonely Heart*, Hitchcock produced even more effective work from him with no apparent effort.

Grant's remoteness and yet his fascination with Bergman's beauty, was nowhere more clearly captured than in the scene in which they appeared to be kissing for considerably longer than the three-second clinch-time the American film production code allowed. As Bergman recalled later: 'We just kissed each other and talked, leaned away and kissed each other again. Then the telephone came between us, and then we moved to the other side of the telephone. So it was a kiss which opened and closed: but the censors couldn't and didn't cut the scene because we never at any point kissed for more than three seconds. We did other things, we nibbled each other's ears, and kissed a cheek so that it looked endless, and became sensational in Hollywood.'

Grant's performance in *Notorious* re-established him as one of the screen's most eligible bachelors: a man who could suffer at the hands of women, but who was also desired by them. Hitchcock had caught his tortured, uncertain admiration of women and turned it into a brilliant screen performance. The eye-brow arching comedian of *The Philadelphia Story* had become a wiser, less frenzied but no less captivating man.

Ingrid Bergman was intoxicated with her co-star's charm. As soon as filming was finished early in 1946 she asked if there was any way they might work together again, and he was delighted at the idea. He admired her determination, her confidence, and her control. They reminded him of another small dark woman he had not seen for nearly eight years, and whom he was now anxious to see again.

Elsie Leach looked only a little older. The strains of bombing, firewatching, doodlebugs, rationing and powdered milk and eggs had left her pale and crotchety but basically the same. Nearly seventy, with the sharp dark eyes that he remembered only too well, she looked up at him awkwardly when they embraced, as if she hardly knew him. And indeed, she hardly did. He was forty-two now, probably handsomer than at any time in his life, and with a sun tan that made him conspicuous in a Britain where most men of his age bore a pallor bred of the hardships and privations of wartime.

'It's been a long time since I saw him,' Elsie told the local paper. 'But he writes regularly, and I always see his films.' She did not tell the paper, or indeed her son, whether she liked them. She said instead: 'I sometimes just wish he would settle down and have a family. It would be a great relief to me.'

Even though he felt slightly uncomfortable with his mother, Cary Grant was convinced that he ought to spend more time with her, and now that the war was over there was no reason why he could not work in England. That might be an ideal way of catching up on the time he and Elsie had lost. After all, in the thirty-two years since she had first disappeared from his life, he had seen her on barely a dozen occasions, and those had been concentrated in the six years before the war. There were few friends to keep him in Hollywood. Randolph Scott had married his own heiress, Patricia Stillman, and had moved into a new house in Beverly Hills; and apart from Howard Hughes, most of his other friends had ties in England, though there was still Noël Coward, whom he adored, and the other English playwright whose company he would always seek out, Freddie Lonsdale, the entertaining author of *The Last of Mrs Cheyney*.

Lonsdale had spent most of the war in America, sometimes in an apartment in New York, sometimes staying with Grant in California; he had introduced Grant to Alexander Korda. Grant called the playwright 'maddening but irresistible', and Lonsdale could well have described the actor in the same way. Both were given to depression, both could cheer the other up. Lonsdale, the son of a Jersey tobacconist, spoke with the assumed accent of Eton and Oxford and was as far from his own roots as Cary Grant was from his. The two men recognized loneliness in each other and ambition. Both were happy to conceal their uncertainty in the wit and contrived jokes of drawing-room comedy. Lady Frances Donaldson, in her biography of her father, said: 'Things that pleased him one day irritated him the next, and it was impossible to predict his reaction to any event. His dearest friends of one day were his enemies of the next and vice versa.' He and Grant had met on the liner taking them to England.

Although Grant knew that he would have to return to America to make a new film for David Selznick, he expected from now on to be back in England regularly. Britain might be austere under the new Labour Government but oddly he felt more affinity for the country than he had since the SS *Olympic* had steamed out of Southampton Water a quarter of a century before. He began to think about making his home in England again, perhaps for part of every year. Sir Alexander Korda had suggested he might make some films in England: Cary Grant was one of the few actors whom Korda did not regard as boring. For his part Grant liked the rascally Hungarian, just as he envied his culture and his confidence. Thanks to Barbara Hutton, though, Grant was no longer terrified of European arrogance, recognizing it as a style that his own upbringing had never offered, but one not to be despised for all that.

The success of Grant's two new films ironically made the prospect of further trips to England more remote. Not only had *Night and Day* opened to long queues at the box office but *Notorious* was also breaking records at the Radio City Music Hall in New York. Only *Life* magazine struck a harsh note among the critics. *Night and Day*, it said, was 'a remarkably complete dossier of all that is wrong with the current musical film ... Monty Woolley, who plays himself, was not a professor when Porter was at college but a fellow undergraduate. Porter himself carries out a largely fictitious war career, during which he is nursed back to health by his future wife from a wound which in fact he never received and composes future hits under circumstances having no relation to the true ones ... It may be of no great consequence that moviegoers are misled concerning the life of a popular composer. But now, when the Hollywood vogue for musical biographies has reached a peak (Chopin, Kern, Gershwin) such disregard for fact destroys the validity of this movie formula.'

But *Notorious* the critics liked. When it opened in New York only a fortnight after *Night and Day* Bosley Crowther in the *New York Times* described it as a 'romantic melodrama which is just about as thrilling as they come – velvet smooth in dramatic action, sharp and sure in its characters and heavily charged with the intensity of warm emotional appeal. But the rare quality of the picture is in the uncommon character of the girl and in the drama of her relations with the American intelligence man. For here Mr Hecht and Mr Hitchcock have done a forthright and daring thing: they have made the girl, played by Miss Bergman, a lady of notably loose morals.'

Back in Hollywood in June, and ready to start filming, Grant was in time for the Fourth of July celebrations; he attended a party at Newport Beach with Howard Hughes and one or two other friends, including Twentieth Century Fox's brand new nineteen-year-old discovery, Jean Peters, whom the studio intended to star in her first film opposite Tyrone Power. Hughes was on the verge of test-flying his company's new military aircraft, the XF-11, but the flight did not go well. Shortly after 6.30 p.m. on Sunday, 7 July 1946, Hughes crashed into the second floor of a house on North Linden Drive, Beverly Hills and almost killed himself.

The rumour in Hollywood that night was that he was tipping his wing to Katharine Hepburn – or Ginger Rogers or Jean Peters – when he crashed, but the reality was more mundane: the plane had simply developed a fault. 'Get well' messages deluged the Good Samaritan Hospital, including one from President Harry S. Truman; but the only people Hughes consented to see in hospital were one or two stars, including his old friend Cary Grant. Everyone else, even the employees of his aircraft company and his two elderly aunts from Texas, was kept out. To the amazement of the hospital's surgical team Hughes began to recover but, as he was to tell some of his friends, 'After the crash I never liked to see people very much again.'

Under the control of Selznick's associate Dore Schary, who had won an Oscar for the screenplay of *Boys' Town* and had gone on to produce for MGM and then for Selznick himself, Grant's new film was based on a Sidney Sheldon story. Originally called 'Too Good To Be True' and now retitled *The Bachelor and The Bobbysoxer*, it had become the vehicle for the seventeen-year-old Shirley Temple as well as for Grant. What plot there was consisted of Temple pursuing a fascinated but still appalled Grant through a series of new teenage rituals, including jitter-bugging and eating ice cream sodas, while her elder sister, played by the magnificent Myrna Loy, looked on.

Uncomplicated, lightweight and with none of Hitchcock's sombre tones, the film nevertheless appealed to Grant. That did not mean, however, that he did not take his usual pains to see that it came up to his standards. To Myrna Loy's consternation he discussed every detail of most scenes before they started shooting. The actress, who had appeared in *The Jazz Singer* and *The Thin Man* and had been called the Queen of Hollywood when Clark Gable was called the King, was taken aback.

As soon as shooting was finished in October 1946 Grant took off for New York with Howard Hughes. Hughes had been determined to fly an aeroplane again as soon as possible after his crash, and had been taking every available opportunity to test his new Constellation, sporting a newly grown moustache to conceal the scars on his lips. On the flight back from New York the two men, who were alone, decided to take an unscheduled trip to Mexico after they had stopped at El Paso. As Grant remember later: 'Howard doesn't like to get embroiled in crowds. So when we landed in El Paso, Howard rolled out to a dark part of the airfield and we sat in the plane drinking coffee, waiting for clearance.'

When they discovered the weather was bad, they took off for Guadalajara, ignoring their established flight plan. Their disappearance provoked headlines across the country. Two days later a reporter in Mexico discovered them. 'Did you fellows know you're in the headlines? You're supposed to be lost,' he said. Grant and Hughes laughed. It was another two days before they returned to Hollywood. As Grant told Hedda Hopper when he got back: 'Being lost suited us fine. We figured that as long as nobody knew where we were we could enjoy ourselves in peace. Howard is a mighty restful person to be around. When we're together we may go for two hours without saying a word to one another.'

Hopper herself added later: 'Cary and Howard Hughes are the closest of friends. Like Cary, Howard's a bachelor; like Grant, he's quiet in public, somewhat of a mystery man, he likes to go places and do things. He's got money, lots more than Cary, who's not exactly poor at a quarter of a million a picture. Together that pair take their fun where they can find it.' What Hopper did not point out was that both men apparently shared a weakness for young bosomy actresses, and that Hughes often asked Grant to organize an introduction to them. That was how Hughes had met Ingrid Bergman; the only time Grant and his co-star on *Notorious* ever went out together in the evening another guest was Howard Hughes. They had gone dancing at El Morocco in New York.

Before he started filming again Cary Grant decided to throw a party. One evening in Mike Romanoff's restaurant in Beverly Hills he met James Stewart, who had just finished making *It's A Wonderful Life* with Frank Capra, which RKO had originally bought as a starring vehicle for Grant himself. Stewart recalls now: 'He said to me, "I'm glad I've seen you because I was thinking that maybe we ought to give a party for all those people who've been giving us parties."

'For some reason it became known as the cads' party,' Stewart remembered, and John McLain and Eddy Duchin became involved in organizing it. Stewart, then also a Hollywood bachelor, was responsible for finding the band. Grant decided it should be held in the Clover Club, and Mike Romanoff did the catering. The room was decorated with two thousand gardenias which Grant bought at a cost of a dollar each. Stewart recalled: 'I took Rita Hayworth, but she was working the next day so I had to take her home about 3 a.m., and she told me to go back to the party. When I got back it was very quiet. Some of the lights were out and I saw Cary. He put his finger to his lips. In a little room off the dance floor the two hundred people who were there were crushed together. Bing Crosby was singing and Hoagy Carmichael was playing the piano, it was magical. Cary had organized that, because Bing didn't really like to do that kind of thing. In those days,' Stewart said, 'there was still the glamour in movies. It wasn't hard, we just had a good time.'

Hitchcock came up with another idea. He wanted Grant to play Hamlet, and asked a professor of the University of California to work on a film script; but the star was not keen. He preferred a new comedy, this time for Sam Goldwyn, which was again to be released by RKO. By now no producer wanted to upset this star who seemed to guarantee success: Grant's last three films had all been big box-office hits. He seemed to feel at last that he could do what he liked, though when he went to the races he still only bet $2 on any horse. Grant had in fact done a spectacular deal with Goldwyn. His agent Frank Vincent had been ill and he had driven the bargain with the producer himself. It guaranteed that he would be paid $300,000 for the picture. Then, dissatisfied – not for the first time – with the showing of director and script after filming had started, he offered to give Goldwyn all his money back if he would release him from his contract. Goldwyn refused, but did finally agree to changes and guaranteed Grant an extra $100,000 to keep him sweet. It was the highest fee any star in Hollywood had ever received for a single film.

Clearly constructed to appeal to the same audiences who had packed Leo McCarey's two hugely successful efforts, *Going My Way* and *Belles of St Mary's*, the new film cast Grant as an angel who arrives on earth to help a Protestant bishop, played by David Niven, to raise money for his cathedral.

The climax of the film, which was called *The Bishop's Wife*, took place on Christmas Eve; and an ever commercially astute Goldwyn had already decided to release it for Christmas.

There were difficulties and indecisions. Robert E. Sherwood, who had just won an Oscar for his screenplay for Goldwyn and RKO's *The Best Years of Our Lives*, produced a version of the script. Then Goldwyn asked Eric Bercovici to do another. The roles of Dudley, the angel, and the bishop had been conceived the wrong way round, with Niven originally cast as the angel and Grant as the bishop. It was Grant who insisted on a change, just as he insisted on debating his role in the film with Goldwyn as they went along. William Seiter started directing, then Goldwyn replaced him with Henry Koster, who had worked on a string of Deanna Durbin pictures.

As his co-star, Loretta Young, recalled later: 'Each morning I would arrive on the stage in wardrobe and make up, ready to go to work, but Cary would start dissecting our next scene with Henry Koster. It made me so nervous I would go into a scene all depressed and unsure. I finally said, "Cary, please, I don't mind you doing this because I know you're trying to get a better film, but please don't do it around me." He apologized to me, and he never did it again – in my presence.' His other co-star, David Niven, took to describing him as 'fey', but left it at that. Not everyone in Hollywood was as generous. *Photoplay* called him 'as contradictory as are his Latin looks to his English blood'.

While he was moodily finishing the picture for Goldwyn, *The Bachelor and the Bobbysoxer* appeared to enthusiastic reviews. *Variety* paid tribute to Cary Grant's 'expert timing', which, it explained, 'proves a terrific lift to an occasionally awkward plot'. The *New York Times* added: 'Being perhaps the most accomplished looker-askance in films, not to mention fumer and frowner, Mr Grant has his opportunities here.' The film became his fourth consecutive box-office success, taking more than $5.5m.

It had hardly left the cinemas when Sam Goldwyn rel-

eased *The Bishop's Wife* to exactly the same rave reaction.
The reviewers called it 'fluent and beguiling' and added that
Grant's playing 'rescues the role from the ultimate peril of
coyness'. Although not quite the equal of its predecessor at
the box office, the film was nevertheless nominated as one of
the best films of 1947 at the Oscar ceremonies in March
1948.

Despite all this, he told one interviewer: 'The fulfilment of
one's ambitions doesn't always lead to happiness, but when
I started out I was eager to explore the idea that success
means happiness . . . Now I know that the success is not the
happiness. The working is.' He had begun to take an interest
in the Chinese religion of Taoism because, he said, 'You just
go along with the rhythm of life.'

At the twentieth Academy Awards in March 1948, *The
Bishop's Wife* lost to Darryl F. Zanuck and Elia Kazan's
Gentleman's Agreement. Ronald Colman won the Oscar as Best
Actor for his performance in *A Double Life*, in a role that
Grant had turned down. Grant's reversion to the idea of
preserving his original image had, on this occasion, cost him
dearly, in prestige at least.

For the moment, however, he couldn't care less about
films. Once again he had fallen in love – or at least was
convinced that he had.

After the filming of *The Bishop's Wife*, Cary Grant had set
off for England again with Freddie Lonsdale. He had two
months free before he was due to start his next picture for
David Selznick, and he wanted to see his mother. He also
had a great deal to discuss with Alexander Korda about his
proposed series of films in England. In the front parlour of
her house near the Downs in Bristol Mrs Leach looked
across at her famous son and frowned. She didn't understand him, but she knew he had always annoyed her.
'Sometimes I'm not sure it would be good for him to marry,'
she would now tell people. 'Archie always was restless, even
as a child. He never likes to feel he's tied in any way.' Her son

smiled distantly, and patted her hand.

The trip went well. Freddie Lonsdale was a marvellous companion. They went to see plenty of the new shows in London, including one called *Deep Are The Roots* which was just completing a seven-month run and had a twenty-four-year-old American actress called Betsy Drake as its female star. They came to the conclusion that the London stage was not at its peak, but there were still interesting things to be seen. At the end of September they went back to America. They were to sail from Southampton on the *Queen Elizabeth*, and both men knew there would be a party of their friends on the ship: Elizabeth Taylor was travelling, in the company of her formidable mother, and so was Lady Korda, otherwise the actress Merle Oberon, and Jock Whitney. They drove down to Southampton in two Rolls-Royces, the front one containing themselves, the one behind brimful of luggage and loaded with two hampers of food and wine for the journey. Not long after the ship had edged out into the Solent, Grant was on his way to the first-class lounge to have tea with Elizabeth Taylor when a short, brown-haired girl with grey-green eyes, sensible shoes and a faintly quizzical expression opened the folding doors of one of the ship's telephone booths and catapulted into his arms.

'Hey, aren't you the girl I saw in *Deep Are The Roots*?' Grant asked her.

In the years to come Betsy Drake would always insist that she was so embarrassed at being thrown into Cary Grant's arms by a lurch of the ship that she couldn't answer a word, but he would maintain: 'I swear a bit of coquetry was going on.' At the time she just blushed fiercely and disappeared in the direction of her cabin.

Next morning on deck Merle Oberon went up to her and said: 'I have a friend, Cary Grant, who would like to meet you. Will you have lunch with us?' Cary Grant was hiding behind a gangway a few yards away, hoping she would not refuse. Both he and Freddie Lonsdale had watched her at dinner the evening before, and both had agreed that she was strikingly beautiful. Indeed, as Grant was to remember:

'Had Freddie been twenty years younger I would certainly have lost her to him.'

For the remaining five days of the voyage, Betsy Drake had every meal with Cary Grant. No-one could separate them. He wanted to find out everything he could about the apparently gauche young actress who stammered slightly when she was nervous. She told him that her father's family had built the famous Drake Hotel in Chicago, but had been ruined by the stock market crash in 1929. She had been born in Paris in September 1923, had two younger brothers, but when she was nine her parents had divorced, with the result that she had had what might best be called a somewhat haphazard education. She had gone to live in New York after studying drama in Washington, had worked in an agent's office, modelled everything from frying pans to girdles, had always wanted to act, and had got one or two small parts before H. M. Tennent's had suggested that she come to London. She had even been offered a contract by Hal Wallis in Hollywood in 1946, but after sitting in a hotel room for two weeks waiting for a screen test she had left for New York, determined to get on with her career. 'She intrigued me no end,' said Grant later. 'She was interested in astronomy and yoga – subjects I'd never investigated myself. She was bookish, but charmingly so.'

By the time they reached New York Cary Grant was convinced that he had met the first woman who needed him as much as he needed her. He was determined to help her with her career, and to teach her everything she would need to know to become a star. It was the greatest gift he had to offer.

'How would you like to be in my next film?' he asked her as they were standing on the upper deck with their collars turned up against the morning air and the liner slipping into the Hudson River. 'It's called *Every Girl Should Be Married*. The part is perfect for you.'

'They'll never give it to me.'

'I'll make them.'

'Oh, you can't. They'd say you were doing it because you – you liked me.'

Grant took her arm. 'They won't say it after they've seen you act. And maybe they'll be a little more perceptive. Maybe they'll say – because I need you so.'

There was nothing to keep her in New York. No part was waiting for her. The chance to make films might be worth the trip to Hollywood, in spite of the Hal Wallis experience, if it helped her to get started. Cary Grant was delighted; Freddie Lonsdale was a little sceptical.

While he started work with Myrna Loy and Melvyn Douglas on *Mr Blandings Builds His Dream House* for David Selznick, Betsy Drake set about finding herself a room in an apartment hotel and seeing whether her career as an actress really would prosper in Hollywood. Some people, she noticed, looked at her a little strangely or nodded at each other knowingly, but she ignored them. She knew that the strangely private man she had met on the *Queen Elizabeth* had always treated her like his daughter, rather than like a starlet.

The first thing Grant had done when they reached Hollywood was to introduce Betsy Drake to David Selznick and Dore Schary. Both men were polite, encouraging and arranged screen tests. Once they had seen them they also became sympathetic. 'Yes,' they told her, 'there is every chance you could have a career in films.' Betsy would never know whether Selznick and Schary were saying that because of the interest in her of one of their most important stars. (What Selznick and Schary did not know was that Grant had carefully coached her to make the best use of the test.) She set her jaw, and made up her mind that she was going to get on in the picture business on her own. As she told Louella Parsons, who was to describe her as 'the most completely determined young woman I've ever met': 'If people say she's made good because of Cary Grant that's bad for him and bad for me.'

Nevertheless Cary Grant certainly made sure that RKO considered her for *Every Girl Should Be Married*, the film he was planning to make after he had finished *Mr Blandings Builds His Dream House*. Schary, RKO's new production head, agreed she might be right. David Selznick agreed to buy half her contract if RKO bought the other half. The studio were not anxious to upset a star who had made four successful films in a row since *Night and Day*, even if they had been thinking of using Barbara Bel Geddes for the part. Betsy Drake's future in Hollywood was settled.

Perhaps another reason why RKO were not keen to contradict their star was that his friend Howard Hughes had just taken over the studio. Early in January 1948, after telling the press he was no longer interested in the movie business, Hughes had flown off to a secret meeting with Floyd B. Odlum, the millionaire president of the $70m Atlas Corporation which effectively controlled RKO. Odlum's severe rheumatoid arthritis meant that he conducted negotiations from the swimming pool of his nine hundred-acre estate near Palm Springs, but Hughes did not mind that. He flew down to see him. By the time shooting had started on *Every Girl Should Be Married* Hughes had bought RKO, and had reassured Dore Schary that he wanted no part in running the studio. That did not last long. By the time Don Hartman had almost finished the film, Hughes had started to interfere. He was even staying in Cary Grant's house to do it.

Dore Schary told the *New York Times* many years later that when he was summoned to see his new boss at the house, 'there wasn't a paper, a cigarette, a flower, a match, a picture, a magazine – there was nothing except two chairs and a sofa.' The only sign of life, he recalled, was Hughes, 'who appeared from a side room in which I caught a glimpse of a woman hooking up her bra before the door closed.' Grant had bought the house looking down over Beverly Hills after he had sold Bellagio Road, but he had yet to move in. After an extraordinary meeting, at which Hughes seemed more interested in where Schary had bought the shoes he was wearing than in the films he was making at RKO, Schary had resigned as production chief. Within a month more than three hundred people in the studio, about a third of the total work force, had been fired.

Every Girl Should Be Married was the last film Grant made for the studio which had first proved he was more than just Paramount's potential matinée idol by casting him in *Sylvia Scarlett*. Before it was released at Christmas 1948, Grant had left America to make his first film with Howard Hawks since *His Girl Friday*. Hawks had decided to make a film in Europe, and to make it another comedy. He had just finished making *Red River*, with John Wayne and Montgomery Clift, and wanted a change of pace; he also wanted to work with Grant again. He was to star opposite a girl he and Randolph Scott had first met when they arrived in Hollywood, Ann Sheridan. Set in Germany after the war, the new film was based on the true story of an officer who was unable to consummate his marriage for six weeks because of army regulations. With a script by Charles Lederer, Leonard Spiegelglass and Hagar Wilde, the film was called *I Was A Male War Bride*.

Cary Grant took Betsy Drake with him to Europe, and stopped off on the way to the location to introduce her to his mother. He was in a cheerful mood. It seemed as though the film would progress without difficulties, and he had always enjoyed working with Hawks. His optimism didn't last. Once shooting started in Germany things began to go severely wrong. First, bad weather stopped filming, and then Ann Sheridan caught pleurisy, which turned into pneumonia. Then Randy Stuart, another member of the cast, contracted jaundice. Hawks began to feel the whole film was jinxed. By the end of November, with the film still unfinished and the company in London, Cary Grant was beginning to complain that he did not feel at all well. Within three days jaundice was diagnosed and a British doctor told him he could do nothing except stay in bed. He was run down, and in need of complete rest.

Lying in bed in London, surrounded by solicitous telegrams, Cary Grant thought for the first time about suicide. He had been depressed before but somehow the sense of isolation he felt at being trapped in a chilly country that was no longer his home left him desolate. Even the telephone calls he made to all his friends did nothing to cheer him up.

He began to lose weight steadily, as if he was no longer interested in the world.

Betsy Drake saved his life. As he said later: 'She nursed me back to health.' She was a revelation to him. Her concern to see him well again convinced him that he had found someone who was prepared to devote herself to him, who was prepared to make his life the most important thing in her own, and who would give him the affection that he had always craved. Gradually his depression subsided, and so did his illness. The reviews of *Every Girl Should Be Married* cheered him up too. Most critics liked Betsy. *Newsweek* said that her 'frenetic charm and windblown naturalness are sometimes nerve-wracking but more often thoroughly appealing' and the *New York Times* added: 'She gives considerable promise of more formidable triumphs on the screen.' Only his old enemy *Time* magazine carped: 'Newcomer Betsy Drake seems to have studied, but not to have learned, the tricks and inflections of early Hepburn.' The film virtually became RKO's only commercial success in 1949, making them more than $750,000 and scoring for Grant his sixth hit in a row. Ironically, since his decision not to make any more serious films after the disappointment of *None But The Lonely Heart*, his success had grown rapidly. He was now finally established as one of the top ten box-office stars in the United States, and even though he had not been one as long as his old rival Gary Cooper, his film *The Bachelor and The Bobbysoxer* had been one of the biggest-grossing films of 1948. Once more, and incontrovertibly, he could console himself with the thought that at least his films made money, even if the critics did not always like them.

Reluctantly Howard Hawks decided there was no point in keeping the company in Europe to finish *I Was A Male War Bride*. The weather in England and Germany was too bad and they would have to finish the picture in Hollywood. Sheridan had just about recovered, but Grant was still weak. He had lost around thirty pounds in weight, and it seemed to the director that his appetite for making films had vanished. He seemed uninterested in anything except getting back to

California and sitting in the sunshine. By the end of February he felt well enough to travel, and decided that going home by the long sea route would give him a chance to recuperate away from the pressures of the movie business, and to think things over. Before he left he told Betsy that he did not need to work. He was not rich, but he had invested his money carefully over the past years and that meant he could afford to turn down any offer he wanted to. He could stop making films altogether. 'I would not miss it.'

'But would you really ever retire?'

'I might,' he told her, 'I might.'

As the Holland-America Line's steamship *Dalerdyck* nosed into her berth in Los Angeles harbour in the soft April air, the crowd of reporters on the quayside began to jostle one another. They knew the small ship's most famous passenger would not take long to disembark; he could see the beautiful girl waiting to meet him. They had already asked Betsy Drake why she was there.

'To meet Mr Grant,' she had told them politely.

Less than five minutes after the ship's bow lines had been secured and the gangplank lowered, they saw Cary Grant walking slowly down it towards them. It took them less than five seconds to ask: 'Have you come back to get married, Mr Grant?' 'Are you and Miss Drake going to get married?'

It was the only question they wanted answered. They knew how well she had looked after him in London, and how she had flown back to California before him to prepare for his arrival.

Looking slightly unsteady, Cary Grant smiled.

'Well, I have asked her. Do you blame me, after getting a look at her?' As she took his arm Betsy Drake smiled too.

'Maybe you can get an answer for me,' Grant called out.

'Well, Miss Drake, are you going to get married? Everyone in Hollywood seems to think you are.'

'I'm too busy concentrating on my next picture right now,' she said quietly.

'The third Mrs Cary Grant,' one of the reporters muttered as he walked towards the telephone box at the end of the pier.

Grant still felt ill, but the worst of his depression had left him. One thing he did not want to talk about, though, was another film. This one seemed to have lasted forever, without a break, and he could not bring himself to think about what he should aim to do next. His agent and old friend Frank Vincent had died the year before, and there were few people he trusted to talk to about his work. For most of the time he preferred to be his own agent. After all, Frank Vincent used to tell him, 'if there's a better agent in Hollywood than Cary Grant I'd like to meet him. There only ever was one better one – Myron Selznick – and he's dead.'

Howard Hawks knew that, which was why he had mentioned to him the idea of making a film of *Don Quixote*, with the Spanish comedian Cantinflas playing Sancho Panza to his Don. The idea was intriguing enough, but after shooting the last few scenes of *I Was A Male War Bride* at the Fox studios and taking another rest in Palm Springs, Grant went into the John Hopkins Hospital in Baltimore for a ten-day check-up, as he had promised Betsy he would. When he came out Howard Hawks invited him to the first preview of the picture that seemed to have ruined his health.

For once Grant was surprised. As he told the *New York Times*: 'Frankly, I approach my pictures with trepidation. But I just saw a preview of the picture here and the audience laughed themselves sick. I've been in many comedies but I've never heard an audience react like this one. I honestly feel it's the best comedy I've ever done.'

After waiting more than a year for it to be finished, Fox were impatient to get the film into the cinemas. By the end of August it was released and Bosley Crowther of the *New York Times* was saying uncertainly: 'The flimsiness of the film's foundations and the disorder of its episodes provoke the inevitable impression that it all fell together en route.' *Newsweek*, however, was adding enthusiastically: 'Under Howard Hawks's direction the end product is one of the most sparklingly original comedies of the year.' Whatever the critics said, the film made a massive impact at the box office. Grant had scored again.

What he wanted most now, though, was to marry Betsy Drake; and even though Freddie Lonsdale had given his warning that it would be bad for her career as an actress, she seemed to want to marry him. By the time they got back to Beverly Hills together in September 1949 they were even talking about the matter to Louella Parsons.

Grant was unusually frank about his intentions. He told Parsons that the date of their marriage was up to Betsy. 'I'm ready at any time, but she feels, and I think she is right, that she wants to have a career, and she wants to do it independently. Of course neither of us can be sure we won't make up our minds to marry, one day, on the spur of the moment. But it looks now as if we would be married around 1 January.' As the columnist wrote afterwards, Betsy Drake had explained: 'If I should marry before I have at least two successful pictures, no matter how good I might be, I would simply be known as Mrs Cary Grant. I hope later to make a picture with Cary, but now I have to do two alone, one a comedy, the other a drama.' She had already started work on *Pretty Baby* at Warners, with Edmund Gwenn and Zachary Scott.

In the end it was Howard Hughes who decided matters. Drama or comedy, films or no films, on Christmas Day 1949 he picked them up in Beverly Hills, took them to Glendale Airport north of Hollywood, put them into one of his own planes, and piloted them to Phoenix, Arizona. He had decided the time had come for them to get married, and they had agreed. For years Cary Grant would say that his friend had made it all possible.

The plane landed in Phoenix at half past one in the afternoon, and within an hour and a half they had been married in the comfortable ranch-house of Mr and Mrs Sterling Hebbard near Scottsdale, Arizona. There were just half a dozen witnesses as the twenty-six-year-old bride, wearing a black and white check suit, looked up at her forty-five-year-old husband while the Reverend Stanley

Smith conducted the brief five-minute service. As Hughes, the best man, was passing the ring he dropped it, but neither the bride nor the groom looked in the least upset.

After a tiny reception Hughes flew the new Mr and Mrs Cary Grant back to Hollywood. Betsy Drake did not even know how many people had watched her get married: she had refused to wear her glasses. As she told her father on the telephone when they got back: 'What girl wants to be married wearing glasses?' Her husband gave her a string of pearls with a diamond clasp for a wedding present, together with a white poodle named Suzie. As the sun settled over the Pacific they talked about making another film together, but they also talked about retiring and sailing round the world. This time, Cary Grant said to himself, he would be happy.

There was just one film for him to make – a new picture he had promised to do for MGM after Christmas. Its producer, Arthur Freed, most famous for his musicals, had guaranteed that it would only take thirty-six days to shoot, and Grant liked the young man whom the studio proposed should direct it, the screenwriter Richard Brooks. Betsy had *Pretty Baby* to finish, but after that they could be together.

Brooks, who had started his career as a newspaper reporter, had been introduced to Grant at the races at Santa Anita. As he recalled later, 'Cary said: "I know that name, there's a script I like called *Crisis*." I said: "Yes, I wrote it; but, Mr Grant, my problem is that I want to direct it too." '

'Well, if you can write it, you can direct it,' Grant told him. And as Brooks maintained from then onwards: 'If it hadn't been for Cary Grant I'd never have been a director.' Brooks, who had written *Key Largo* for Humphrey Bogart in 1948, became one of Grant's staunchest supporters in Hollywood. As he told the *Los Angeles Times*: 'Those stories about him being stingy are far from true . . . I bought my present house and spent all my money on it and had no furniture. One day a truck arrived and it was filled with furniture. It was from Cary. I called him and said, "I can't take this." He said, "Listen, I have to pay storage for it in a warehouse.

You're not going to charge me storage if you keep it are you?" '

One of Grant's co-stars on *Crisis* was to be José Ferrer. This versatile Puerto-Rican-born actor had been nominated for an Academy Award in 1949 for his portrayal of the Dauphin in the screen version of *Joan of Arc*, playing opposite Ingrid Bergman, but had lost it to Walter Huston. Ferrer recalled that he was pleased to get the part in *Crisis* because it was a good step forward in his career, and remembered that when the filming started 'We were all a little excited because it was Richard Brooks's first directing job and we were all rooting for him.' Of Grant he said: 'He had a keen sense of the comic and the ridiculous and it made working easy and pleasant, and I also remember that he had a very clear idea of what he wanted to do and how he wanted to do it, and on at least one or two occasions quietly made his wishes known and imposed his will.'

Basically a flimsy story of a respected brain surgeon who is kidnapped while on holiday in a Latin American country and forced to operate on its sick dictator, *Crisis* bore a strong resemblance to the British film *State Secret*. The straight-forward plot seemed to appeal to Grant, as did the fact that it was all to be shot in Hollywood on just five sets. As soon as *Crisis* was made, he returned gratefully to his house in Palm Springs, settled in with his new wife, and put motion pictures out of his mind again.

That did not prevent there being a great deal of talk about films he *might* make. David Selznick was considering adapt-ing F. Scott Fitzgerald's novel *Tender Is The Night* for Grant and Jennifer Jones, and asking George Cukor to direct it; and all sorts of other scripts were delivered to the star's door every day. But he was interested in none of them. As far as he was concerned, the only important thing he wanted was to make his marriage work. If he could simply concentrate on his new wife, and convince her that he did indeed like being married, then nothing else really mattered.

Crisis came out in June to respectful reviews, although the critics seemed a little surprised that Grant should have broken away from comedy for the first time since *Notorious*. They did not know that one of the young actresses he had tested for the leading role was Nancy Davis, later to become Nancy Reagan. Grant contented himself later with remarking that she was probably lucky she didn't get the part. The film was a commercial disaster.

For the rest of 1950 he and Betsy Drake spent little or no time in Hollywood. There was a trip to England to see his mother, a good deal of riding in Palm Springs, and some tennis and swimming, but there was no talk of films. Cary Grant was learning that his wife had considerably more intellectual ambitions than had appeared. She wanted to write, and had an idea for turning *Mr Blandings Builds His Dream House* into a radio series. Meanwhile Betsy was discovering that her husband was more than happy to take an interest in anything she advised. She gave him books on natural history, discussed new and original diets with him, and introduced him to new kinds of music. He made the radio series with her, and although it was not a success he did not mind. 'What does one more bad Mr and Mrs Show on radio matter?' he asked his friends.

Perhaps, had it not been for Joseph L. Mankiewicz, Cary Grant would have remained in Palm Springs. But the screenwriter-turned-director, who had won four Oscars in the past two years for successes including *A Letter to Three Wives* and *All About Eve*, wanted to make his next film with Cary Grant. He had a play he thought would guarantee success, and Darryl F. Zanuck at Fox believed him.

Reluctantly Grant began to consider making a film again. He knew that the number of television sets in American homes had doubled in the past year – he had one himself, and had grown to like it – and that cinema audiences were falling fast. But he also knew that Mankiewicz seemed to have the golden touch. It meant that the percentage of the profits he always looked for would make the experience of going back into the studio just about bearable.

All About Eve had told the story of an ageing Broadway star and an ambitious young actress, and now Mankiewicz was aiming to do the same thing for the medical profession. Based on the play *Dr Praetorius* by Kurt Goetz, which had been made into a film in Germany but had never been released in the United States, it set out to explore the pressures on a crusading doctor who falls in love with a pregnant but unmarried girl who has just tried to commit suicide.

Grant liked the script, which was now called *People Will Talk*, and he took the pains he always did to learn exactly what it would be necessary for him to know as a doctor, taking professional guidance from a New York heart specialist, insisting that the settings be as authentic and convincing as possible. Shot at Fox in the spring of 1951, the picture was completed and prepared for release quickly while Mankiewicz's Oscars were still fresh in people's minds. It was launched at a spectacular première at Graumann's Chinese Theater in Hollywood in July. Sadly, what had worked for George Sanders did not seem to work for Cary Grant. The film was not the compelling portrait of *All About Eve*. The *Hollywood Reporter* noted sadly: 'The slick production comes up with a collation of observations that run the gamut from cynical and shocking to delightful and plumb foolish.' Even the old-fashioned movie première, which was attended by Norma Shearer, Joan Crawford and Mitzi Gaynor, as well as by Grant and his co-star, Jeannie Crain, did nothing to help. *Newsweek* described him as giving 'one of the most intelligent performances in his nineteen-year Hollywood career', but the film did not capture the audience's imagination. It was Arthur Freed's musicals at MGM like *An American in Paris*, *The Great Caruso* and *Showboat* which were doing that.

Disappointed, Grant agreed to do another film with Betsy Drake, this time for Warner Brothers. Howard Hawks's idea of making *Don Quixote* had fallen through, but in the meantime Warners had found a script which had a part for both the Grants. His fee was to be ten per cent of the gross revenue of the picture, with a minimum guarantee of

$100,000, while Betsy was to be paid $25,000. Cary would have the special dressingroom and telephone that he always asked for now, although they did not allow him free long-distance calls. The studio also allowed him to continue to appear in the radio series of *Mr Blandings*, and they had accepted that he wanted to get the picture over quickly so that he could work with Howard Hawks again.

Room For One More was based on a bestseller about a city engineer whose wife likes to look after unwanted children as they have none of their own. It seemed to echo Grant's own life; all Hollywood was beginning to wonder if he might at last become a father. For once he looked calm and cheerful on the set. He even took to telling anyone who asked him: 'The only place we go nights is home. Domesticity is a great invention, more people should relax and enjoy it. Somebody's always asking what we do with ourselves and I always answer "Enjoy life" but that never seems to be enough. I feel sorry for people who don't take pleasure in their homes. They apparently don't understand those who do.'

He even seemed pleased when his wife made 8-mm home movies about the filming. She was encouraging him to learn French, and he gave her a guitar for her birthday. They both gave the five children in the picture presents. This was nothing like the nervous, overwrought star that some of the crew at Warners remembered. Betsy Drake had taken up painting as well as amateur photography; on Sundays she and her husband would play tennis, swim and sit beside the pool at the Beverly Hills house although, as she told one interviewer, 'We don't always see as much of our friends as we should, but the truth of the matter is that we seldom entertain.'

Room For One More seemed to capture the cheerfulness its stars were both feeling. *Variety* called it 'happy' when it was finally released early in 1952, and the *Hollywood Reporter* added: 'A delightful domestic comedy.' Even *Time* magazine admitted grudgingly: 'The movie's handling of child behaviour is unusually sound for a Hollywood film, fairly free of obvious tear jerking.' But the film was nothing like the success of *Every Girl Should Be Married*. Disheartened, Grant realized again that he did not enjoy making films any more. Betsy was telling him that perhaps it was time to take a complete break from Hollywood, and he agreed with her. He had promised Howard Hawks that he would work with him a fifth time, but he did not feel much pleasure at the prospect. The story Hawks had for him was simple. An absent-minded scientist experimenting with chimpanzees accidentally discovers a youth drug that makes him act like a young man. The screenplay had been written by his old friends Ben Hecht and Charles Lederer, with some help from I. A. L. Diamond. Originally called 'Darling I Am Getting Younger', the film had its title changed by Hawks and Fox to *Monkey Business*.

Although the inspired frenzy of *Bringing Up Baby* was there in some of the big scenes, all too often the new script meandered, and Grant was left feeling uncomfortable. This time there was a chimpanzee called Peggy rather than a leopard called Nissa for him to contend with, and even the presence of his old friend Ginger Rogers playing his wife, and the new discovery Marilyn Monroe as the secretary with whom he rediscovers his youth on the roller-skating rink, failed to reassure him. After it was over even Hawks was prepared to admit that perhaps it had all gone too far. 'I don't think the premise of the film was really believable,' he said, 'and for that reason it was not as funny as it should have been.' Bosley Crowther pointed out in the *New York Times* that it was a curiously old-fashioned picture. The conventions of 'screwball comedy', so appropriate and timely in the depression of the 1930s, seemed strained and out of place in a Hollywood that was making *Death of a Salesman*, *Come Back Little Sheba*, and *High Noon* in the 1950s.

Grant too felt that the time for his kind of films had come to a close. 'It was the period of blue jeans, dope addicts, the method and nobody cared about comedy at all,' he said morosely. That year's Oscars went to Vivien Leigh and Karl Malden for *A Streetcar Named Desire*. Still, even though he believed that his career was nearing its end Grant agreed with Dore Schary at MGM that he would make just one more picture for him.

Schary wanted to recreate the success of *The Bachelor and The Bobbysoxer*, and he had got Sidney Sheldon, who had won an Oscar for scripting that, to work on an unpublished story called *Dream Wife* in order to do it. He convinced Grant that it was worth trying, and they both agreed that Sheldon should direct it. But in spite of their hopes the alchemy of the first film could not be repeated. Not even the talents of Deborah Kerr and Walter Pidgeon could make *Dream Wife* a success. Made while MGM were also filming *Mogambo* with Clark Gable and Ava Gardner, and *The Band Wagon* with Fred Astaire, it turned out to be another uncomfortably old-fashioned comedy. Amiable and fluffy, it seemed altogether contrived. The *Hollywood Reporter* called it 'stretched out far beyond the value of its basic premise' – and the *Hollywood Reporter* was right.

Grant really did not mind. Almost exactly twenty years after he had driven into Hollywood in his Packard he decided it was time for him to retire from the movie scene. He and Betsy could travel if she wanted to, perhaps go round the world on a tramp steamer, forget about motion pictures, and forget the character called Cary Grant. Perhaps he might even start to find out who he really was and what he wanted to become.

PART THREE
The Haunted Star

'If I give the impression of being a man
without a problem in the world it is because
people with problems always try to give that
impression. We are all the opposite of what we
appear to be.'

Cary Grant

IO

A Tiny Private World

'Style is self-plagiarism.'

Alfred Hitchcock

There were tears in George Cukor's eyes. It was the finest performance he had ever seen Cary Grant give, but he suspected he would be the only person in the world ever to witness it. Beside the swimming pool of his house Cukor watched the nearly fifty-year-old actor read part of Moss Hart's script for the film he was planning, and become the middle-aged star, Norman Maine, whose career is slowly disintegrating while his new young wife's begins.

'At least think about it, Cary,' Cukor said. 'It's a terrific part.' But the director knew his persuasion was never going to work. Grant had already told him he wanted to retire and that he had no intention of changing his mind. Even if he did he was far from sure that he would want to make a serious film, and he didn't know how it would work out for him to play opposite Judy Garland.

Cukor didn't answer. He knew that nothing would persuade Cary Grant to appear in his new version of *A Star is Born*. Both men knew, but neither put into words, that there was an unspoken reason for Cary Grant's refusal. The film plot seemed strangely to parallel the actor's own life: his new young wife was just starting on her career, while his seemed to be ending with a number of films which had not had quite the success which many had hoped. It was asking a great deal to expect Cary Grant to live out his private fears on celluloid. When Betsy Drake had found out that her husband had been reading for Cukor she told the director to leave him alone, and now he knew that Cary Grant would never appear in the part. It was a loss. Garland wanted him; she and her husband Sidney Luft had spent weeks tracking him down. But the film would survive. If Garland behaved she could even win an Oscar for it, and if she did, she would deserve it.

On the steamer to Japan, on the first leg of their cruise around the world away from Hollywood and the picture business, Cary Grant looked across at Betsy and reminded himself how lucky he was.

'If you'd known me when I was young,' he told her, 'you wouldn't have liked me and I wouldn't have liked you.'

Slightly surprised, she looked up from her book, 'Why ever not?'

'When I was young I was conceited and impossible. I was so conscious of my clothes and the way I looked. I never knew there was another actor on the set. I thought only of my lines.'

Betsy Drake shook her head, and her husband reached across to her.

'Now I know how completely unimportant it is to have well fitted clothes in an ill-fitting performance! You're the most honest person I know. Simple. Direct and intelligent. When I was young I wouldn't have appreciated your qualities. I was too self-centred.'

He felt as if his life had only just begun, as though he had always been waiting for this moment. It was all he had ever wanted, to travel in the company of a woman who cared for him. There were no films dragging either of them back to Hollywood, and people could think whatever they liked. They could say he was the meanest actor in Hollywood, the man who never entertained anyone at his home. He cared nothing for that – Howard Hughes never entertained much either. He and Betsy would be all right. He felt free for the first time in his life. There were so many things to discover together, so many books to read, so much to see and so much to understand. He could not think why he had not retired before.

Besides, the Hollywood they had left was changing. Suddenly everyone was accusing everyone else of being a Communist, or a Communist sympathizer. Hughes had got all worked up and had rushed off to Washington to support Senator Joe McCarthy's attacks on the Communists in the film industry, but Cary Grant did not intend to get involved. Bogart and Bacall could protest if they wanted to, but he would not be dragged in. There were people he knew who seemed to be getting a rough deal, like Donald Ogden Stewart, who had written *The Philadelphia Story*, and that was a shame; but it was not his concern. Let Howard fight his battles alone, or fight them against Chaplin, whose new picture, *Limelight,* he was now refusing to back. When they got off the steamer in Tokyo, a reporter asked Grant about Chaplin; the question took him a little by surprise. After a moment's thought he had simply said: 'He has given great pleasure to millions of people, and I hope he comes back to Hollywood. Personally I don't think Mr Chaplin is a 'Communist'. Whatever his political views are, they are secondary to the fact that he is a great entertainer.' What had puzzled Grant was that, so far as he was aware, Howard Hughes had never had any political views in the past; Grant did not even know if he voted Democrat or Republican. So his friend's decision to cut down production at RKO in the spring of 1952 while he 'cleaned house' of the Communists in the studio had come as something of a shock.

Not that Grant thought all that much about it. He liked the new life on the steamer; it seemed simpler than when they were at home in Beverly Hills, where Betsy's endless piles of books, perched on every chair, got on his nerves, as did the clutter of her cameras and her tripods. 'I suggest you take some hobbies that don't take up so much space,' he told her once. 'I suggest from now on you learn to write on the head of a pin.' To the handful of passengers travelling with them, the tall, dark-haired actor and his sensible, pretty young wife seemed locked in their own private world, full of its own idiosyncrasies, and with their own private language. It was not the baby talk of some young couples, but a strangely archaic vocabulary of their own invention. 'My, you look thoughtative,' he had a tendency to say, before describing himself as 'happily tearful'.

They shared a fascination with hypnotism. Betsy had brought along Leslie LeCron's book *Hypnosis Today* and had become so entranced with the subject that she had persuaded her husband to let her try and hypnotize him into giving up smoking sixty cigarettes a day as he had for years. It had worked. 'She put me into a trance,' Grant would tell anyone who expressed an interest, 'and planted a post-hypnotic suggestion that I would stop smoking. We went to sleep and the next morning when I reached for a cigarette, just as I always did, I took one puff and instantly I felt nauseated. I didn't take another one that day and I haven't done since.' They also tried health diets together, and Grant had told his friends: 'I'm sick and tired of being questioned about why I look young for my age and why I keep trim. Everyone wants to keep fit – so what do they do? They poison themselves with the wrong foods, they poison their lungs with smoking, they clog their pores with greasy make up, they drink poison liquids. What can they expect?'

'Do you know,' he would say to his wife from time to time, 'we might just be called those crazy people who live on a hill.' He liked to stay at home watching television in the evenings when they were not travelling. He liked his wife to consult him about her clothes. He liked those clothes to be either simple or 'ethnic', as the description would be today, like the twenty Indian saris that Barbara Hutton had sent her for a wedding present. If there were people back in Hollywood who maintained that he was only happy when he had someone to fuss over and manipulate, he did not mind. Betsy seemed happy to be with him. She was with him all the time, and he wanted to do everything with her.

One thing she could not do was to cure him of his depressions, of the misery which occasionally swept over him like a cloud. At times he became obsessed with saving every cent he could, in the belief that he would be left penniless; at others he became a prey to an extraordinary bitter envy – that was at its worst on the night of the Academy Awards. In short, Cary Grant was still the same as he had always been. His debonair manner in the company of others vanished as soon as the door to his own home closed and their slow trip around the world did nothing to ease his problems. Even his experiments with yoga, which Betsy encouraged, did not calm him completely. On the contrary, his disconsolate, morose moods began to last longer and longer, and although he could slip into his carefree character from time to time, he would soon slip out of it again.

By the time they got back to Grant's Mexican-style house in Palm Springs, with its simple furniture and thick adobe walls to protect its occupants against the fierce desert temperatures, Betsy had begun to wonder whether in fact her husband actually missed the business of making motion pictures, no matter how often he complained about it. He still seemed interested in box-office returns, and each day there were telephone calls from people in the picture business, like Alfred Hitchcock, whom he had known and worked with. Sadly, in the midst of the long silences, Betsy realized that her husband's memories of the cinema were too strong to be put aside. Their plan for a happy, peaceful life away from the pressures of Hollywood began to fade.

Less than a month after his fiftieth birthday in January 1954 Cary Grant decided that he would start making films again. It had been nearly fifteen months since he had left the set of *Dream Wife*, but he did not seem able to get the business out of his mind. He was a star, and he was not ready to slip into a vague obscurity. He was no Garbo. He wanted to be alone, but he also wanted to be noticed.

Perhaps the two could be combined. Alfred Hitchcock had told him about a novel he had just bought called *To Catch a Thief*. Written by David Dodge, it was set on the French Riviera and told the story of a retired jewel thief and cat burglar who, suspected of a new wave of jewel thefts, sets out to clear his own name. Hitchcock wanted to make the picture that summer, and he was thinking of making it on location in the South of France. Not even Leo McCarey or Howard Hawks could have persuaded Cary Grant to look at a script, but he still liked Hitchcock, and he knew that the director wanted to make a spectacularly successful film, that he would let him improvise as he had always done. Grant dithered. He talked to Betsy; she looked a little sad, but assured him that if he wanted to make the picture she did not mind. When he told her she could come on location with him, she looked down, before murmuring quietly: 'If you want me to.'

But it was Grace Kelly who finally drew Grant back into films. As he put it later: 'I didn't want to do the film. It was only when Hitch told me I'd play opposite Grace Kelly that I did accept.'

Hitchcock was just finishing off *Rear Window* starring Grace Kelly opposite James Stewart, and he wanted to use her again in *To Catch a Thief*. Her apparently chilly manner, as he had found in his last two films, concealed a passionate, intelligent mind, which fascinated him. He had never fallen in love with her, as he had with some of his leading ladies, but he had never been able to intimidate her, as he had intimidated some of them.

Bob Cummings, who had played opposite her on her first Hitchcock film, *Dial M for Murder*, remembered later that the script had called for him to kiss her a good deal during the filming but: 'I think she said no more than fifty words to me outside the script, the hairdressers would refer to her as the princess, she wouldn't sit and talk, she was a very private person like Ingrid Bergman.' The daughter of wealthy Irish-Catholic parents from Philadelphia, Kelly had started making films only in 1950 after a brief spell on Broadway and some experience in television. But although she was best known in Hollywood for her cool and aloof elegance, she had just finished making an untypical film for her, *The Country Girl*, opposite Bing Crosby, in which she had played a frumpy harridan desperate to encourage her drunken husband to resume his singing career.

Grant, like Hitchcock, was fascinated by Kelly. She seemed to him to be the one untouchable woman, the blonde beauty who could be admired from afar but who, close to, was far more than that. Knowing that John Michael Hayes's script for the new film promised that he was to become the object of Kelly's affections, Grant could not resist the combination of Grace Kelly and summer on the French Riviera. He decided to go. There were other reasons. He still wished to prove to himself that he deserved the audience's praise; and he still had the feeling, which he had noticed in himself before, that when he was single he wanted to be married and when he was married he wanted to be single.

As he packed for France, he really felt that he had finally found the film he wanted to make. As he told one interviewer: 'I think comedy must have a certain grace and that involves living with a certain grace, which very few people – writers or anyone else – do these days.' He certainly managed to do so in Cannes. With Grace Kelly, at that time being escorted by the designer Oleg Cassini, Grant and Alfred Hitchcock settled into life on the French Riviera with all the style that Paramount's generous budget allowed.

Grant's contract stipulated that he should stop work no later than six o'clock each evening, and he firmly adhered to the rule. He may have returned to the movies, but he had no intention of returning to the slavery of the studios. Besides, as he had said, to make films with grace one had to live with grace.

Grace Kelly captivated him. 'She was the most beautiful woman I'd ever known,' he said later. 'She had the most incredible ESP about me. She could almost read my thoughts. She was cool and reserved, but then she'd say something about my own mood or attitude and it was like she was completely tuned in.' Whatever his fantasies about their relationship, however, he also said: 'It seemed like the only passionate words of love I ever spoke to her were with Hitchcock staring in my face.'

The irony of the situation may have been in Hitchcock's mind from the start. Certainly he made every effort to make their relationship one of the most openly sexual in any of his films. The script was heavy with an innuendo still unusual in a Hollywood-financed movie which had to exist within the moral confines of the Production Code. Kelly's sudden unexpected kiss on Grant's lips in the corridor of their hotel was unquestionably the most openly aggressive suggestion any of his female co-stars had ever made to him. It was capped, even more crudely, in the course of their picnic lunch, when the dialogue had her say to him: 'I've never caught a jewel thief before. It's so stimulating' – and then add, as she offers to help him to cold chicken: 'Do you want a leg or a breast?'

He replies: 'You make the choice,' and she says, 'Tell me how long has it been?'

'Since what?'

'Since you were last in America.'

The repartee became one of the most notorious innuendos in the American cinema.

While Hitchcock became increasingly excited about the filming, Betsy found herself spending more and more time alone, uncertain what she should do next. Her husband was already talking about making his next film, and it seemed as if he was simply determined to disappear on location either with this beautiful actress or another one just like her. She felt isolated and increasingly resentful. In contrast Cary Grant was unusually cheerful on the set, and unusually relaxed too. Hitchcock was always telling him: 'The best screen actor is the man who can do nothing – extremely well.' The elaborate over-reactions Grant had so often relied on in his earlier films were triumphantly phased out, to be replaced by responses infinitely more interesting. With Hitchcock's help he began to refine his own screen character into something more sophisticated than the eyebrow-arching hero of the 'screwball' comedies, delightful though these had been. In its place stood a man who could survive whatever happened, a man still attractive to women, but highly resilient. Hitchcock himself described the effect many years later. 'I've always taken the average man and got him involved in the extraordinary. That's how a man like Cary Grant has been cast, because they represent someone with whom the audience will identify and rather worry about.'

The only thing Grant was nervous about was wearing a swimming costume. Hitchcock's veteran costume designer, the incomparable Edith Head, explained later that he was very embarrassed at the idea of appearing on the screen wearing swimming trunks. When she told him that was what Hitchcock had in mind, he looked stunned.

'Good Lord,' he told her, 'I can't go out there looking like that. I'd feel as if I had nothing on.' Head said later that it took endless urging to persuade him to put the trunks on. 'Then he looked at himself in the mirror, and went very red,' she recalled.

When the filming was finished, towards the end of the summer, Grant went back to Bristol on a visit to his mother. She was approaching her eightieth birthday but still lived on her own, looked after her own needs, and proudly took a walk most afternoons across the Downs towards the Clifton Bridge, just as she had when she was young. She still, also, looked disapprovingly at her son, and tended to turn away her face when he bent down to kiss her. The habits of a lifetime were not forgotten. Yet beneath everything she was extremely proud of her boy, even if she found it difficult to tell him so.

On the journey back to California Grant reflected that perhaps he would return to Palm Springs and the quiet life that he and Betsy had been leading before he had left for France. To do so would cheer her up and, he was, moreover, not so anxious to go back into films that he was prepared to work in a studio again. If he were to be tempted, it would have to be something quite exceptional. And besides, Hollywood had grown so terribly serious. With falling production and falling cinema attendances, the old kind of razzamatazz and showmanship that had been the industry's stock-in-trade for three decades now seemed oddly out of date. Howard Hughes had tried to recreate it by taking two hundred journalists to Florida to look at a preview of his new Jane Russell film *Underwater*, and persuaded them to watch it twenty feet under water themselves by providing them with aqualungs. But that sort of stunt was rare. The film industry seemed intent on making harsher, more dramatic films, aimed at the one clearly defined part of the cinema audience that did not seem to be declining. Pan Berman was producing *The Blackboard Jungle* with Richard Brooks as director at MGM; Susan Hayward was playing an alcoholic singer in *I'll Cry Tomorrow* for the studio; and Ernest Borgnine, writer Paddy Chayevsky and director Delbert Mann were planning the transfer of their realistic television success *Marty* to the screen at United Artists.

One man in Hollywood, however, was not intimidated by the apparent fashion for dramatic films. Mike Todd had no appetite for such things. Born Avrom Goldenborgen in 1907, Todd was a Broadway producer with a taste for spectacular productions. He was convinced that Hollywood needed his sort of showmanship, and he had decided to produce a film which would prove it. He intended to assemble the largest collection of stars the industry had ever seen together in a single film, and to link them together with a simple story. He even knew the story that he wanted to film. It was Jules Verne's adventure, *Around The World in Eighty Days*.

Boundlessly energetic, relentlessly persuasive and eternally optimistic, Todd, who had recently married Elizabeth Taylor, had decided that the one star who would be able to carry his story was Cary Grant. Todd saw Grant as one of the old Hollywood stars who believed films should be witty and entertaining rather than solemnly thought-provoking, and whom audiences would instantly recognize as signifying an entertaining film. So he set out to persuade Grant to be the principal among his forty-eight stars, the centrepiece of his massive film. The ebullient producer waxed as lyrical as ever. There would be all the money they needed, they would be filming all over the world, there would be spectacular sights for the audience to see as well as the story to keep them interested, and there was no need to worry about the script: S. J. Perelman, John Farrow and James Poe were working on it.

But Cary Grant was by no means certain. From the way Todd was talking it seemed to him as though all that mattered was the fact it was being filmed in exotic locations all over the world. There didn't seem to be much room for him to create a character and now he didn't want to be just an elegant bystander, even if the magnificent offer which Todd was making him meant that he would virtually own half of the proposed film, and half its potential profits. So for what seemed to him entirely sensible reasons he turned down the offer, and the part was finally offered to his old friend, David Niven.

So, as Howard Hughes finally sold the RKO studio he had bought in 1951 to a subsidiary of the General Tire and Rubber Company, Cary Grant sat quietly at home and wondered what to do next. Betsy still seemed to be a little bit unsettled, but at least she was pleased he was not filming any more, and he thought she would be additionally pleased he was not about to dash off around the world with Todd. When *To Catch A Thief* opened in New York in August the reviews were not as good as he had hoped. The *Saturday Review* called it a 'little bit of a mess', and *Variety* added: 'As a mystery it fails to mystify. This one won't enhance the prestige of either the stars or the producer-director.' Bosley Crowther in the *New York Times* was kinder. The film, he said, 'does nothing but give out a good exciting time'. At least the box-office appeal of Grant himself, starring in his first film for two years and his first ever on the new wide screen which Fox had pioneered with *The Robe*, had emphatically not waned. In spite of the reviews the film became one of the year's successes. Just before it was released, Grace Kelly won an Oscar for her performance in *The Country Girl*, defeating as she did so, to the considerable surprise of

Hollywood, Judy Garland in *A Star Is Born*; so the combination of Hollywood's newest Oscar winner and oldest heart throb carried the film past the critics' scepticism.

For Grant, sadly, that year brought the sudden deaths of two of the few people he regarded as his friends and the idea of death stayed with him. Dorothy di Frasso had died on a train going from Las Vegas to Los Angeles. He and Betsy had stayed with her coffin throughout the night before her funeral because, as they explained: 'She hated to be alone; we didn't want her to be tonight.' Not long before that, Freddie Lonsdale had collapsed and died in a London street on his way home from Claridge's. Almost the last letter he had received had been from Mrs Cary Grant.

Cary Grant and Betsy did not entertain very much. When they did Grant liked to have dinner served by their butler on a tray so it could be eaten in front of the television set. It was a habit that utterly astonished one noted English director who visited him in Palm Springs. For years afterwards this man would tell his friends: 'There we all were, the three of us; Cary, Betsy and I, sitting in black tie in front of the television set while the butler served dinner on trays on our knees.'

What Grant really preferred to do in the evenings was to talk to his few old friends on the telephone, especially when he could not sleep. The insomnia he had suffered for years still plagued him, and although Betsy had helped a little with her attempts at hypnosis, the restlessness he had always felt was at its worst after the half light of the Californian night had fallen across the desert. It was then that he brooded on the films he should have made, and the reputation he should have had. He knew he was one of Hollywood's greatest stars, yet he also knew only too well he had never really dominated the list of top box-office draws, hugely successful though he had been, and that he had never won an Academy Award. In the early morning hours Grant decided that he wanted to go back to making films again, to prove to Hollywood that he was a star.

There were plenty of offers to occupy his mind. The success of *To Catch A Thief* had brought a deluge of scripts for him to consider, all of them sent with persuasive letters from hopeful producers; but most of them he just laid aside, or looked at briefly. On top of that the new television networks were also asking him to appear on their shows but their requests were not even considered. 'No television' he told any producer who asked him, even though they pointed out that he had made a brief appearance on a Dave Willock and Cliff Arguette show in 1951. 'Television men are a fast trading group and I don't want to get involved with them.' It was a decision he never changed.

Sam Spiegel was getting together a picture at Columbia, however, that sounded interesting. The English director, David Lean, was planning to make a film about British prisoners-of-war in Burma, forced to work on a railway and to build a bridge over the River Kwai. Spiegel and Lean had already cast Alec Guinness as the English commanding officer, but they wanted Grant to play one of the party sent to destroy the bridge. It was a good part: dramatic, convincing and well written by Carl Foreman. But Grant was not altogether sure that he wanted to spend a long period on location in Ceylon, where the film was to be shot. 'Meanwhile,' he said later, 'Columbia, knowing me, had also sent a script to Bill Holden. Holden read the story, decided it was magnificent, which it was and said he'd do it. By then, of course, I realized what a great part I'd lost.'

He still saw Howard Hughes regularly. He had introduced him to Stewart Granger and Jean Simmons; and Hughes had arranged their elopement and marriage in Arizona in December 1950 in much the same way that he had arranged Betsy's and Grant's. Since then Hughes had developed a passion for the dark-haired Simmons, rather to Stewart Granger's and her own despair. Grant enjoyed introducing beautiful women to the reclusive Hughes, and there was no denying that Hughes delighted in it. He was too shy to arrange the meetings himself, but he never objected when Cary Grant did it for him. After all, that was how he had met Ingrid Bergman.

But Betsy knew exactly what Stewart Granger meant when he said: 'Cary Grant is exactly not what he appears to be. He isn't carefree, debonair and relaxed at all; in fact he's the opposite.' Her husband's depression still seemed to hang round his shoulders like a shroud, and his only real pleasures seemed to come from looking at the financial returns on his films and remembering the deals he had made. Gradually she realized that their marriage was leading nowhere. If he was going to start making films again, she felt she had better go back to work herself. Perhaps that would make their life together easier; they would see less of each other, but at least they would have more to talk about. As she told Hedda Hopper nearly a decade later: 'I gave up my career when I got married. I couldn't be an actress and a housewife too, and if I were married now I wouldn't be acting.'

But this was hindsight. All that seemed certain to Cary Grant and his wife, at the beginning of 1956, was that the life they thought they had wanted to share, away from films, was satisfying neither of them. Almost without discussing it they came to the conclusion that Betsy would return to making movies too. Frank Tashlin at Fox was putting together a project which might appeal to her, while Stanley Kramer, the forty-three-year-old producer of the Oscar-winning *High Noon* and *The Caine Mutiny*, wanted Grant to appear in the film he was planning to produce and direct based on C. S. Forrester's Napoleonic story, *The Gun*.

Kramer had it in mind to win a belated Oscar for Grant. Sam Spiegel had produced Forrester's story *The African Queen* only four years earlier to win one for Bogart, and Kramer felt sure he could do the same. Grant was the first person he had approached for the film, which was to be retitled *The Pride and the Passion* and shot entirely on location in Spain. 'Cary had some reservations about leaving his usual pattern of roles,' Kramer recalls now, 'and he was not entirely easy with the idea of playing an English naval officer whose hair is tied with a bun at the back.' Nevertheless the project appealed to him and he agreed to make the film.

Kramer was not certain who to cast as the woman in the story. His first thought had been Ava Gardner, but then he switched to the new Italian actress Sophia Loren, who at only twenty-one was already famous in Europe, though she had never made a film in English. Kramer offered Carlo Ponti, Loren's forty-year-old lover and manager, $200,000 for her services, which he was happy to accept.

'Originally Cary objected to Sophia,' Kramer says now. 'He thought she was too commercial a ploy, but I arranged a meeting and he looked at two of her films, and he changed his mind very quickly.' The meeting Kramer arranged was at a cocktail party for the start of filming. As Loren recalled later, as soon as he was introduced to her Cary Grant started to tease her by calling her Miss Lolloloren and Lorengida, but she went on: 'He exuded charm, and he was even more handsome and debonair than he appeared on the screen. I immediately felt at ease with him and after a few minutes of lively banter I could tell from the look in his eyes that I had passed muster.' She had done considerably more than that. She had fascinated him.

As he recalled later: 'She was half way between stardom and starstruck. That was half her appeal. She never had an air of self-importance. She was a totally honest woman. Between takes she'd eat spaghetti out of a tin plate with insatiable gusto.' When any reporter asked if he was in love with her, he would reply: 'Who wouldn't be? She's an adorable flirt.'

Loren was perceptive about Grant. 'As I got to know him,' she wrote later, 'I began to realize that he had an inner conflict of wanting to be open and honest and direct, and yet not make himself vulnerable . . . And slowly as our relationship grew and his trust in me grew, he came to realize that trust and vulnerability went hand in hand; when his trust was strong enough he no longer bothered with his mask.'

After having dinner with Loren alone every evening on

location Cary Grant fell in love; he told her he was prepared to give up everything for her. 'We can start a new life together,' he declared. Loren was flattered, delighted and yet confused; she thought she still loved Carlo Ponti, and she knew that Betsy Drake would visit the location soon.

The closeness of Grant and Loren had its effect on the film's other principal star, Frank Sinatra. One evening in the large mess tent the company used while they were filming, Sinatra stood on his chair and shouted across to his co-star: 'Sophia, you'll get yours.' The actress did not quite understand what Sinatra meant, and asked the person next to her to explain. When he did, she shouted back at the actor: 'Not from you, you Italian son of a bitch.' In the closed community of a film set on location the atmosphere became distinctly tense. Filming had not gone smoothly. Grant had suffered sword wounds in his back, and Sinatra was desperate to get back to New York as quickly as possible. Disagreements broke out between Kramer and Sinatra and finally Sinatra left before filming was completed. 'It hurt the picture desperately,' Kramer maintains now.

Working in Hollywood, Betsy had no idea what was happening in Spain. She simply waited for her husband to call her from the location and ask her to visit him. 'It was agony always waiting for him to ring to say come,' she wrote later. 'I wanted to go but I always had to wait for him to ask.' Finally, late in June, he called. In Spain Betsy got an inkling of her husband's feeling for Loren. He left her to her own devices and she consoled herself by writing a memoir of what she was seeing and recording it on home movies.

She had never had cause to doubt her husband's generosity or concern for her. He had bought her more than $200,000-worth of jewels, though she would have preferred less ostentatious tributes. Whatever her feelings, Betsy did not interrupt her husband's work while she was with him, she simply looked after herself.

Towards the end of July she prepared to go back to Hollywood to start work on the Frank Tashlin picture, *Will Success Spoil Rock Hunter?* She was to sail on the flagship of

Italia line, the *Andrea Doria*, which was due to arrive in New York at the end of July.

On the night of 25 July, in patchy fog less than two hundred miles off the coast of Newfoundland, the *Andrea Doria* was rammed by the Swedish liner *Stockholm*, slicing open seven of her eleven decks. After the collision the Italian liner heeled over so quickly to starboard that barely half her lifeboats could be launched, and the 1,134 passengers on board were forced to abandon ship within half an hour. Survivors were picked up by the *Stockholm*, and the French liner *Ile De France*, which had been only some forty-four miles away when the collision occurred. In spite of their efforts forty-three people drowned. Betsy was among the survivors. She had been forced to leave the ship wearing only a simple dress, leaving the $200,000 worth of jewellery she had taken with her to Spain, as well as her manuscripts and photographs. She was picked up by the *Ile De France* and taken back to New York. When she landed she sent a cable to her husband which ended, 'Your safe, sound and rescued wife.' As she put it afterwards, 'I don't think I have ever loved Cary quite so much as I did the night I thought I would never live to see him again.'

But Grant did not go straight back to see her. His infatuation with Loren was more or less complete by now and he talked more and more urgently about the possibility of their getting married. As Loren recalled later: 'With every passing day, he said, he was more sure that we belonged together, that he finally had found in me someone to whom he could totally relate. Finally someone to whom he could commit himself and to hell with being vulnerable. "I trust you and love you and want to marry you," he said. I never doubted for a second that Cary loved me as much as I could hope to be loved by a man.'

On the last night of their filming together, just before Loren was to leave for Greece to start work on her new picture *Boy On A Dolphin*, opposite Alan Ladd, and Grant was to return to Hollywood to begin a new film with Deborah Kerr, she told him: 'I wish I weren't so mixed up

241

and confused. But one day I am pulled one way and the next day another. I don't know what's going to happen.' Grant told her, 'Why don't we just get married and discuss all this afterwards?'

A confused, trembling Sophia Loren set off for Greece the next morning, while Cary Grant began the long trip back to California and Betsy. When he arrived at Los Angeles airport to meet her, his wife was wearing a polka-dot dress, a firmly set smile, and her hair had been restored to its original brown colour rather than the blondeness that he preferred.

Cary Grant had been away from Hollywood for seven months but the movie industry had not forgotten him. He had worried that it might, and that the pompous stiffness of his dramatic role in *The Pride and the Passion* might persuade some people that he wasn't interested in comedy any longer, but his fears proved groundless. Every studio seemed to want him to work for them. As he shot the last few scenes on Stanley Kramer's picture in California, using a coathanger to speak to in place of the absent Frank Sinatra, that thought cheered him. It was not the only good news. There was also the prospect of seeing Sophia Loren again, for she too had to finish her film in Hollywood, and he had read that she was discussing a contract with Columbia.

In the meantime he had decided to waste no time before making another film, and although it would not be a straightforward comedy it would be directed by Leo McCarey. In the past few years the ebullient but accident-prone director had struggled to make a film. His health had not been good, and his enormous successes in the 1930s and 1940s had not guaranteed him the right sort of niche in a Hollywood now increasingly dominated by 'method' actors and 'message' pictures. His light touch seemed out of place and his favourite explanation of the sort of work he liked to do – 'I'll let someone else photograph the ugliness of the world. It's larceny to remind people of how lousy things are and call it entertainment' – did not endear him to the new breed of Hollywood producer.

But it greatly appealed to Cary Grant, especially when McCarey told him that he intended to remake *Love Affair*, the film he had first made at RKO in 1938 with Charles Boyer and Irene Dunne. It was the story of a couple who meet on board ship, fall in love and then part. McCarey explained: 'I want to do it because a lot of people say its the best love story they have ever seen – and it's my favourite love story.' Grant could still remember visiting the set of the original picture to talk to Irene Dunne and wishing he had been playing in it.

When they came to work together again, what amazed McCarey was the new-found cheerfulness of his star. The tense, haunted man of *The Awful Truth* and *Once Upon A Honeymoon* seemed genuinely to have turned into a calm, generous actor who enjoyed making the film and working with his co-star Deborah Kerr – even if he did tell the producer, Jerry Wald, that the cabin boy's buttons they intended to use were wrong and must be changed. During the filming Grant seemed to blossom again; as McCarey was to put it later: 'The difference between *Love Affair* and *An Affair to Remember* is very simply the difference between Charles Boyer and Cary Grant. Grant could never really mask his sense of humour – which is extraordinary – and that's why the second version is funnier.' Nevertheless the elated director put in a joke at his star's expense. During the shooting, he added to the script a line for a cabin boy to say to Grant:

'I've heard so much about you.'

When his star asked the boy what he'd heard, McCarey had him reply:

'I don't know. Whenever they start to talk about you they make me leave the room.' As he explained: 'That way I could tell the audience the opinion people had about Grant without having to underline it – and get it from a character they liked.' Overall McCarey preferred his original version of the film and felt that Boyer had given a better performance than Grant, but the director knew well that Grant meant infinitely more to the average cinema audience than Boyer had ever done and that his presence in the new version would almost certainly guarantee its success.

There were two other reasons for Grant's uncharacteristic relaxation. Sophia Loren was in Hollywood, and not only was he telephoning her every day, he was also sending vast bunches of flowers to the Beverly Hills Hotel, where she was staying with Carlo Ponti. Still more significantly, he had started psychoanalysis; and the experience had begun to transform him.

At Betsy's suggestion he had visited two Beverly Hills psychiatrists, Dr Mortimer A. Hartman and Dr Arthur Chandler, who were carrying out experiments with the hallucinogenic drug Lsyergic Acid (or LSD 25), which they gave to their patients to facilitate the process of psychotherapy. Betsy had tried the treatment, and she had encouraged her husband to try it. He could hardly refuse, because, as he admitted later, 'I felt I had to do something; I'd already had two unsuccessful marriages and now this one was threatened.'

The Hartman and Chandler treatment was distinctly experimental. Nevertheless Cary Grant had gingerly begun to attend sessions. Like the other hundred and ten patients taking part in the experiment, he would lie on a couch wearing a shield over his eyes, and with wax or cotton plugs in his ears would take LSD and then try to re-live the past. Whatever the medical establishment might think of the practice, this experience changed his life.

Not that Harman and Chandler gave him the drug straight away. Before they allowed any of their patients to take it they carried out a detailed psychiatric examination; but they were convinced, as they put it in the American Medical Association's Archives of General Psychiatry in March 1960, that 'certain drugs on which we have done research have the capacity to broaden the patient's spectrum of awareness. If a patient uses this enhanced capacity to look inward, he is often enabled, particularly in the case of LSD 25, to see and experience many effects, childhood memories, conflicts and impulse strivings which were previously blotted out by the repressive forces.' Hartman and Chandler came to the conclusion that Cary Grant would certainly benefit from the drug; and he became one of its most enthusiastic supporters. He would lie for up to four hours at a time in their consulting-room in near darkness every Saturday afternoon with classical music playing in the background, and remember his past.

When each session was over he was never allowed to drive himself home, and was occasionally given a sedative to calm him down. 'Patients were required to write up the sessions between twenty-four and forty-eight hours later in a free associative manner,' Hartman and Chandler wrote. 'Occasionally a pillow will be pounded or thrown, or a magazine torn up . . . but no physical assaults or property destruction occurred.'

In the next eighteen months Grant attended more than sixty Saturday sessions and took LSD every time he did so. As he was to write only three years later: 'I passed through changing areas of horrifying and happy thoughts, through a montage of intense love and hate, a mosaic of past impressions assembling and re-assembling; through terrifying depths of dark despair replaced by heavenlike religious symbolism. Session after session. Week after week.' Before he started the sessions, he maintained, 'I was always professing a knowledge I didn't have. I was an utter fake, a know-all who knew very little. I was very aggressive, but without the courage to be physically aggressive. I knew I was a bad-tempered man, but I hid it . . .'

To the average cinemagoer in 1957, the knowledge that Cary Grant was a bad-tempered man, who was experimenting with LSD, and undergoing radical psychotherapy for several hours most Saturday afternoons, would have come as a profound shock. The relaxed, handsome figure they saw in front of them on the screen, perpetually tanned, looking at least a dozen years younger than his fifty-three, for ever attractive to women, and never at a loss for a worldly, witty line of dialogue, seemed only to be acting himself. That was the very cornerstone of his appeal. It was to be some years before he himself began to admit that the reality was quite different. In the meantime he seemed intent once more on making films in which he acted exactly as his audience expected him to.

Soon after the McCarey film was finished, Grant learnt that *Around the World in Eighty Days*, the film he had turned down, was on the way to becoming a massive hit at the box office. What he could not yet know was that both *The Pride and The Passion* and *An Affair to Remember*, were destined to do very nearly as well. McCarey might say his judgement of a film was still not all that good, but his appeal at the box office was stronger than it had ever been. So, as MGM gingerly followed the lead of Warner Brothers and Fox and heralded the first intrusion of the smaller screen into Hollywood by selling some of its films to television (including *The Wizard of Oz*) Cary Grant went back to work, once again at Fox and once again with Jerry Wald as producer. This time the thirty-three-year-old Stanley Donen was director and Fox's new contract star, Jayne Mansfield was Grant's co-star. Based on Frederic Wakeman's best selling novel *Shore Leave*, which was later turned into a play by Luther Davis, *Kiss Them For Me* had run for 111 performances on Broadway in 1945. Julius Epstein had now written a film script, one that Grant felt happy with.

Before he could start on the new picture, however, Grant had to have a small, benign tumour removed from his forehead. He had been advised in England that it might take him anything up to a month to recover from the operation, but, as he put it, 'I couldn't spare that amount of time.' So he persuaded Betsy to hypnotize him so that the surgeon would only need to use a local anaesthetic and he would recover more quickly. To Hollywood, with its addiction to everything artificial, this decision seemed strangely eccentric. Thus, with hardly any delay Grant was able to start work on *Kiss Them For Me*, and its simple story of Navy men on shore leave. He had grown to like the young Donen, whose earlier films as a director had all been musicals, including the uninhibited *Seven Brides for Seven Brothers* and *The Pajama Game*, and the filming itself was easy. Jayne Mansfield and his other co-star, the model-turned-actress, Suzy Parker, were amenable enough to work with, but Cary Grant's real thoughts were still with Sophia Loren. He wanted to see more of her and he still wondered if they would ever get married. One thing was certain. Now that Paramount had signed her to a four-picture contract, he would do everything he could to work with her again.

By July 1957, when *An Affair to Remember* was released to unenthusiastic reviews – the *New Yorker* called it 'awfully maudlin' and *Time* commented, 'Only sensitive acting from Deborah and Cary saves this saccharine trifle from suffocating in its sentimental wrappings' – and *Kiss Them For Me* had just finished shooting, Grant had found the film he wanted to make with Sophia. Jack Rose and Mel Shavelson, who had worked on the script for *Room For One More* which he had made with Betsy at Warners, had come up with a script for the new woman in his life. Almost the only significant difference between the two films was that in *Room For One More* the children in the story were orphans, while in the new story, *Houseboat*, they had lost their mother but still had their father.

Rose and Shavelson described the plot of their new script simply enough. 'Sophia Loren plays the misunderstood daughter of a harassed father who runs away and meets a misunderstood seven-year-old son who is running away from Cary Grant . . . Because of her own experience she is able to bring father and son together, and what she learns in the meantime of Cary's problems brings her closer to her own father – and so close to Cary that marriage is the only solution the Motion Picture Production Code will accept.' It was also a solution that Cary Grant wished for yet, ironically, it was to be denied him just as it was about to take place. Directed by Shavelson and produced by Rose at Paramount, *Houseboat* was virtually completed when Loren's future was decided for her. While she and Carlo Ponti were staying in a bungalow in the select Bel Air Hotel in Beverly Hills, Louella Parsons reported that two Mexican lawyers in Juarez, some thousand miles to the south, had not only finalized Ponti's divorce from his wife, but had also executed his marriage to Sophia Loren. Whether they realized it or not, Sophia and Carlo Ponti were now legally man and wife.

Yet again, Grant's screen life seemed mysteriously to echo his own, for there, on the set at Paramount, less than two days after her actual marriage, a white wedding ceremony was conducted for Sophia and Grant, the last sequence of *Houseboat* to be shot. When she came on the set he said to her simply: 'I hope you will be very happy,' and kissed her on both cheeks, but filming was intensely difficult for both of them. As Loren recalled: 'I was aware how painful it was for him to play this scene with me, and to have the minister pronounce us man and wife, to take me in his arms and kiss me.' As the Mendelssohn Wedding March echoed across the Paramount set Grant knew he had to do something. He was in love with a woman who had been married by proxy, just as she was 'marrying' him on the screen, and he doubted whether he could face life without her. Betsy was marvellously friendly and kind, but some of his friends had begun to notice that she herself did not seem to be happy either at work or back with her husband at home. As Clifford Odets said later: 'Their marriage dissolved into a brother-sister relationship. At no point in the last few years did I feel they were truly man and wife.' Once again Cary Grant decided to leave Hollywood. He wanted to see his mother in England, and Stanley Donen had a project which might mean he could make a film while he was there. Gratefully, he began to plan his escape.

Ingrid Bergman had not made a film in Hollywood since 1949, when the uproar surrounding the revelation that she was pregnant by the Italian film director Roberto Rossellini while still married to her first husband had forced her to leave the United States. As the *New York Times* reported years later: 'Suddenly the American public that had elevated her to the point of idolatry cast her down, vilified her, and boycotted her films. She was even condemned on the floor of the United States Senate.' But Cary Grant had not forgotten her, and he had always wanted to appear with her again. In March 1957 he had promised to stand by at the twenty-ninth Academy Awards ceremony in case she won for her performance in *Anastasia*, which had been filmed in England. She had won, defeating both Katharine Hepburn and Deborah Kerr and, as he collected her gold statuette, Cary Grant declaimed to the audience in the ornate Pantages Theater on Hollywood Boulevard: 'Dear Ingrid, wherever you are in the world, we, your friends, want to congratulate you, and may you be as happy as we are for you.' Their friendship, which had always been close, was even more firmly cemented by this gallant speech.

Donen thought that he could persuade his friend, Norman Krasna, whose light comedy *Kind Sir* had been playing on Broadway, to move the location of his story from New York to London and to adapt it so that Cary Grant and Ingrid Bergman could play it there. Then he suggested to Grant that they form their own company, Grandon Productions, to sell the film to Warner Brothers and, of course, guarantee him his now customary fee of $300,000. Once the deal had been agreed, and Grant had incidentally persuaded Jack Warner to provide him with a Rolls-Royce in London during filming, he and Donen settled into the Connaught Hotel while preparations for shooting began. In the meantime, however, Ingrid Bergman's liaison with Roberto Rossellini had publicly broken up. When she arrived at Heathrow airport, a tumultuous crowd of reporters were there to meet her. But so also was Cary Grant. As she was ushered into a packed press conference she found him already there, and he shouted to her: 'Ingrid, wait till you hear *my* problems!'

As Bergman recalled: 'That broke the ice. Everybody burst into laughter. He held them at bay in such a nice way.' In particular he kept telling the reporters: 'Come on, fellas, you can't ask a lady that. Ask me the same question and I'll give you an answer. So, you're not interested in my life? It's twice as colourful as Ingrid's.'

Although no one in the room was aware of it, his life was indeed at least as colourful as his co-star's, and he was about to go through exactly the same painfully public separation from his partner as she had. But in the banter of the press conference no-one suspected that Cary Grant might have been concealing his own feelings. He seemed as he always seemed, handsome, charming, cheerful, and very protective of a beautiful woman.

'*Indiscreet* was a light comedy,' Bergman wrote later. 'I played a famous wealthy actress: Cary Grant was an American diplomat protecting his bachelor status by pretending he was already married.' The line of dialogue which captured the spirit of the plot, and in which Bergman challenged Grant by saying: 'How dare you make love to me and not be a married man?', had been suggested by Grant himself. He believed that single line made every other line in the picture funnier, and Bergman agreed with him. 'It ended happily ever after,' she remembered. 'And that's what I wanted to be. I was in love with Lars Schmidt [a successful Swedish theatrical producer] and we wanted to get married.'

For Cary Grant, however, things were not to progress so smoothly. By the end of 1957, as the filming of *Indiscreet* was drawing to a close, rumours about his own marriage were growing. Betsy had already spent some time in London appearing in the play *Next to No Time* opposite Kenneth More, and she was about to make *Intent to Kill*, a film with Richard Todd, at Pinewood Studios; but her relations with Grant were now strained and distant. At Christmas he took her to Monte Carlo, where they spent two days on board Aristotle Onassis's yacht, the *Christina*, and had dinner with Grace Kelly and her new husband, Prince Rainier. But even there the troubles of the past few years, and the memory of Sophia Loren, took their toll. On the surface Grant was the debonair, relaxed guest, but in quiet moments when he thought no-one was watching him, he was in despair.

Once again, however, he hesitated before doing anything. First he took a weekend trip to Moscow with producer Sam Spiegel and novelist Truman Capote; then he returned to Bristol to see his mother on her birthday. Even when he got back to Hollywood and the previews of *Indiscreet* had shown that he almost certainly had another success on his hands,

Grant was still struggling to understand his own attitudes. He knew that he could not go on with Betsy, but he did not know what to do instead. Once again Alfred Hitchcock saved him, in company with the Beverly Hills psychiatrist, Dr Mortimer Hartman.

For the first time in his life, Cary Grant was made publically conscious of growing old. He had fought against the wrinkles and the folds of skin by taking massage, rest, a careful diet and the occasional resort to cosmetic surgery. Although he was fifty-four he believed he looked at least ten years younger. Suddenly, however, it had begun to dawn on him that he could not remain one of the cinema's most romantic leading men for ever. After *Kiss Them For Me* had been released in November 1957, Bosley Crowther in the *New York Times* had commented tartly of Grant that he 'seems somewhat over-age for this kind of assignment', and a year later had described him in *Houseboat* as 'leathery' and 'old enough to be the kid's grandfather'. To Grant's fragile confidence, these judgements were deep wounds.

He had also seen Sophia Loren leave Hollywood married to Carlo Ponti, ten years his junior. It seemed as though he had to accept that he would not be able to continue making films for much longer, at least if he wished to remain one of the cinema's lovers. He was well aware that Gary Cooper had not done himself much good with the critics in his recent film, *Love in the Afternoon*, opposite the young Audrey Hepburn. One or two of them had mentioned that he had looked too old to be convincing as Hepburn's romantic attachment and Cary Grant tried never to commit his old rival's mistakes. So, even though he had just been voted Hollywood's most attractive man, Cary Grant began to say: 'I'm getting to the stage when I have to be very careful about love scenes with young actresses.'

Saying goodbye to Sophia Loren had been particularly difficult. He had persuaded Alfred Hitchcock to create a part for her in the film they were planning together, and her downright refusal to accept it annoyed him. He could not understand why she wanted to go back to Italy to make a film about two women, neither of whom was beautiful or seductive. 'That man will ruin her career,' he told his friends. 'Here she could have been in a Hitchcock picture seen by millions, now she will go into that small Italian picture. It will ruin Sophia, such casting.' In fact the film she left to make, *Two Women*, won her an Oscar, the first ever to be awarded to an Italian actress in a foreign language film: and the person who telephoned her from Hollywood with the news that she had won was Cary Grant.

The part Grant had originally suggested for Loren was the tantalizing government agent in Hitchcock's new film which the director had been planning for more than a year. The screen writer, Ernest Lehman, who had written *West Side Story*, had been working on it for months, basing it on Hitchcock's idea of a chase across America which would end inside the nose of the massive stone face of President Lincoln in Mount Rushmore, South Dakota. One of Hitchcock's first titles for the film had been 'The Man in Lincoln's Nose', although he had later amended that to 'In a Northerly Direction' and then to the elliptical *North By Northwest*, a point on the compass which does not exist.

Hitchcock was determined to make the centrepiece of his film the character that Cary Grant had created over the years. The plot he and Lehman had in mind depended on the audience identifying totally with Grant as a man to whom terrible things happen, but who nevertheless still seems never to lose control. Hitchcock wanted it to be the American version of his acclaimed English thriller, *The Thirty-Nine Steps*. After Loren's departure Hitchcock and Grant agreed that Eva Marie Saint, who had won an Oscar as Best Supporting Actress in her first film *On The Waterfront* without ever having set foot in Hollywood, might be suitable for the government agent. Intelligent and superbly controlled, she fell very much into the Grace Kelly mould; cool, blonde and intensely attractive, her restraint still giving the impression of hidden passions.

This time, Grant was not particularly relaxed during the shooting. He insisted on contributing some of his own dialogue to Lehman's script, and a third of the way through the filming he told Hitchcock: 'It's a terrible script, and I still can't make head or tail of it.' The director ignored his star's complaints, to which he was now well used (though afterwards, he said that it was 'a relief to be working with birds'). James Mason recalled that he hardly saw his co-star when they weren't shooting together, and Eva Marie Saint remembered later that she found him very attractive but did not see very much of him. Cary Grant had begun to retreat into himself again, wary of any invasion of his privacy.

Hitchcock knew that the role that Grant was playing on the screen was a precise parody of his own image. While the director delighted in transforming Saint from her customarily drab roles into an unexpectedly glamorous Mata Hari, he was depending on Cary Grant to seem himself, the man the audience recognized. Hitchcock even had him tell Eva Marie Saint towards the end of the film: 'My wives divorced me. I think they said I led too dull a life.'

It was a bleak self-commentary. The shooting had not finished when Cary Grant and Betsy Drake finally announced that they were separating. The marriage that Howard Hughes had arranged on Christmas Day 1949 came to an end in October 1958 with a brief statement, which Grant had drafted himself. It read simply: After careful consideration and long discussion we have decided to live apart. We have had, and shall always have a deep love and respect for each other, but alas, our marriage has not brought us the happiness we fully expected and mutually desired. So since we have no children needful of our affection it is consequently best that we separate for a while.' And it ended: 'We have purposefully issued this public statement through the newspaper writers who have been so kind to us in the past in order to forestall the usual misinformed gossip and conjecture. There are no plans for divorce, and we ask only that the press respect our statement as complete and our friends to be patient with, and understanding of, our decision.'

Lysergic Acid Diethylamide

'A star is authentic: you never doubt him; he
is real – *not* an actor, not even, any longer,
someone playing himself. He simply is.'

Peter Bogdanovich

Outside on Wilshire Boulevard the cars were streaming
home from the beach in the late afternoon sunshine, but in a
small dark room in Beverly Hills Cary Grant was crying.
The tears had been running down his cheeks for more than
an hour, and he could not stop them. The face he had
studiously kept tanned and lean for fifty-five years was
blotched, and his mind was struggling with the effects of the
LSD he had taken that morning.

In the past four hours every fear he had ever remembered
had become a nightmare. He had been to other sessions on
other Saturday afternoons over the past year but today had
been the breakthrough. He felt that he had actually travelled
down from his mother's womb into the chill air of that
January night in 1904 and as if his whole life since then had
passed in front of him. The loneliness of childhood; the
self-conscious search for affection as an adolescent; the
adoption of a character and the fitting of the mask; the
obsession in middle age about money and the screen image;
and the final recognition that Cary Grant, film star, was a
stranger to himself, unable to love women or, it seemed, to be
loved by them.

The session had left him dazed and exhausted, but when
he was driven home in his Rolls-Royce, he was ecstatic. At

'I think of us as the same age' : Barbara Harris, almost fifty years younger than Cary Grant, whom she married in April 1981.

(above) Now seventeen, and as striking as her father at the same age, Jennifer Grant is close to her father and stepmother and is with them regularly.

(left) No public performances since 1966 to speak of, but Cary Grant still keeps a piano in his home in Beverly Hills.

Fatherhood - actress Dyan Cannon became the fourth Mrs Grant in 1965 and presented him with his first child, a daughter, Jennifer, in February 1966. He was sixty-two.

Proud parent or not, it took a long and painful series of court battles to establish his right to see his daughter Jennifer after his separation from her mother.

'Here hold them . . . they're the most beautiful
thing in the world, and the one thing you can't resist':
Grace Kelly was referring to her jewels in the 1955
film, To Catch A Thief, but there were millions of
cinema-goers who did not believe her.

*The bride that might have been: Sophia Loren
and Cary Grant may have considered marriage, but
they actually wed only on the screen in their 1957
film,* Houseboat.

last, he felt, he was beginning to understand why he had always been so miserable and so afraid. He could hardly wait for next Saturday to come round. The LSD and the quiet tones of Dr Hartman's voice seeping through into his mind had proved, literally, a revelation. On the Saturday following he seemed to spend the entire four hours talking about his parents and his attitude to women, and once again, on the way back to his house in Beverly Hills, he felt like shouting for joy, stopping the car and telling everyone he passed on Rodeo Drive what had happened to him. It might startle his friends, but they did not know what he'd been through, they did not know he could change. Only Betsy would understand. She would know what it felt like.

Cary Grant had always confided in Betsy. He had been doing it ever since they had first met, and even though they had separated three months ago he saw no reason why he should stop doing so. She lived in a Spanish house on Mandeville Canyon in the hills north of Sunset Boulevard, and although she had lost patience with him during the last months of their marriage, he knew she was one of the few people he could trust. She herself had had LSD sessions, though she had since given them up. So she would appreciate how he felt. He talked to her, and then, cautiously, to a few of his other friends. All of them told him the same thing: 'If you think you've changed, then you should tell other people about it, tell everyone what's happened.'

Sitting in the small study of his house, looking through his collection of scripts and contracts, photographs and cuttings, Grant resolved to do so. There were likely to be plenty of opportunities in the weeks to come. He was already working on his next film, and when the unit went on location in Florida, the set was bound to attract reporters from all over the world. He would make sure that it did.

He had never worked at Universal before, but they had approached him about making a film with Tony Curtis and the idea had appealed to him. He had seen Curtis's spectacular impersonation of him in Billy Wilder's new film, *Some Like It Hot*, and he had heard that the young actor had

255

learnt it in the submarine service during the war – the crew had only had his old film *Gunga Din* to watch, and to keep themselves amused they had trained themselves to play all the parts. Tony Curtis had always played Grant, and had perfected a fine imitation. The idea of playing opposite Curtis in turn seemed rather attractive to the older star. Perhaps he could imitate *him*.

The film, called *Operation Petticoat*, was originally intended to star Curtis and Jeff Chandler, but neither would agree to give the other top billing. Eventually Universal asked Curtis who he would accept as a star over him, and his reply was – only Clark Gable or Cary Grant. Gable had just finished making another submarine picture, *Run Silent Run Deep*, so it seemed better to approach Grant, who, ironically, had turned down Gable's role in the other film. Grant liked Robert Arthur, who was to produce the new film, and he also liked the studio which, though smaller than some, was prepared to look after him. They agreed to let him have a bungalow on their lot just off the Hollywood Freeway going north, about twenty minutes from his house, and to provide him with a secretary. They originally offered him a flat $750,000 as an advance against ten per cent of the gross profits, but he preferred to take $300,000 in advance and a seventy-five per cent share of the profits; that way, if the picture was a hit, he would benefit not the studio. The script was entrusted to Stanley Shapiro, who had won an Oscar for *Pillow Talk*.

No matter what the benefits of Hartman's treatment in other ways, Grant on the set was the restless perfectionist he had always been. Robert Arthur remembers now that 'Cary did not want new clothes made for his role as the sub-marine's commander. He wanted the wardrobe department to find the leather jacket he had worn for *Destination Tokyo*, because he thought that was precisely right.' He was none too happy that Tony Curtis intended to have his clothes specially made and, even worse, to wear shorts in the picture. 'Cary didn't think that would actually have happened and that worried him,' Arthur recalled.

The unit was due to spend five weeks on location in Key West, off the coast of Florida, where President Truman had had a house and where there was still a large naval base, before coming back to Hollywood. Universal wanted the whole thing wrapped up by September, intending to make the picture their major Christmas release. The weather on Key West was perfect, and the shooting went fairly smoothly. Robert Arthur had been asked to intervene only now and again, and the director, Blake Edwards, then in his midthirties, seemed to get on well with both stars. Grant once or twice demanded changes in the script, but in general seemed distinctly cheerful. One of the girls in the picture, Madlyn Rhue, seemed to be taking a particular interest in him.

But he was still determined to spread the good news about LSD. As the shooting continued on Key West and reporters were ushered on to the set to interview him, he started to talk about the changes that had come over him. In particular he told both Lionel Crane of the London *Daily Mirror* and Joe Hyams, a columnist based in Hollywood, exactly what had happened to him.

'I have been born again,' he told Hyams confidentially, as they sat on the deck of the pink painted submarine that was the heart of the picture. 'I have been through a psychiatric experience which has completely changed me. It was horrendous. I had to face things about myself which I never admitted, which I didn't know were there. Now I know that I hurt every woman I ever loved. I was an utter fake, a self-opinionated bore, a know-all who knew very little.' Hyams was astonished. He did not know whether or not to believe what he was hearing, and certainly could not guess whether he would be able to print it. This was the star everyone in Hollywood knew *never* talked about himself, avoided the columnists and who, so the jokes ran, was 'always on' [that is, on stage] 'and when he isn't on he's depressed.'

'I found I was hiding behind all kinds of defences, hypocrisies and vanities,' Grant told Hyams. 'I had to get rid of them layer by layer. The moment when your conscious meets your sub-conscious is a hell of a wrench. With me

257

there came a day when I saw the light. I know that's a cliché, but clichés are clichés because they're true.' The columnist, who had started to tape record the conversation, said that Grant went on: 'Each of us is dying for affection [but] we don't know how to go about getting it. Everything we do is affected by this longing. That's why I became an actor – I was longing for affection. I wanted people to like me, but I went about it the wrong way, almost all of us do.

'Every man is conceited,' Grant continued, 'but I know now that in my earlier days I really despised myself. It's when you admit this you're beginning to change. Now everything's changed. My attitude towards women is completely different. I don't intend to foul up any more lives.' As Hyams said later: 'It was an astonishing interview and I was tense with excitement as I turned off the tape recorder. I was convinced by much of what he said: Cary's new frankness, compared to his old taciturnity, bespoke some profound changes in his personality.'

'May I publish what you've just said?' he asked.

'Not yet, but the time's coming and I'll let you know when I'm ready.'

The two men went on to talk about other things, including Cary Grant's habit of wearing women's nylon panties because they were easy to pack and wash, it was a trick he said he had picked up on location. Sitting on the submarine, with a small aluminium sheet attached to his neck to catch the best of the sun's rays and increase his suntan, he looked completely relaxed, and very much the new man he told Hyams he felt. He told Lionel Crane almost exactly the same things. Within a matter of days the first public revelation that one of Hollywood's most enduring stars had started to experiment with LSD, and had found himself a changed man, began to appear in England.

When Joe Hyams heard that, he asked Cary Grant if he could now write up his own interview for America. One night at the Hartford Theater in Hollywood, when they sat beside each other, with Betsy Drake only a little farther away and accompanied by someone else, Grant told Hyams that he had no objections. 'As long as you use only the quotes I approved for Lionel's article.' But the secret fear that Grant had harboured for more than a quarter of a century had not totally disappeared in Dr Hartman's consulting room. He had always wanted to become a star, and he had always been determined never to do anything to endanger his place as one of Hollywood's most famous names. The fear that his achievements could suddenly now be taken away from him had not left him and neither had his habit of changing his mind and his mood from moment to moment.

On the day before Hyams's series of articles were due to appear in the *New York Herald Tribune*, Grant called the columnist and told him:

'You can't run the articles.'

'Why not?'

'Because I don't want them run in America.'

When Hyams explained that they were already being run off the presses in New York, Grant simply said:

'I can't help that. You better find a way to stop them or you'll be discredited. I'll tell the press I haven't seen you at all.'

'But that's ridiculous and you know it.'

'It's your word against mine, and you know who they'll believe.'

Grant rang off and within a few minutes Hyams was telephoned by Stanley Fox, his lawyer and adviser, who told him:

'You'd better do something about killing the series.'

When Hyams repeated that there was nothing he could do, Fox went on:

'You must do it. Cary tells me he hasn't seen you for two years, which means that you've made the whole series up or pirated it from another source.'

Hyams was unable to stop his articles, so on the morning of Monday, 20 April 1959, barely two months before *North by Northwest* was scheduled to open in New York, newspapers throughout America were reporting that Cary Grant was being treated by a psychiatrist and that he had experimented with LSD. They were also reporting that Cary

259

Grant himself was firmly denying the story, and saying: 'I've never had an interview with Joe Hyams on any subject. The article is completely erroneous.'

The denial did nothing to lessen the public interest. The series had Grant admitting: 'I've just been born again. I've been though a psychiatric experience which has completely changed me . . . Before this happened I was in a fog. Afterward I was given eyesight to see everything as it is . . . I have been married three times, but never had a child. Now I am fit for children. I hope I will beget some . . . I am no longer lonely. I am a happy man.' The follow-up article reported him as saying that after his psychiatric treatment he had discovered that he and Betsy Drake 'loved each other more than we'd ever done before' and continuing: 'Now I know that I hurt every woman I loved and they tried to hurt me too, but the faults were mine, always mine.'

On the third morning Grant was saying in print: 'I'm bored by that word charm. It was tacked on to me some years ago. Now I'm sick of it,' and concluding: 'Heaven knows I needed to change. I left it late but at least I did it. There are some people who go screaming in ignorance to their graves.'

Grant's revulsion from his own indiscretions was swift. Cary Grant, the star of more than sixty films, was not someone who felt he should talk about psychiatry or hallucinogenic drugs, no matter how much Archie Leach may have wanted him to. Angry and resentful, he retired again to the small dark study of his house in Beverly Hills and tried to forget the world outside. Within a month Joe Hyams had issued a suit for slander against him claiming $500,000 in damages, and shortly after that Universal Studios sent Hyams a photograph of the two of them talking to each other on the set of *Operation Petticoat* in Key West. Within four months Grant had withdrawn his denial of the interviews and had settled the slander action out of court. He had even agreed to co-operate with Hyams in the preparation of his life story, but that was not to happen in the form that either man envisaged.

Whatever Cary Grant's private fears, in fact the public revelations about his experiments with psychiatry and LSD did nothing to detract from his appeal in *North by Northwest*. When the film opened at the end of July 1959 *Newsweek* said enthusiastically that it 'resoundingly reaffirms the fact that Cary Grant and Alfred Hitchcock are two of the very slickest operators before and behind the Hollywood cameras. Together they can be unbeatable.' Even the *New Yorker* admitted that Hitchcock's film was a 'brilliant realization of a feat he had been unintentionally moving toward for more than a decade – a perfect parody of his own work'; and *Variety* called it 'The mixture as before, suspense, intrigue, comedy, humour; but seldom has the concoction been served up so delectably or in so glossy a package.'

Rumours about Grant continued none the less, to swirl back and forth in the American newspapers. It was said that he was not going to stay in Hollywood any longer because he disliked the smog; that he had spent the entire Cannes film festival dancing with Kim Novak; that he had fallen in love with Sophia Loren's stand-in, a Yugoslavian actress named Luba Otesevic, who bore an uncanny resemblance to her. There were even reports that his former chauffeur, Raymond Austin, had had a relationship with Betsy Drake and would be cited in their divorce suit. Grant issued a statement to the press saying that, 'As far as Mrs Grant and I can gather the young man is denying something of which he has never been accused. So since neither of us has any way to defend ourselves against such publicity we have decided it is best to make no other comment either upon the story or its ridiculous implications.'

The reason for the interest in him was clear enough. At the age of fifty-five, and after one abortive attempt at retirement, he had become one of the most popular film actors in the world. His enthusiasm for LSD had not waned. He had agreed to tell *Look* magazine about his experiments, and to allow the magazine to talk to Dr Hartman about the treatment. *Look*'s reporter, Laura Berquist, did not find the task easy. For the more she talked to the actor's friends about him, the more confusing the picture became.

'I discovered many baffling and contradictory Grants,' Berquist wrote in September 1959. 'The Lone Wolf who can't bear to be alone; the Simple Grant, happily relaxing in Levis at "The Dump", his Mexican adobe retreat in Palm Springs; the Perfectionist, who drove one director to a hospital with nervous exhaustion; the Evangelist for new enthusiasms. There is also Grant the Tycoon, bargaining his six-figure earnings with a mind like an IBM machine; Grant the Tastemaker; and, of course, Grant the legendary charmer.' Even Betsy, who had never collaborated with an interviewer in the past, did nothing to alleviate the confusion. She told Berquist: 'Who knows? He may come back to me, or not marry at all, or marry somebody quite different from me. He's dizzy! Enormously stimulating! Younger than many young men I know.'

On one point Cary Grant was clear to Berquist – the benefits of psychotherapy with LSD. He told her: 'I know that all my life I've been going around in a fog. You're just a bunch of molecules until you know who you are. You spend all your time getting to be a big Hollywood actor. But then what? You've reached a comfortable plateau and you want to stay on it, you resist change.'

'All my life I've been searching for peace of mind,' he went on. Nothing really seemed to give me what I wanted until this treatment. I'd explored yoga and hypnotism and made attempts at mysticism. Now people come to me for help. It's amazing, but young women have never been so attracted to me. All my life I've been running from what I wanted most. I've shied, for example, from women who look like my mother.' He was even prepared to admit: 'I used to love a woman with great passion, and we destroyed each other. Or I loved not all, or in friendship. Now I'm ready to love on an equal level. If I can find a woman on whom I can exhaust all my thoughts, energies and emotions, and who loves me that way in return, we can live happily ever after.'

By the time Berquist's analysis appeared in *Look*, Cary Grant had fled the United States, and was safely hidden from anyone who wanted to ask him where he might find a new woman. He was beginning to wonder whether he had already found her in Betsy Drake. In the months since they had officially announced their separation he had spent more time with her than ever before. Three times a week for almost a year he had sent her a spray of orchids for her bedroom, and twice a week they had had dinner together, though their lawyers were discussing the details of their divorce settlement. Certainly he always discussed any problem he had with her, and he had begun to tell his friends that 'We never loved each other when we were married as we do now.'

The one solid fact was his continued appeal at the box office. Hardly had the massive queues for *North By Northwest* subsided than new ones started for *Operation Petticoat*. In spite of its flimsy plot about a wartime submarine forced to pick up a group of female officers, the picture opened at the Radio City Music Hall in New York in December 1959 to good reviews and enthusiastic audiences. *Variety* called Grant 'a living lesson in getting laughs without lines . . . It is his reaction, blank, startled, always underplayed, that creates or releases the humour,' and the *Los Angeles Examiner* suggested that he was the 'motivating keynote that held together the whole movie'.

By the beginning of January 1960 he had become the first star in the history of the movies whose films had grossed more than $10m in one single cinema, the Radio City Music Hall in New York. *Operation Petticoat* took $8m at the box office and made him almost $3m as his percentage of the profits, more than he had ever made from a film before.

With his success at the box office his urge to prove his attraction to young actresses seemed to increase, and so did the number of his appearances in the world's press. It was as if Cary Grant had come to believe that there was no woman in the world who would not be attracted to him. The stories of his reported conquests grew day by day, and yet at Christmas when he visited his friend and former director Clifford Odets, he refused to stay, because he wanted to spend the holiday with Betsy. As Odets recalled: 'He had a bag packed for a visit. Her house wasn't a twenty-minute drive from his but he wanted to move in.' Not long afterwards, when he flew out of Los Angeles to make a film with Stanley Donen in London, Betsy was there to see him off.

'I wish you were coming too. You will think about it, won't you?'

'Yes, I'll think about it.'

As soon as he arrived he started to telephone her every day to persuade her to 'Come on over,' even though the London papers were reporting that he was spending his evenings in the company of the singer Alma Cogan, whom he described to one reporter as 'one of my closest friends'.

Finally Betsy did agree to come, and he booked a suite for them both at the Savoy. It seemed as though they had decided to try to resurrect their marriage. Certainly they acted like honeymooners. The Rolls-Royce he had demanded as part of his fee for *Indiscreet* was still in London, and in the evenings he would take his wife out for a drive; they would get out and he would instruct the chauffeur to follow discreetly behind them. If his wife noticed that it was precisely the same manoeuvre he had used to entrance the beautiful Ingrid Bergman in the film itself, she did not mention the fact.

One person who was keen to see Cary Grant and Betsy Drake reunited was Elsie Leach. When he had taken his wife down to Bristol to see her, early in 1960, as the Donen picture got under way in England, she had told her son firmly: 'When are you two going to stop all this nonsense and get back together again?'

'Maybe soon, Mother, maybe soon,' Grant had replied.

Betsy, however, did not see any need to dispel the confusion in other people's minds. 'Why should we make a reconciliation announcement?' she asked one fan magazine interviewer stiffly. 'We might not be together tomorrow. He might decide to go somewhere I don't want to go, or I might want to go somewhere he doesn't enjoy. But as long as we enjoy doing things together we will be together, because we are in love.' In fact they had decided to resume living together, but not to restrict each other's freedom. The American press called it 'marriage on the instalment plan', and a 'wildly Utopian idea', but neither Betsy nor Grant seemed in the least concerned. Their reconciliation went without a hitch; or so it seemed.

The film Grant had come to London to make was a version of the English stage success, *The Grass is Greener*. It seemed to Grant to be just the kind of light comedy that suited him best, the sort of frivolous story and elegant setting that he had always felt most comfortable with, expensive surroundings which allowed him to look elegant and the women to look both stylish and beautiful.

When they had first discussed it, Grant and Donen had decided that Kay Kendall and her husband Rex Harrison would be perfect as two of the other stars, and that Deborah Kerr would be ideal for the fourth main part. They calculated that the distinctive Englishness of all three would act as a balance to Grant's obvious Americanness in a story set among the British aristocracy. But Kay Kendall's sudden and tragic death at the age of thirty-three had forced them to revise their plans. They had talked about asking Ingrid Bergman to take over Kendall's part as the Countess of Rhyall, but when Deborah Kerr had suggested that she might play it herself, Grant and Donen had gratefully agreed.

To take over Deborah Kerr's original part Grant wanted Jean Simmons, whose marriage to Stewart Granger was on the verge of collapse; and Donen suggested that they use Robert Mitchum as the other leading man. Grant's old friend Noël Coward had told Donen that he would be interested in playing the part of the literary butler when they made the film, but after some thought Donen eventually turned down his offer and decided to use the English actor, Moray Watson, who had created the part on the London stage. He was the only member of the London stage company, which had included Celia Johnson and Joan Greenwood, to appear in the film version.

As shooting began everyone on the set became aware that Cary Grant was not at ease. He was having some difficulty in remembering his lines, and every shot seemed to be lined up so that only he would be cast in the best light. Deborah Kerr remained loyal, but even she told her friends privately that a change seemed to have come over him since *Dream Wife* and *An Affair to Remember*. Robert Mitchum was less diplomatic. 'I had a girl at the side of the set who told me when to say "Why? Really?" whenever Cary Grant came to the end of a speech.' Some things had not changed, however. Grant was still obsessed by the tiniest detail of the production, but now he seemed to oscillate alarmingly between elation and depression. It was a curious performance, as if he hated the business of playing the role he had created for himself and yet was hypnotized by it.

Moray Watson remembered that when he asked him if he thought he would ever come back to England permanently, Grant had told him:

'I doubt it. I've kind of got used to the climate in California, and besides I can't understand your electricity system over here. Why don't you have simple plugs?' The two men spent a lot of time together during the filming, going over their lines and talking about the past. Watson remembered being slightly surprised when Grant talked about women. 'He talked about himself as if he were an exhibit, not a man at all.'

Certainly he had not lost the habit of introducing himself to anyone he met with the words, 'Hello, I'm Cary Grant,' just as he had not lost the habit of looking at himself persistently in the mirror. Part of his unhappiness was rooted in his age. In *Sylvia Scarlett* in 1935 Katharine Hepburn had preferred Brian Aherne, but that was the last time he'd been 'rejected'. Ever since then it was Grant who had got the girl at the end of the film. Now he knew that that would not be the case much longer.

As if to compensate for this unpalatable realization, off the screen he seemed almost desperate to prove he could still charm any woman he chose. By the time shooting was finished on *The Grass is Greener* several American newspapers had reported his appearance at Alma Cogan's birthday party, and as the columnist Sheilah Graham put it, they 'held hands' and Cary Grant 'generally looked like a man in love'. Another columnist even quoted him as saying that Cogan was 'the sweetest girl in the world. She has brains, talent, a sense of humour and a wonderful sense of understanding.' The columnist concluded: 'Cary has neglected to mention whether his third wife Betsy thinks Alma is wonderful too.'

Within a week Louella Parsons had reported in Hollywood that Betsy Drake had suddenly left London, and Sheilah Graham had added that Grant was developing a crush on another actress, Agnes Laurent. In the next few months other beauties of the screen, like Haya Harareet and Nancy Kovacs, were also reported as being among his close friends. But by the middle of August he was back in Hollywood with Betsy. To the amazement of the press they held hands at a sneak preview of *The Grass is Greener* and again at a party for her birthday in September, but soon he was back in England again for a little extra work on the film, and Louella Parsons was reporting his friendship with actress Jackie Chan. In Hollywood once more, he was reported to be escorting another actress, Ziva Rodann, but when he went back to England for Christmas, he travelled with Betsy.

Radio City Music Hall had planned to make *The Grass is Greener* their Christmas attraction, solely on the strength of Grant's appeal at the box office, but they changed their minds after seeing the first version of the film and when it was shown in Hollywood, the trade press were distinctly unimpressed. The *Hollywood Reporter* called it 'pseudo-Coward', a film in which the 'stars do not glitter, or even glow', and *Variety* had said that it was a 'generally tedious romantic exercise'. When the film eventually opened at Christmas 1960 even harsher criticism came from the *New York Times*. Bosley Crowther said: 'Mr Grant and Mr Mitchum try hard to create the illusion of being moved by love and passion. But they both appear mechanical and bored.' But *Time* magazine came closer to revealing Grant's strength and the film's weakness when it commented: 'He is the only funny man in movie history who has maintained himself for close to thirty years as a ranking romantic star. He wears only one expression: the bland mask of drawing-room comedy. He plays only one plot: the well-pressed, elegantly laundered, masculine existence that finds itself splashed by love's old sweet ketchup. About that situation Grant has nothing important to say, no social or moral message to deliver. He creates in a vacuum of values, he is a technician only, but he is a technician of genius.'

Now, whenever he went out in Hollywood, Grant made sure that he appeared as the star. He attended only the very best parties, the smartest openings. On these occasions he was the movie industry's perfect ambassador, elegant, charming, debonair, with a faint fey smile in his eyes; the man whom every woman in the room felt that she alone could finally make happy. He acted the part the industry had come to expect of him, and he did it as carefully and as professionally as if he was on the set. In fact, he went out less and less. As 1961 began and he celebrated his fifty-seventh birthday, he knew there could only be a handful of years left for him as the romantic lead; he did not want to tarnish the end of his long career by getting a reputation as a lascivious old man unable to grow old with dignity and charm. Cosmetic surgery would not solve the problem either. Cinema audiences were growing younger as the older generation stayed at home to watch television. The curtain was falling on his career because he did not want to play any other part than his perennially debonair self. So when Jack Warner asked him if he would be interested in playing the lead in the film version of Meredith Wilson's Broadway musical *The Music Man*, Grant told him the person he should ask was Robert Preston, who had played it on Broadway.

He looked at the vast pile of scripts that gathered for him in his bungalow at Universal but few of them appealed. In fact, it was the man who shared his bungalow, Robert

Arthur, the producer of *Operation Petticoat*, who finally helped him decide what to do next. Arthur had realized that Cary Grant liked to work with people he knew and trusted, that only then did he feel comfortable enough to give his best performances. He had also long wanted to put him together with Universal's other major star, Doris Day. Day's string of hits included *Pillow Talk* and *Lover Come Back*. Both pictures had been partly written by Stanley Shapiro, who had scripted *Operation Petticoat*. Robert Arthur suggested that Shapiro should continue the series, only this time write a film especially to feature Cary Grant. The film he came up with was *That Touch of Mink*.

The blonde, freckled Day, a former dance band singer now aged thirty-eight, had established herself as the virginal sweetheart of America, naive, endlessly enthusiastic, but with a girlish twinkle in her eye. Marty Melcher, her second husband, and manager, who was also to be the new film's co-producer, demanded for his wife a fee of $750,000 to make the picture. Cary Grant was prepared to take a lower initial fee of $600,000 as an advance against a ten per cent share of the gross receipts.

Filming started in the summer of 1961. Day told me later: 'I really didn't get to know him very, very well. I always had a feeling that there were lots of things about Cary I didn't know.' In the script he was to play a millionaire; he insisted on not only changing the doorknobs Universal had designed for his office on the set but also on adorning it with paintings from his own home. He brought in some of his Boudins, which Universal had to have specially guarded to satisfy their insurance company. 'If I'm meant to be a millionaire I should look like one,' Grant explained. 'A hundred little details add up to an impression.'

Day also said of the experience: 'I think he is a very private person, but then maybe we all are. But he has got great taste and I admire that.' Certainly she trusted him enough to allow him to take her to New York for a week to choose a wardrobe for the film. He wanted Norman Norell to design her clothes. There was only one major point of disagreement. Cary Grant still disliked being photographed from the right – he always had done – but so did Doris Day. Finally he allowed her the privilege – occasionally.

Doris Day's film career was not destined to last long after her film with Cary Grant, but she remembers him with affection: 'I trusted his judgement, he had an innate sense of what is right for a film. He's definitely the most underrated actor in Los Angeles. He's really just himself and that's the most difficult thing to be.' As always, Cary Grant insisted on wearing his own clothes during the filming. The film's director, Delbert Mann, recalled: 'He was very conscious of every detail. I'd never come across an actor like that before: he always struck me, though, as being a bit of a loner. He was always affable, jovial, professional, but I never thought I got to know him.' In fact Mann believes that 'the challenge of acting seemed to have gone out of things for him. He was just playing Cary Grant, and nobody does it better than he does.'

Glossy, inconsequential, rooted in farce and making few demands on the audience, the film was a recreation of a Leo McCarey story. A wealthy bachelor not interested in marriage meets a smalltown girl working in New York after his Rolls-Royce has splashed her in the rain, and after an on-and-off romance in the style of *The Awful Truth*, they finally marry. Although *Variety* called the film 'essentially threadbare', when it opened in June 1962 at Radio City Music Hall, the old screwball comedy formula still had its charm. Brendan Gill in the *New Yorker* remarked that it was 'identical to Delbert Mann and Stanley Shapiro's earlier film *Lover Come Back* except that in *Lover Come Back* the Cary Grant part was played by Rock Hudson and in *That Touch of Mink* the Cary Grant part is played by Cary Grant.' No matter what the critics thought, the film was a huge success, taking more than $1m at Radio City alone, the first film in movie history ever to gross more than a million dollars in a single cinema. It earned Grant another $3m as a result of his share of its receipts.

Off the set, his reconciliation with Betsy had mystified

Hollywood. They appeared to see each other regularly, and were often noticed deep in conversation together, but Grant's appetite for beautiful young actresses did not seem to have diminished, even if he courted them in a rather eccentric way. One of the girls he took out was Greta Thyssen. She recalled later: 'Cary was fifty-eight when I knew him, and yet I was never conscious of the fact that he was older than my father. He is as romantic and virile as any younger man I've ever dated and never acts or does anything to make you aware of his age. According to him – and this is a viewpoint he expressed over and over again – he has full rights to love all attractive people he meets.' A former Miss Denmark, who had first gone to Hollywood originally to take part in the Miss Universe contest, Thyssen later admitted: 'I knew that Cary's philosophy was only a highly refined version of many lines I had heard. Yet, all the same, I really felt he believed it and still does. At least when he says, "I might love you today but I can make no promises if I find someone as pretty as you tomorrow," you know how you stand and build no false hopes for the future.'

Thyssen regularly visited Grant at home, and when she did he would usually offer her dinner on his bed in front of the television set. The housekeeper served it to them on a tray, and after they had finished they would continue to watch television. It was not exactly what Hollywood expected from its leading man. If they went out together – which was not something he liked to do – Grant usually just took her for a long drive in the Rolls-Royce, through the Hollywood Hills towards the Pacific Ocean, much as he had taken Barbara Hutton twenty years earlier. There were hardly any candlelit dinners in expensive restaurants, and very few parties to go to; he didn't shower Thyssen with flowers or expensive presents – 'just records and stuffed animals', she said later. Sometimes they would visit Tony Curtis for dinner, but Grant preferred to be at home in bed early. 'On weekends he sometimes does nothing but stay in bed, resting, reading and just taking it easy,' Thyssen said, 'so he is always watching his health, his youth and his rest.

271

Sometimes he will talk to people only on the phone, but not see them for days at a time.'

Thyssen also recalled that Grant disliked anyone disagreeing with him, that he 'wants his domestic help to be perfect', that he would tell her which clothes to wear and ask her not to wear make-up. Although he never introduced her to LSD, there were certain other girls to whom he would extol its benefits. At one stage he had paid for a girl to have sessions. However, by the summer of 1962, Dr Hartman's experiments with the drug had fallen foul of the Californian Board of Medical Examiners. In August 1961 they placed him on ten years' probation and instructed him to take an oral examination before they would allow him to practise again. In October 1961 they formally suspended him from practising in California after he had failed the oral examination three times. He was forced out of California, and went to practise in the Eastern United States, but insists now: 'All the hundred and ten patients in the experiment that we ran were volunteers. We never intended it to be a particularly deep psychological examination. We were interested to see how the volunteers responded to the drug itself.' He admits: 'There were always a lot of people against the drug. But I think I underestimated the power they had, because they finally banned it. I considered my experiment a success. There never were any accidents with it in our experiment, although I know there were in some others. The reason was that we were very careful.'

In July 1962, at Santa Monica Supreme Court, the long-suffering Betsy Drake finally filed for divorce; with reports of her husband's many attachments multiplying in the press, she had almost no alternative. Like Barbara Hutton before her, she claimed that Cary Grant had subjected her to 'grievous mental suffering' until the break-up of their marriage in 1958.

At the formal hearing a month later a composed but depressed Betsy told Judge Edward R. Brand that her husband had 'left home for long periods', that he was 'apparently bored with me', and that he 'preferred watching television to talking to me'. She testified: 'He told me he didn't want to be married. He went away for long periods of time – not in connection with his work. He also showed no interest in any of my friends.' After being granted a divorce, Drake told the hubbub of reporters waiting outside the courtroom: 'I was always in love with him and I still am.' More than fifteen years later she told the *New York Times*: 'I divorced the whole town as well as Cary, and they divorced me.' The bookish actress saw her film career evaporate. She turned to studying psychotherapy, went on to teach psychodrama, and finally became a writer.

Hardly had the divorce been granted than Cary Grant planned another trip to Europe with Stanley Donen. He was now, at fifty-eight, the biggest box-office star in the world, took seventy-five per cent of the profits of all his films with Universal, and was entitled to have the negatives revert to him after eight years. As *Time* magazine had noted tartly: 'All this has made him so rich that he could, if he chose, join NATO,' and had gone on to add: 'He also has virtually every nickel he has ever earned.' Embittered by the rumours about his meanness and eccentricity, Grant responded by becoming even more remote from Hollywood. The standoffishness that had grown out of his shyness long before became the central feature of his character. It was the audience in the Radio City Music Hall that had made him, and kept him a star, he told himself. He owed his allegiance to them, not to the newspapers, magazines or to their columnists.

On his way to Paris to meet Stanley Donen and start work on their new film *Charade*, Grant stopped off in Philadelphia to see a performance of the touring version of the Broadway comedy, *The Fun Couple*, a visit that had nothing to do with the play. He had gone to see a young blonde actress who was appearing in it. Her name: Dyan Cannon.

Grant had first set eyes on her while sitting alone on his bed one evening watching a forgettable television series and he had been hypnotized by her. Within an hour he had discovered who she was, and had telephoned her agent,

273

Adeline Gould, to ask if she would be prepared to talk to him about making a film. It was an old Hollywood ploy – the ageing star asking the well-endowed young actress if she would like to make a picture with him – but Gould had taken it seriously enough to call Cannon, who was filming in Rome.

Cannon was interested but not prepared to come back to Hollywood unless Grant was willing to pay her air fare. It was not until the summer of 1962 that Gould finally ushered her client into Cary Grant's bungalow at Universal. That day they spent an hour and a half talking to each other without a word being said about a film, and the next day Cary Grant called her to ask for a date. Cannon made one but broke it. He asked again and she broke it again. She broke the next seven dates they made. It was not until the ninth time he asked her that she allowed Hollywood's most successful male star to take her out to lunch, and not until the tenth that she allowed him to take her out to dinner. She said later: 'He brought me home and then, outside the house, I asked him to kiss me goodnight. I had never asked a man to kiss me. Never had to . . .'

The twenty-three-year-old actress with blonde hair and hazel eyes, had been born Samille Diane Friessen in Tacoma, Washington, the daughter of an insurance salesman who was a deacon in the Baptist Church and his Jewish wife. At seventeen, she had arrived in Hollywood to get engaged to a businessman – an insurance salesman like her father – and although her mother had persuaded her that she was too young to get married, she had decided to stay on and try her luck at becoming an actress. Like a legion of Hollywood starlets before her, she had been eternally hopeful. She had worked as a drama student, a model and a Slenderella beautician while awaiting her opportunity. Finally, she had been offered a screen test by the producer Jerry Wald which had led to more than two hundred television parts and some stage work.

At their first dinner together Cannon recalls that she was 'enchanted by Cary, I was charmed in the true sense of the word, we talked for a couple of hours. It was a marvellous conversation. I was completely smitten with him, and with his ideas.' By the end of that summer Dyan, who had at one stage been the close friend of the comedian Mort Sahl, had become the most important of the young actresses with whom Cary Grant occupied his time. As always, the couple watched television at Grant's home, and rarely went out. Grant began to suggest that Dyan wear less perfume, less make-up, and that perhaps she might consider wearing different clothes. As she put it later, theirs was a 'pygmalion relationship'.

But Grant was not prepared to play Professor Higgins in public, even if he was considering doing so on the screen. Jack Warner had paid $5.5m for the film rights to the Lerner and Lowe Broadway musical, *My Fair Lady*, based on George Bernard Shaw's play *Pygmalion*. He wanted Grant as Higgins, whom Rex Harrison had portrayed on Broadway, and George Cukor as director, and he had pursued Grant for months about the prospect. The studio were convinced that the film would be an enormous success, and were prepared to give Grant almost any terms he wanted, as well as offering him his choice of co-star. Jack Warner had been so anxious to get him that he had signed Audrey Hepburn for a fee of $1.1m to play Eliza Doolittle, rather than Julie Andrews who had played the part on Broadway, because he knew Grant liked her and had just arranged for her to appear with him in *Charade*.

To Warner's disappointment, after months of uncertainty Cary Grant turned the part down, telling him: 'No matter how good I am I'll either be compared with Rex Harrison, and I don't think I'll be better than he is, or I'll be told I'm imitating him, which isn't good for him, or for me.' So Warner turned back to Rex Harrison to play the role.

His refusal was certainly not prompted by any dislike of the gamine Hepburn, who had started her career in England only to win an Oscar for her first major film in Hollywood, *Roman Holiday*. He thought she could well become the last of his great leading ladies, a successor to her namesake,

275

Katharine Hepburn, to Grace Kelly and Ingrid Bergman. Planning *Charade*, he and Donen were convinced she would be perfect for the part of the chic but naive Unesco translator, Reggie Lambert. Based on an original short story by Peter Stone and Marc Behan, which the thirty-two-year-old Stone had turned into a screenplay, the film was heavy with echoes of Grant's earlier work with Hitchcock. Once again he would be presented as every woman's desire but someone who was probably not quite what he appeared. Grant wanted it to open at Radio City at Christmas 1963. He had no doubt that it would appeal to the audience there just as much as *Suspicion* had done twenty-two years before.

Filming in Paris went well. Hepburn proved every bit as good as Grant thought she would be, and the only thing he disliked about the experience was the cold; it reminded him why he could never return permanently to England. He sent Dyan Cannon a crystal ball from the set and telephoned her regularly, and he crossed the Channel to England to celebrate his mother's eighty-sixth birthday with her in Bristol. Among other things, they discussed whether it might not be time for her to move out of her house and into a nursing home. Although Elsie Leach was never prepared to admit that she was any less in command than she had always been, she agreed that such a move might make her life a little easier. Grant told her he would keep the house on if she moved, so she could always come back to it. She said to him: 'Why don't you dye your hair? That grey makes you look old.' He did not quite know what to say.

In spite of the Parisian cold, and in spite of Dyan, he was not especially keen to return to California. The life story that he had agreed to tell Joe Hyams after their slander action was about to be published in the *American Ladies Home Journal*. He had worked on the series of three articles himself after Hyams had submitted them to him, and the columnist had agreed to remove his byline and share his $125,000 fee with him. But Grant was still not anxious to see his past life dragged out into the open, and his experiments with LSD publicized again. In the end the repercussions were not as bad as he had expected. He had mainly restricted his reminiscences to his early life, with little about his various wives, although he did say: 'I've never clearly resolved why Betsy and I parted. We lived together, not as easily and contentedly as some, perhaps; yet, it seemed to me, as far as one marriage can be compared with any other, compatibly happier than most. I owe a lot to Betsy.'

He did, however, launch an attack on the world's press for associating him with 'all sorts of ladies: some I've never met, some whose names are unknown to me, and some who don't even exist,' and the articles also gave him an excellent opportunity to defend the taking of LSD. 'Orthodox psychiatrists using the slower customary methods resisted its usage,' he said, 'and it's unlikely that it will be reintroduced until some brave, venturesome and respected psychiatrist speaks publically out in its favour. Meanwhile the authorities have banned its use: at least for therapeutic purposes. Although how men can be authorities on something they've never tried mystifies me.'

Back in the affluent vacuum of Beverly Hills, Grant returned to the seclusion of his house, and the quiet restrained life that he had come to prefer. There were only one or two alternations to his daily routine of going to bed before ten o'clock in the evening, sleeping in late, and spending the day resting, looking at his investments and talking to his friends on the telephone. He had been rather surprised to be telephoned by President John Kennedy. When it had first happened, he had been convinced that someone was playing a joke on him, but when the President had convinced him he was real, Grant had thought he wanted to invite him to a White House dinner. To his surprise the young President had told him simply that he and his brother Bobby had 'just wanted to hear his voice', and they both took to calling him regularly, until in the autumn of 1963 Bobby Kennedy invited him to Washington to help him launch a project to stop America's high school children dropping out. His gilded role as Cary Grant, Hollywood's suavest ambassador, seemed more spectacularly successful than ever.

As the publicity for the opening of *Charade* began he was still the irresistible star. As *Look* magazine put it: 'He is the tall, dark, handsome, charming, lovable, considerate, dependable, athletic, day and night dream man who lurks deep in most women's fantasies . . . who has wooed a *Who's Who* of glamour.' Not a word was breathed about his experiments with LSD, his meanness, his vanity, or his depression. To John F. Kennedy and to most of America, he was still what he had always been, one of the most attractive men in the world. Yet privately he was troubled. When Clifford Odets was dying at the age of fifty-seven in Hollywood, in August 1963, Grant had wanted to see him and had been refused. As Margaret Brennan Gibson revealed in her 1981 biography of the playwright, the man who had directed *None But The Lonely Heart* from his own script had denounced Cary Grant to his friends as 'Mr Hollywood' and had called the bunch of carnations that he had sent to his hospital room 'phony' – a wounding insult from a dying man whose intellect Grant had so publicly admired.

Variety's assessment of Grant's fortune as more than $15m did not please him either. For one thing, there were other, richer actors – Bob Hope for example; and for another he just took no pleasure in being compared with William Holden, Gregory Peck and Doris Day. If he preferred to handle his own business deals, with the aid of his experienced adviser, Stanley Fox, that was his affair; and if he demanded control over everything that affected a film he was working on, that was simply common sense. He believed he had earned his wealth. He had worked hard for more than thirty years, he had released sixty-nine films. Now, he had decided to produce his next film himself. His choice was a picture based on another script by Peter Stone and once again the studio would be Universal. He knew they were grateful to him for saving them from a slump, and would gladly concede his seventy-five per cent of the gross receipts. The enthusiastic reception that *Charade* was already beginning to receive would make them keener on the project than ever.

Charade was the twenty-sixth Cary Grant picture to play the Radio City Music Hall in New York when it opened in December 1963, and it was the fourth of his previous five films to play there at Christmas, as he had planned it would. Not that the *New York Times* was all that enthusiastic. Bosley Crowther warned his readers, 'I tell you this light-hearted picture is full of such gruesome violence' and went on: 'Mr Grant does everything from taking a shower without removing his suit to fighting with thugs, with all the blandness and the boredom of an old screwball comedy hand.' *Time* was no kinder. It pointed out that Stanley Donen had let the film degenerate from a sensible idea 'into a bloody awful farce, the sort of shaggy dog story in which the customers are the real victims – they are inexorably gagged to death.' But to Grant's relief *Newsweek* had called the picture an 'absolute delight'. He knew the audience enjoyed it: he stood at the back of the theatre and watched them. In its first week the film took more than $170,000, a record for the Music Hall, and once again Grant knew that he could cheerfully ignore most of the critics. What was interesting him now was who to choose as leading lady for his own proposed film, *Father Goose*. Audrey Hepburn was unavailable but he was considering Leslie Caron: he had just seen the French-born actress in her film, *The L-Shaped Room*, and thought she looked rather like Hepburn.

Caron had not enjoyed the happiest of times in Hollywood. She had made a brilliant start with Gene Kelly in *An American in Paris*, but after her husband, the English stage director Peter Hall, had named Warren Beatty as the 'other man' in their divorce action things had not gone quite as well for her. Small, slight, and with her native French accent still intact, she had been nominated for an Oscar for *Lili* in 1952, but *The L-Shaped Room* had marked her return to acceptance in Hollywood. She was being tipped as likely to be nominated for an Academy Award again for her performance in the picture. Grant's plans to produce the film himself did not go smoothly. David Miller, who had just completed the comedy drama *Captain Newman MD* with Gregory Peck and Tony

279

Curtis, and whom he had hired as director, had not settled comfortably, and in fact left the film in March 1964, not long after his sixtieth birthday. Finally, Grant accepted defeat, he went back to Robert Arthur, and asked him to take over the production for him. Together they agreed on a new director, the talented Ralph Nelson, whose career had begun with great distinction in television – he directed the award-winning *Requiem for a Heavyweight* with Jack Palance – and they settled on the locations in Jamaica.

More than anything else what had appealed to Cary Grant in the script of *Father Goose* was that it allowed him to be old, unshaven, grey-haired and eccentric, yet still to win the heart of his co-star at the end of the picture. For the first time in seventy feature films he was not to look impeccably groomed: he was to wear dirty jeans, a week's beard, and straw sandals as the history professor who rebelled against society and escaped to a Pacific island, only to be caught up in World War II and find himself the protector of Leslie Caron and seven children. Perhaps he also felt that his performance might win him an Oscar just as Humphrey Bogart had won one for his dishevelled river trader in John Huston's *The African Queen*. He had been nominated no more often than his young co-star, Leslie Caron and could not escape a feeling of resentment as he remembered how many Oscars his films had won for their directors, co-stars and writers. Within a year, he would see Rex Harrison win one for the part he had turned down in George Cukor's *My Fair Lady* and Peter Stone win for the script he was just about to film.

Once more he began talking about giving up films, or at least retiring again for a period. 'After all,' he told Roderick Mann of the London *Sunday Express*, one of the only journalists he had ever trusted, 'I am quite an old fellow to some young people. But to be honest with you I don't know what I will do. Maybe I will quit . . . That's why in *Charade* I insisted on putting in so many references to my age. I anticipated a lot of people's reactions.' Mann noted that Grant was still studiously having a massage every day, and

resting as much as he could to remain 'lean, suave, incomp-
arably tanned', as well as being 'rich and famous'. But
Mann added that the one thing Grant would miss from the
filming he had just finished was the seven children who were
Leslie Caron's charges.

Cary Grant was seriously thinking about having a child, and
so was wondering whether he should get married again. He
was now sixty, Dyan Cannon was twenty-five. He was still
seeing her, and they talked about having children.

In January 1964 he had celebrated his sixtieth birthday by
flying to see her perform in the touring version of the comedy
How To Succeed in Business Without Really Trying. In the next
two months he had paid for her to fly back to Los Angeles at
weekends, and in April she had left the cast to be with him.
Cary Grant's friends, like Tony Curtis and Howard Hawks,
watched his attachment to the tawny blonde girl grow, and
were pleased that she was clearly fascinated by him,
although, as she explained, 'he didn't want to get married
because, he thought, if we did it would ruin our relationship.
I can't be married, he said, I've tried, I ought to know.'

Dyan would not accept that. As she explained: 'Cary and
I talked about having a family when we were going together.
I knew somehow that if we both willed it we would have a
family. I don't think he really wanted them enough to have
them before. I believe that when he wanted a child he
decided to have one.' It was a view shared by some of his
friends, who believed that he had never considered having a
child of his own before because he was too involved in the
meticulous planning of his career. Grant and Dyan had
started talking about getting married a month after their
first meeting, but had dropped the subject. 'After that,' she
said later, 'we'd bring it up and consider it, and then it
wouldn't be brought up again for months.' They would
occasionally drift apart, but never for very long, and never
because of the differences in their ages. 'Neither of us was
concerned about age,' she said. 'I was so taken, so smitten,
so enamoured of, so much in love with him that – oh, I

281

didn't, couldn't see anything else. Of course, I wanted a child, his child. So after that he asked me three times. The first time he was so nervous he came down to my house and cracked up his car in the garage. I said, okay, I'll marry you, but nothing happened. So, after a while, I said it doesn't look like we are getting married, so I'd better check out. He didn't like that, so he asked me again. And again.'

Cary Grant dithered throughout 1964, and while *Father Goose* was prepared for its Christmas release at Radio City in New York, he was still not sure. When the film opened Bosley Crowther in the *New York Times* was more complimentary than he had been about *Charade*. He wrote that it was 'Mr Grant's blustering and bristling in his filthy old clothes and scraggly beard, rising in righteous indignation and shooting barbed shafts of manly wit that make for the major personality and most pungent humour in the film. It is not a very deep character or a very real one, but it is fun.' Brendan Gill, however, declared in the *New Yorker*: '*Father Goose* offers us a surly, slatternly, unshaven and hard-drinking Cary Grant in a part that would have suited Humphrey Bogart to a T but suits Mr Grant only to about a J.'

Grant also dithered about his career. He was attracted by a proposal to remake a George Stevens film, the 1943 Columbia picture *The More The Merrier*, about a housing shortage in Washington during World War II and to set it in Japan at the 1964 Olympic Games. But a lot depended on his marriage plans. He had taken Dyan Cannon to see his mother who had finally, at eighty-eight, left her house and moved into a nursing home. Dyan thought Elsie was 'incredible', a woman 'with a pysche that has the strength of a twenty-mule team'. Grant was gratified by his mother's reaction to Dyan, even if she did keep calling her Betsy. Finally, as the spring of 1965 passed into summer, Cary Grant made up his mind. He went to visit Dyan's parents and, early in July, he invited them to their wedding.

It took place in Las Vegas, Nevada. Grant had an arrangement with the Dunes Hotel whereby he acted as their adviser and host from time to time, and in return for his services the hotel and casino provided him with a suite when he needed it. As secretive as his friend Hughes, he decided it would be the best place to get married if he wished to avoid the attentions of the press. So, on Saturday, 22 July 1965 Justice of the Peace James Brennan conducted exactly the same three-minute ceremony he had already provided for six thousand other couples in Las Vegas that year; Cary Grant and the former Miss West Seattle, Dyan Cannon, were duly married. Brennan recalled afterwards that Hollywood's most popular male star 'had a quiver in his voice and a tear in his eye'. Only a dozen people were present in the small suite and all of them were sworn to secrecy. The ceremony was hardly over when the new Mr and Mrs Cary Grant left Las Vegas for a honeymoon in England. Cary Grant wanted to make sure that one person knew before anyone else that he had married for the fourth time – his mother. The only other person he told was his old friend Roderick Mann, but soon the news broke and Grant and Dyan – for whom he had not even bought an engagement ring – were besieged by reporters and forced to leave the single rooms they had booked at the Royal Hotel, Bristol, by climbing out of a back window at three o'clock in the morning and escaping to stay with friends. Grant did not intend to give interviews or information about his plans, but he rang up Jack Garland of the *Bristol Evening Post*, the photographer with whom he had worked many times before, and asked him if he would like to come to the Bristol Zoo, where he and Dyan would pose for one or two pictures. Garland recalls that 'They got out of an old Austin Cambridge like fugitives. It was very strange, but they were almost the only pictures anyone took of them on their honeymoon.'

When they got back to California, they had hardly settled into his Beverly Hills house when Dyan told him she thought she was pregnant.

'You have to find out,' he had told her nervously, before calling the doctor in what looked to his fourth wife like a very young man's panic. 'You have to go down there right now. We must know.' When she got back, her pregnancy confirmed, he took her out to celebrate the impending birth of his first child. They went to a night baseball game at Dodger Stadium, and he bought her a hot dog.

PART FOUR
Retreat into Privacy

'I have spent the greater part of my life fluctuating between Archie Leach and Cary Grant; unsure of either, suspecting each.'

Cary Grant

12

The Final Bow .

'It's hard for a star to take stock of himself.
There he is sixty feet tall on the screen.
Women fall in love with him; he lives in a
world of special consideration.'

Richard Brooks

If Dyan Cannon had thought she could change Cary Grant,
she soon realized her mistake. Despite his growth through
LSD she was, like her predecessors, the companion of a
pernickety, obsessed man haunted by the fears of his childhood, desperate to avoid poverty and to protect his secrets.
He saved the string from parcels and the tinsel from the
Christmas tree, cut the buttons off the shirts he was about to
discard in order to save them for future use; he marked the
wine bottle to make sure that none was drunk while he was
not there, shouted abuse at the television set when he saw
someone he was jealous of; and he was capable of putting his
new young wife, pregnant or not, over his knee and spanking
her if she wore too much make-up or too short a miniskirt.
Dyan Cannon discovered what perhaps she should have
guessed before, that her husband's only too famous public
charm was left at the parties or the dinners they sometimes
went to; it seldom accompanied him home.

She found herself living in a rented house in the San
Fernando Valley with a man who still liked to stay at home
and watch television rather than go out, and who preferred
to eat sitting on his bed. When they did go out to a baseball
game or to the races there was no dinner afterwards at one of

287

the exclusive Beverly Hills restaurants – the Bistro, say, or La Scala or Ma Maison. Instead, Grant would stop at a hamburger bar or a drive-in for a quick bite on the way home. Some of Cary Grant's friends wondered quite how he had come to marry a woman thirty-four years younger than himself who was apparently addicted to loud parties, short dresses and elaborate make-up. And surely, they said, Dyan must have known what her sixty-one-year-old husband was like. He had never enjoyed going out and he had always been careful with money; she had even laughed when she had explained he had never given her an engagement ring. 'Are you kidding?' she told Sheilah Graham when the columnist had asked to see it.

In the first few months of their marriage, however, while he was planning his new film *Walk Don't Run* and she was growing more and more obviously pregnant, it hardly seemed to matter that they did not go out very much. They were both more concerned about the welfare of their future child. Grant started to read books on childbirth and motherhood; soon after he had announced publicly that they were expecting a child, he had begun to visit maternity hospitals all over Los Angeles to check what they were like. With his invincible appetite for detail he had begun to look at each hospital's delivery room and labour wards, medical care and surgical record. He was every bit as determined as his mother had been that any child of his should survive.

He was just as determined that neither he nor the child should become public property. Universal's recent decision to run tours of their studio for members of the public had enraged him. The tour buses came past his bungalow throughout the day; he could hear the guides say, 'That's Cary Grant's bungalow,' and 'That's Cary Grant's car.' This made him so angry that he refused to eat in the studio's restaurant, and took his lunch instead far away on the backlot where no one could see him. 'I'm not an animal in a zoo,' he told Universal. He decided that his next film would be produced for another studio, Columbia.

Besides teaching Universal a lesson for allowing his privacy to be invaded by tourists – which seemed to him the equivalent of giving free performances on television – Grant had another reason for moving to Columbia. The studio owned the rights to George Stevens's 1943 hit comedy *The More The Merrier*, which had originally starred Jean Arthur, Joel McCrea and Charles Coburn and had been nominated for an Oscar as the Best Picture of its year. Though it had lost, Coburn had won an Oscar for his performance as the older of the two men whom a kindly young girl in Washington allows to share her apartment. The studio hoped a re-make might do the same for Cary Grant, and asked Sol Saks to update the original script with him in mind. However, in addition to the change of setting from Washington to Tokyo, and from World War II to the 1964 Olympic Games, there would be one even more significant innovation. For the first time since 1936, Cary Grant was not going to get the girl: his career as the cinema's longest lasting matinée idol had come to an end.

Originally Grant had hoped to take Dyan with him on the location in Tokyo, but she had decided finally that she should stay at home to rest – even though the child was not due until the late spring of 1966 and she seemed to be in the very rudest of health. Her husband was relieved in some ways although he was distressed to be alone. In Tokyo Grant began to explain once again in public that his days as leading man were probably over. He repeated to Sheilah Graham what he had said half a dozen years earlier: 'I honestly think that young people, who are the bulk of the movie-going public, prefer young men to make love to young women.' He also confessed, in another rare interview: 'This may be my last film – I don't know.'

Grant's co-stars in *Walk, Don't Run*, as *The More The Merrier* was now renamed, were to be the young English actress Samantha Eggar, who had recently finished filming in the screen version of John Fowles's novel *The Collector*, and who also had just given birth to her first child, and the tall American, Jim Hutton. Eggar recalled that Grant treated her wonderfully. 'I'd only had my son three weeks before I arrived in Tokyo and I got there with a forty-two-inch bust, rather than my more normal thirty-one and so I had to squash myself into my costume.' Eggar had never met Grant before the filming started. 'I remember he really impressed me by showing me all sorts of comedy moves for the camera. I got the impression he was involved in everything. He insisted that I had to change my hair, and chose my dress, just as he brought all his own props. He was on top of everything.' But she also admitted, 'I didn't really get to know him. He kept himself to himself. Besides, he was being wined and dined by the head of Sony. He really didn't open up personally at all, even though I was a friend of Dyan's.' Directed by the veteran Charles Walters, who had made his name with musicals like *Easter Parade* and *High Society*, the new film was to be photographed by Harry Stradling who had worked for Cukor on *My Fair Lady* and had won an Oscar for that. Grant had asked for him particularly, and Sol Siegel, who was producing the film, having gone independent from Fox, had been happy to provide him.

Overcautious though it may have appeared, Cary Grant's concern for his wife's health turned out to be justified. Hardly had he returned to Hollywood from Tokyo than Dyan felt the first pains of labour. At seven o'clock on the morning of Saturday, 26 February 1966 Cary Grant ushered her out into the warm morning air and helped her into his car for the drive to St John's Hospital in Burbank, north of Hollywood, where he had decided that their child should be born. The journey took just eighteen minutes. As they waited for Dr Abner Moss, the obstetrician Grant had chosen, they held hands.

Moss, who had delivered all three of Bing Crosby's younger children by his second wife Kathryn, examined Dyan and told them both that the birth might well take some time. The only thing they could do was to wait; he would be back to see them regularly. While Dyan settled into her room her husband slipped out to telephone the head of publicity at Columbia, John Flynn.

'How is she, Cary?'

'Marvellous, you've never seen a girl as brave. But you know how premature this is, there's a possibility of complications. This may not even be the day.'

'Is there anything I can do?'

'Pray for us, John.'

'I'm with you,' Flynn told him.

'Incidentally, I've asked the hospital to refer all calls to you.'

Walking nervously up and down, Grant gave a perfect performance of a father-to-be; and when the nurses suggested he move to the hospital's Fathers' Waiting Area while his wife was taken into the delivery room he kept it up, to the amazement of the men already there.

'Didn't you just come back from Japan?' one asked him.

'*Walk Don't Run*. We shot in Tokyo.'

'Yeah, yeah. With Samantha Eggar. Lotta good love scenes?'

A distracted Cary Grant smiled. 'Samantha Eggar and Jim Hutton. You've probably seen me in my last picture as a romantic lead. I'm too old for that stuff.'

'You look great.'

'Feel great, but I'm playing my love scenes in private life.'

At last, shortly after eight o'clock in the evening, Moss came into the waiting-room and told him: 'Mr Grant, you're the father of a healthy four-pound eight-ounce baby girl.' It was forty-two days after his sixty-second birthday, and he had been married for just seven months. Much more significantly, there was now another woman in Cary Grant's life who was destined to become as important to him as his mother: his daughter. A jubilant Grant went to see the new baby in the incubator where Moss had put her, and then went on to see his wife. Within a few hours they had agreed she would be called Jennifer, just Jennifer. 'If she wants another name she can add it herself,' he explained. He did not want her struggling under the weight of unfortunate names, as he had done himself.

When they got back to their rented house in the San Fernando Valley, Grant became even more obsessive than he had been on film sets during the past thirty years. He went to his daughter's room at 7.30 each morning to gaze down at her; he supervised the warming of her bottles and the sort of food that she could be weaned on to; he made certain that he would always be back from working on the editing of *Walk Don't Run* in time to see her seven o'clock feed in the evening. 'I like to be part of that,' he told *Look* magazine.

He took innumerable photographs of his daughter and tape-recorded her first sounds. 'She's the most winsome, captivating girl I've ever known, and I've known quite a few girls,' he said. 'She's probably the only completely perfect baby in the world.' The only thing he wanted to do now was to show her to his mother, and determined to take her to England as soon as she could travel. 'Because I don't know how much longer I shall have a mother in my life,' he told the *Los Angeles Times*.

Cary Grant's fascination with every detail of his daughter's upbringing came to irritate Dyan, but his ability to lose his temper suddenly and fly into an uncontrollable rage terrified her. While they had been watching the Academy Awards together she had seen him suddenly jump up and down on their bed screaming insults at the actors as they took their awards, his hands trembling almost uncontrollably. She had also been astonished when he had taken the keys to their three cars to stop her going out. He had locked her into her room, and threatened to spank her. Before boarding the *Oriana* on 1 July 1966 to visit England and his mother, they had even argued about whether to take any special formula milk for Jennifer's bottle. But however she felt, Dyan had to smile at the photographers who had gathered at San Pedro to see them embark. It was the first time Grant had allowed anyone to photograph Jennifer, the fact that it was just before the release of his new film obviously affecting his decision. When *Walk Don't Run* finally opened, the notices were all flattering. Even the normally sceptical *New Yorker* commented: 'Mr Grant has never looked handsomer or in finer fettle,' and went on to say that if it 'proves anything it is that his attempted abdication as a screen dreamboat is premature and will have to be withdrawn: he is a good ten years away from playing anyone's jolly, knowing uncle, and as for lovable Mr Fixit, he should be ready for that role in about the year 2000.'

But Grant's seventy-second film mattered much less to him than his daughter Jennifer, and in England he made sure that her grandmother could see as much of her as possible. He also preoccupied himself with looking for the most hygienic, safe, and private places to stay. He spent less time wondering why his wife seemed to be getting steadily more and more depressed. All Dyan knew was that her husband seemed to wish he had never married her: he did not trust her to bring up their daughter, and he seemed pleased when she was miserable. Even in her worst moments she had never envisaged that married life would turn out to be so difficult, or so painful. By the time they returned to Hollywood in October 1966, Grant too was facing the fact that once more he might have failed. At Rosalind Russell and Freddie Brisson's twenty-fifth wedding anniversary celebration at Las Vegas that October, all he could do was to sit and cry. Russell said later: 'It seemed even then his marriage was on the rocks.'

Dyan explained: 'He thought that LSD would help. I was a very troubled girl and Cary told my family that I was on the verge of having a nervous breakdown and that he hoped I would have one because the new me rebuilt through LSD would be a much healthier being. He really believed that. I remember my father came down from Seattle and told him, "You mustn't," and Cary got very upset and said, "You're her father and I'm her husband and I'm the one she answers to now." My father said: "I would tell my next door neighbour not to take LSD, let alone my own daughter." ' Dyan did indeed take LSD to please her husband. 'When I stopped taking it, it became one of the things he became very unhappy about. But we had Jennifer and I didn't want to admit failure, and when Cary said, "I want a divorce," I said, "No, let's go to a doctor, let's go to a marriage counsellor," and we had already been to doctors and all that. And then Cary said no, and I said okay, and I moved out.'

Three days after Christmas their neighbours noticed that Dyan and Jennifer seemed to have left the rented house, and so had Cary Grant. A terse note had been left for the milkman telling him to 'Stop further deliveries until further notice.' The rumour was that Grant had gone to stay with friends in Westwood while Dyan had taken Jennifer back to her parents. It was not until the end of January, almost four weeks later, that Cary Grant acknowledged officially that his fourth marriage, and the only one to bring him a child, had foundered, that he and Dyan had separated. Once again this most publicly attractive of men had been forced to acknowledge the fact that his 'romantic appeal did not continue beyond the warm glow of a movie studio's klieg lamps.

But no sooner had Dyan left the house than her husband wanted her back again, and particularly he wanted his daughter. The gloomy evenings they had spent bickering about his meanness and her desire for a more interesting and more glamorous life were suddenly forgotten. Grant telephoned anyone whom he thought might see her, with messages about how much he loved her, and how everything would be different from now on. He sent flowers and presents for Jennifer. He even talked to one or two newspaper columnists, like Sheilah Graham, so desperate was he to salvage this latest marriage. For he knew he was growing old, and the realization that from now on he might never see his only child for more than a few days a year was torture.

'The thought of being separated from your child is intolerable,' he told his friends Connie Moore and Johnny Maschio, with whom he was staying. 'I don't want to miss a bit of her.' As he said it his head would drop down towards his chest, and he would produce a photograph of his daughter lying on the lawn in front of his house: a tiny wide-eyed baby clutching a pink rabbit.

He telephoned Dyan every night, pleading with her to start again.

'Everything will be different.'

'I doubt it.'

'You'll see, of course it will.'

But Dyan had heard that before, and she did not believe it.

'There's no point, Cary! We've been through all that,' she would conclude. She felt she had been her husband's mother, sister, girlfriend rolled into one, but never really his wife.

'But we've got to stay together for Jennifer's sake,' Grant told her again and again.

'When there's dissension and heartache in the house you stay apart,' she said later in an interview. 'Otherwise it's just a cop-out. Like you're saying, I don't have to make a decision, I'll let my kid be the football, and she'll take the brunt of all the anger I feel and all the anger he feels. The child of ours would have been all mucked up.'

'After Jennifer was born Cary suddenly became an expert on child-raising. Well, I'd never had a child either. But what makes him a better expert than I? And I at least was at home all the time. I didn't have a career to pursue as well!' She had given up her career and she believed she had suffered enough at the hands of a man who was never what he appeared and who never knew what he wanted. She no longer trusted him, and she was determined to make her own way in the world again.

'Cary is a very demanding man,' she went on. 'In a peculiar way. He's such a perfectionist and has such strong ideas of his own about everything – even about things that women ordinarily are concerned with. He meddles in what should be women's work.'

But Grant was not to be put off. He offered his wife the leading role in an original script he was working on with MGM, *The Old Man and Me*, written by Isobel Lennart. He told the studio he would do it only if they signed Dyan without a screen test. Frank Sinatra was planning to make the film *The Detective* with Mia Farrow, so there was no

295

reason why Grant and Dyan could not appear together as well. MGM were hesitant and Dyan did not want to be given the part only because of her husband. She wanted to go back to the stage in New York, and had been offered a part in a play called *The Ninety Day Mistress*. She had every intention of accepting it.

Grant was distraught. If the play was a success then Jennifer would be in New York for months, and he would be able to see her even less than he did now. He had agreed to pay his wife $4,000 a month in maintenance, and she had given him access to their daughter for limited periods in return, but all that would change if she went to New York. Jennifer would not have the garden and the beach, the riding in Palm Springs and all the other things that he had planned for her. In despair Grant began to plan an action for custody of his daughter. After all, he told his friends, he would be able to spend much more time at home with her than his wife would, for in fact he did not ever need to work again.

He became more and more pressing. When Dyan took Jennifer to New York for a visit he turned up at the airport with a seat on the same plane. When she checked into the Croydon Hotel with their nanny, he booked a suite just down the corridor. When she went out to dinner with friends he 'happened' to be there too. When she went to the theatre he would be just down the row. 'Just keeping an eye on things,' he would tell her. 'An eye on the baby and you.' Dyan was furious. She told him he had to move out of the hotel and that he had to 'stop bothering us'. He had no intention of doing so. His daughter was the only thing that mattered to him now. He would be ready to fight for her when the divorce hearings started.

They began in September 1967, barely two years after the wedding in Las Vegas. Dyan told the Los Angeles Domestic Relations Court that she needed 'reasonable' support of $5,470 a month for herself and Jennifer, and claimed that her husband was worth at least $10m, with an annual income of more than $500,000. As he had done on the three previous occasions, Cary Grant did not go to court and he did not make any public statement about his divorce. During the last months of 1967 Grant lived in New York with his friend, the public relations consultant, Bob Taplinger, visiting his wife when she would let him, but mostly staying in the house quietly talking to his friends on the phone, watching television and wondering how he was going to survive the rest of his life alone. There were some people who told him he was a natural bachelor, pointing out that he had spent less than fifteen of his sixty-three years with his four wives, but he refused to admit the truth of this. He still needed to be loved. When the respected Producers Guild of America announced in October that they had decided to give him their coveted Milestone Award for his 'historic contribution to the motion picture industry' in succession to Louis B. Mayer and Adolph Zukor, he was sitting disconsolately in New York, not knowing how much he would be allowed to see his daughter. The movies, and the award, could not have mattered less.

Throughout the winter the battle over how often he could see his daughter, and whether she would ever be allowed to stay with him overnight, raged on. Dyan was firm. He could see Jennifer occasionally, but she could not stay overnight. He offered to hire a nurse to look after her when she was with him, but his wife was adamant. She also wanted her divorce. There was nothing to talk about any more. If her husband would not accept her decision then she would go back to Los Angeles and state on oath just how difficult life had been as Mrs Cary Grant.

The prospect of this terrified him. Yet he did not see why Dyan should be allowed to dictate to him how often he could see his own daughter, and if he had to suffer in public to get more time with her, then he would. But as he set off for Kennedy airport on that wet Tuesday afternoon of 12 March 1968, to go back to Los Angeles for the divorce hearings, he was gloomy, even though the presence of the beautiful twenty-three-year-old heiress Gratia von Furstenburg, who had ridden out to the airport with him in the limousine, cheered him up a little. No-one would ever sympathize with him. Once

297

again he would be portrayed as the villain in a divorce.

Grant never made the plane for Los Angeles, or the divorce court. On the Long Island Expressway two trucks travelling in the opposite direction collided; four wheels flew across the central divide and crashed into his car. The next thing he knew he was in hospital in the suburb of Queens, with his nose broken and fierce pains stabbing through his chest. As he came round he saw that he had a drip leading into his arm, and realized that he could barely move. It was some days before he would discover that he had been luckier than Gratia von Furstenburg, who had a broken leg and a broken collar bone. The tiny St John's Hospital had never had such a famous patient, and it could hardly cope. The switchboard was jammed almost continually with telephone calls from all over the world enquiring about his progress. Eighty-seven bouquets of flowers had arrived on the first day. From his bed Grant asked Bob Taplinger to hire a security guard to protect him from visitors and told the hospital to put through telephone calls only from people who asked for 'Count Bezok'.

His nose had been broken and his upper lip badly cut, but as the worst of the pain began to subside and it seemed that his face would not be permanently damaged, Grant realized that his stay in hospital would bring him one small benefit. He would not have to travel back to Los Angeles and watch the worst of the accusations about him fly back and forth across the courtroom. Though it would all be reported in the press and on television, what went on three thousand miles away never seemed quite so bad.

A week after Grant had been admitted to St John's Hospital Dyan Cannon walked into Santa Monica Superior Court in Los Angeles to tell Judge Robert A. Wenke and a packed court room that life with the world's most famous romantic film star had been a 'terrifying, unromantic nightmare'. As she stood in the court's pine witness box she looked frail and tired, but clearly determined that no one should be in any doubt that Cary Grant had not only beaten her up and locked her in her room but that he had frequently dissolved into 'fits of uncontrollable temper'. She told the court quietly that he was 'outlandish, irrational and hostile'. When her lawyer, Frank Belcher, asked her why she thought her husband behaved like that, she told the court softly: 'I attribute it to LSD.'

'He told me he had been taking the drug for about ten years and suggested I try it,' she went on. Belcher asked her how often she had seen Grant take the drug.

'About once a week.'

She announced that he had urged her to try the drug and had even telephoned her after their separation and told her he was 'on a trip'.

'He had a habit of admitting publicly his use of LSD and suggesting that his friends try it,' she volunteered.

Then she described how her husband had announced that he wanted a divorce. 'I suggested he see a marriage counsellor but he refused,' she said, even though she admitted that after their separation he had sent a lawyer to suggest to her that after a divorce 'they could go back to living together and announce publicly we had remarried'.

But the bleak list of Cary Grant's failings was not at an end. Cannon went on to explain to the court how 'he would yell and scream and jump up and down. Sometimes all it would take would be if I said: "Please pass the sugar." ' She said that when they had watched the Academy Awards ceremony together 'he had become violent, jumped up and down on the bed and carried on. He yelled that everyone on the awards show had their faces lifted, and he spilled wine on the bed.'

Finally she alleged that Grant had twice beaten her because she wanted to wear a miniskirt and had invited their servants to watch as he did so; that he had bolted the gates of their house and locked her in her room; and that he had accused a psychiatrist he had urged her to visit of trying to seduce her.

'I couldn't please him, no matter what I'd do or say,' she concluded. 'He criticized everything I did – the way I carried the baby, the way I fed the baby, the way I dressed and the way I dressed the baby. I couldn't do anything right.'

Then came the final blow. She demanded that any visits Grant might make to their daughter must be conducted in the presence of a third party, because 'In my estimation he is an unfit father due to his instability.'

It was the most damning public criticism of any Hollywood star since Fatty Arbuckle, and it was not over yet. The following morning his wife told the court:

'He said he hoped I would have a nervous breakdown because when I got over it there would be a new me – that the new me would be a wonderful person and that this could be done with LSD.'

Then Dyan's agent, Adeline Gould, explained that Grant had even suggested LSD to her husband as a cure for migraine. She testified that when Dyan had rung her from her room, after Grant had locked her in, the actor had picked up the phone and screamed, 'Stay out of my marriage, I'm going to break her like a pony. She's not going to leave until I break her.' Another of Cannon's friends, Mary Gries, added that Grant had told her he hoped Dyan would have a nervous breakdown so he could 'remake her into a new girl with the aid of psychotherapy and LSD – then she would be a wonderful person'.

It was a chilling exposition of the dark side of a shining image. Grant's lawyers replied that what he had actually said was that 'She was heading for a nervous breakdown and nervous breakdowns are usually self-made and that rest would be good for her.' Then they got down to the main point of their client's case.

They told the court that they were not opposing the divorce, only the demand for substantial financial support and the refusal to agree to regular visiting rights.

In particular they called to the witness stand two psychiatrists. Dr John Marmon of the University of California told the court that he had examined Cary Grant in September 1967. The actor who had starred in seventy-two films had told him he had used LSD regularly, but he

(Marmon) had 'found no organic defects in Grant's brain as a result'.

'Mr Grant is an emotional individual, as seen in many actors,' Marmon said calmly, 'but there are no irrational effects to prevent him from being a loving father or to make him endanger his daughter.'

The second psychiatrist was Dr Sidney Palmer, of the University of Southern California. He also testified that he had examined the actor and concluded: 'I found nothing irrational or incoherent about him, he shows a great concern for his daughter's welfare, he reveals a deep love and affection for the child. I found nothing indicating his behaviour would be dangerous to the child.'

In his final statement Dyan's lawyer told the court: 'We are not dealing here with an adventuress who walked into a rich man's life, then walked out again. We have a woman who married a man because she loved him, then gave him a child – something he could not get with three previous wives. But she ultimately was driven from her home because of the conduct of her husband.'

Lawyer Harry Fain's response on Cary Grant's behalf was quiet and unemotional. He told the court: 'We don't have a naive little lamb coming into marriage and not knowing about her husband . . . He, at the age of sixty-four, wants to devote the rest of his life to making his daughter happy.'

Judge Robert Wenke then gave his decision. He saw no reason to deny Cary Grant reasonable access to his daughter whatever amounts of LSD he might have taken in the past. Granting Dyan a divorce and ordering that she be paid $4,250 a month in maintenance, he concluded sternly: 'Violence is a serious matter, but in this case it seems to be directed only towards the wife. This could have been due to LSD, and it may no longer be a problem . . . The evidence shows that Mr Grant is no longer using LSD and he appears to be a loving and devoted father. He should be entitled to visiting rights.'

Wenke ruled that Grant should be allowed to see his

daughter 'sixty days of each year,' and to keep her overnight 'at reasonable times'. Dyan's plan to separate her daughter from her ex-husband had failed.

In hospital in New York Grant sat motionless. He could not but realize that what the court had heard was the most brutal condemnation of a Hollywood star in modern times and the most telling catalogue of a distinguished actor's failings ever to be made public. He watched his former wife telling the television reporters outside the court room: 'I'm sorry all this had to be aired,' but he vowed he would never take revenge on her or do anything to endanger his right to see his daughter. Instead he would do precisely what his lawyer had told the court that he intended to do. He would devote his life to Jennifer. He wanted to be for her exactly what he had always hoped his own parents would be for him, affectionate, supportive, and loving. Cary Grant knew he would never make another film.

A week later, he walked out of St John's Hospital, New York, still a little unsteady on his legs, but looking as tanned, as relaxed and as handsome as he had ever done on the screen. He joked with the nurses on the doorstep, told every photographer who asked him that 'this is the best place to be ill if you've got to be,' and waved at everyone who had come to see him. It was a performance any actor would have been proud of.

He flew out of Kennedy Airport on a private jet owned by George Barrie, the president and founder of the successful perfume company Rayette-Fabergé. Grant and Barrie had only recently been introduced by Bob Taplinger, but they had talked about the possibility of his joining the board of the company, which had sales of $124m in 1967. Now they discussed further what Grant could do for Fabergé. 'George's enthusiasm, endless curiosity and self-criticism fascinated me,' Grant was to say. 'He'd started out in life as a musician, spent years in show business and spoke its lingo.' On the trip across the continent in the privacy of the jet, the two men were on the brink of a deal.

Short, formidably intense and given to impromptu jam sessions in the company's boardroom – he had once played the saxophone for a living – Barrie believed Grant could give his company a superb image of class and style. He knew the star had always been interested in the business side of film-making, and he saw no reason why he should not enjoy making perfumes every bit as much. Barrie had even launched a bid to take over Twentieth-Century Fox the year before. It had failed, but he might be tempted to try the same sort of thing again; Cary Grant would be a help if he decided to. Less than seven weeks later, to the amazement of Hollywood, Grant accepted Barrie's offer to join the board of Rayette-Fabergé; its stock rose two points on the New York Stock Exchange at the announcement. Even *Time* magazine was mildly surprised that the actor should associate himself with something as mundane as a perfume company, and it noted that he had not announced his actual retirement from films. 'The last of the great matinée idols, he symbolized male impeccability and the kind of ageless elegance everyone dreams of attaining.' Grant maintained there was indeed not much difference between the film business and the perfume business. 'They find a fragrance as we find a story. They find a title for it that's merchandizable and saleable. They find an advertising campaign for it and we do. They ship it out in cans. We ship it out in cans. They ship it to department stores. We ship it to theatres.' To anyone who had only seen Cary Grant the elegant comedian, all this was quite a surprise.

While his ex-wife went back to court to claim an increase in her maintenance payments on the grounds of his 'extreme wealth', Grant turned to Barrie for moral support. The two men spent the summer travelling together, talking about what Grant would be doing to help Fabergé, and trying to forget the miseries of the divorce.

Whatever he was doing and wherever he was, however, Grant now made a point of flying back to Beverly Hills to see Jennifer when he was allowed to, and he would always visit her if her mother took her away for a trip. The play Dyan had wanted to do had flopped on Broadway but he still went to see Jennifer in New York; and as the little girl started to run and play he became prouder and prouder of what he called 'my greatest production'. For the first time in his life he decided to settle down in one house. He wanted to build a nursery Jennifer could stay in on the nights he was allowed to keep her.

The house he chose was the one Howard Hughes had always admired. The millionaire had tried to swap his own for it on one occasion, and he and Katharine Hepburn had each rented it at different times. It was not large – a swimming pool, three bedrooms, a small set of rooms for a butler and a cook. There was no tennis court but the grounds were spectacular, looking down across Los Angeles from the heights above Beverly Hills. In the evenings Grant could sit on the terrace and look out across the city from one of the most expensive and select vantage-points on earth. Behind him was the Spanish-style mansion that had once belonged to Charles Boyer, in front Harold Lloyd's old villa, and beyond that Valentino's house Falcon's Lair. But none of those was too close. The large garden and the tall gates in front of Grant's house made the others seem miles away. As well as providing a home for Jennifer, Grant wanted a place too where he could store all the souvenirs he had kept so carefully for more than forty years. He wanted to construct a vault in his house where all those records of his life would always be at hand for him to look through. He wanted a place for the memorabilia of Archie Leach.

As he told the columnist James Bacon: 'I had lots of problems over the years but mostly they were Archibald Leach's problems, not Cary Grant's. You might say that Archie Leach sat in a movie one day and said, 'Why don't I relax like Cary Grant.' That was precisely what he now intended to do.

He had also decided to help Dyan get work in Hollywood rather than in repertory companies all over the country. He telephoned his old friend, Mike Frankovich, Columbia's head of production, and said:

'Mike, you know you promised me that you're going to give my wife a crack at it . . .'

A slightly bewildered Frankovich replied:

'A crack at what?'

'You're making this picture *Bob and Carol* and . . . There must be a role in it for her.'

Frankovich said he would think about it, but when he talked to Paul Mazursky, the film's writer and director, the young Englishman told him: 'We've already interviewed her and turned her down.' At Frankovich's insistence Mazursky talked to Dyan again, and finally cast her. The job kept Jennifer and her mother in Los Angeles for some months, but Grant could not stop Dyan looking for whatever roles she could find wherever they were offered, nor could he prevent her from taking an interest in more and more experimental forms of psychiatry, including that propounded by the Esalen Institute, a group psychotherapy centre in Northern California that featured in her film *Bob and Carol and Ted and Alice*. She also tried Arthur Janov's primal scream therapy which called for her to shut herself in a padded room and to scream whenever she felt tense.

The thought that his daughter might be shuttled relentlessly round the country, dumped in hotel rooms or looked after in rented houses, depressed Grant greatly. Harry Fain went back to court to try to modify the custody agreement Judge Wenke had handed down at the time of Grant's divorce, and in October 1969 he was successful. He negotiated a new agreement with Frank Belcher, Dyan's lawyer, whereby Grant would be allowed to have Jennifer on alternate weekends from Friday evening until Sunday afternoon, as well as every Monday afternoon between three and six o'clock. She was also to be allowed to stay with him for half the Christmas holidays, for one month of each of her summer holidays, and for all the Easter holidays on alternate years. It was more than he had dared hope for. Even more significantly, however, the court accepted Grant's suggestion that neither he nor Dyan should be allowed to take Jennifer out of California without the specific permission of the other, or of itself, and without providing precise details of where they were going. So from now on, if Dyan wished to spirit his daughter away to Europe, or just to New York, he would have to know about it. If he did not, his wife would be breaking the law.

After the judgement Cary Grant told one inquisitive reporter in Boston: 'I have no commitments for the future and anticipate none. It would have to be something very special to get me out of my "retirement"!' Gradually Hollywood realized that Cary Grant would never again walk on to a sound stage to make a film. As if, unofficially, to mark their acceptance of this fact, his friends in the movie industry recommended he be given a special honorary Oscar at the forty-third Academy Award ceremony, due to be held in the Dorothy Chandler Music Pavilion, on 7 April 1970. Gregory Peck, as President of the Academy, was organizing the awards, and he had asked Grace Kelly if she would make the presentation. The gold statuette would bear the special inscription: 'Cary Grant – for his unique mastery of the art of screen acting, with the respect and affection of his colleagues.'

It was a distinction the Academy had bestowed on few in the past. Greta Garbo had been given a special Oscar 'for her unforgettable screen performances' in 1954, and in 1969 the producer Arthur Freed had been honoured. It was, perhaps, not quite as good as winning in competition but still it was some recompense for the Oscars he had seen others win in his films. As Peter Stone said when he collected his own Oscar in 1965 for the script of *Father Goose*: 'Thank you to Cary Grant who keeps winning these things for other people.' When he heard of the proposed tribute Cary Grant was delighted. The ghost of the neglected outsider had finally been laid.

As so often before, when everything seemed settled and going nicely, something unpleasant occurred. In the first weeks of 1970 Grant heard that Cynthia Bouron, a former actress who had worked for a time as a producer at Universal, was claiming that he was the father of the child to which she was about to give birth. Bouron, a thirty-five-year-old with two children from previous marriages, announced that if her baby was a boy she was going to name him Cary Grant. She had already named her English collie dog after him.

As the Academy Awards drew nearer rumours about the story swirled around Hollywood. Grant, however, was in Manhattan at the Fabergé offices, or visiting his mother in England, or staying in Jamaica with Noël Coward – anywhere, in fact, except at home. All Hollywood held its breath. The Los Angeles newspapers kept silent for six weeks, but on 20 March, less than three weeks before the Oscar ceremony, the *Los Angeles Times* reported Cynthia Bouron's claim, and disclosed that she had actually given birth to a baby girl, whom she had christened Stephanie Andrea Grant. On the birth certificate, the paper reported, she had given the name of the father as Cary Grant – age: sixty-six; occupation: actor.

Once again Grant kept silent. Stanley Fox, his lawyer friend, merely announced on his behalf: 'As far as I'm concerned there is no validity to the charge.' Then gradually the details of Cynthia Bouron's life began to emerge. First married in Paris to a dentist, she had taken as her second husband the actor Milos Milocevic, once a stunt man working for the French star, Alain Delon. Milocevic had murdered his girlfriend, Mickey Rooney's wife, Barbara, in January 1966, when she had threatened to leave him, and had then killed himself. Not long afterwards Bouron had been arrested for burglary but had subsequently been found not guilty. One former friend called her a 'conwoman'; others said merely that she was one of those women whose lives were spent following movie stars around. As these facts became public, most people in Hollywood believed Cary Grant should ignore the scandal. Nevertheless, barely a week before the ceremony, he asked the organizers of the Academy Awards to withdraw his name. Sheilah Graham reported that he had given 'personal reasons' for his decision, and that there were those in the Academy who thought the award should not be made. But Gregory Peck stood firm.

'We don't take back the award if the recipient isn't going to be present,' he said – and set about doing all he could to persuade Cary Grant to change his mind.

The Hollywood press were in no doubt. 'He should not distinguish the muckraking by not making an appearance,' the *Citizen News* said angrily. 'The real tragedy is that Cary Grant, because of these scandalous stories, not even worthy of a weekly tabloid, has been deprived of accepting an Oscar he so rightly deserves.' In the end it was Howard Hughes, the one man whose advice Cary Grant had always sought and whose attitudes to privacy and secrecy he had long shared, who persuaded him to accept the Oscar. Now growing increasingly reclusive, and living on the top floor of The Desert Inn Hotel in Las Vegas protected by Mormon guards and communicating only on the telephone, Hughes told his old friend that there was every reason for not turning it down. He deserved it. He should have had it before. Hang the publicity. Nervously Cary Grant returned to Los Angeles. Other Hollywood stars had lived through paternity suits and paternity claims, and he accepted that now he might still have to do the same. As he said later: 'I'm lucky, I guess, I don't get it as badly as some – Frank Sinatra, for example, or Errol Flynn, poor Errol.' He spent the night before the ceremony rehearsing his speech with Dyan.

As he stepped forward to accept his Oscar from Frank Sinatra, whom Peck had persuaded to stand in for Kelly when she was prevented from attending and who had come to Los Angeles specially for the occasion, the singer told him: 'It was awarded for sheer brilliance of acting.' The tears mounted to Grant's eyes as Sinatra went on: 'Cary had so much skill that he makes it all look easy.'

Cary Grant looked down at the polished wood dais in front of him, away from the television cameras and paused. The vast television audience as well as the crowd of actors in the arena in front of him did not know what he would say. Few of them had ever seen him say anything that was not in a script. Slowly he started to speak: 'You know, I may never look at this without remembering the quiet patience of the directors who were so kind to me, who were kind enough to put up with me more than once – some of them even three or four times. There were Howard Hawks, Hitchcock, the late Leo McCarey, George Stevens, George Cukor and Stanley Donen. And the writers. There were Philip Barry, Dore Schary, Bob Sherwood, Ben Hecht, dear Clifford Odets, Sidney Sheldon and more recently Stanley Shapiro and Peter Stone. Well, I trust they and all the other directors, writers and producers, and leading women, have all forgiven me what I didn't know.' As the audience got to its feet to give him a standing ovation, he concluded: 'You know, I've never been a joiner or a member of any – of a particular – social set, but I've been privileged to be a part of Hollywood's most glorious era.'

As he received his special Oscar, that glorious era came to an end. The days of light comedians, elegance and style, of beautiful costumes and dazzling women, of heroes and villains belonged to a past age, to a part of the movie industry that had imperceptibly died. Motion pictures never again offered their audiences such gentle and delicate pleasures. After Grant had walked off the stage John Schlesinger's *Midnight Cowboy* was awarded the Oscar as Best Picture of the Year. Dyan had lost only by a narrow margin as the Best Supporting Actress of the Year for *Bob and Carol and Ted and Alice*. Cary Grant did not know this. He simply knew that he had given his last professional performance. In the back of his car on the way home to Beverly Hills, he slipped on his black-rimmed glasses and thought of Jennifer.

On the beach at Malibu Cary Grant walked slowly along the Pacific, his bare toes curling in the cold morning surf. He smiled pleasantly at the few people exercising their dogs, or doing limbering-up exercises in the chill air, but did not pay them much attention. He was gazing instead at the small wooden house with its vast glass windows perched on the edge of the sand. Dyan had moved into the exclusive Malibu Colony, which had a permanent guard on its gates and where even the beach was fenced against intruders. He had rented a house there himself just to be near his daughter. As he stood watching the surf surge towards him, she and her mother would be having their breakfast. Some mornings he would wave at no-one in particular, hoping Jennifer would see him. He had retired into the privacy he had always cherished. Even when he travelled for Fabergé, shaking hands effortlessly with department store perfume buyers and turning on his accustomed charm, he was thinking of the beach and his daughter. On the afternoons she stayed with him he would curl up with her on the bed to encourage her to take a nap. This tall man of sixty-six, the star of more than seventy films, would lie with the tiny child curled in his arms for hours, and if anyone asked him why he did it he would simply reply: 'If it helps her to sleep, it's worth it.' On the weekends when she stayed with him he would take her back to the house in Beverly Hills, and the nursery he had built for her, but when it was not his turn to have her he would stay at the beach, hoping to catch a glimpse of her as she ran down to the ocean.

He had become even more cautious and more discreet as he had grown older, less prepared to be seen with beautiful young women who might be attracted to him. He preferred to stay at home and look after himself as carefully as he had always done. He did not want any more Cynthia Bourons. Grant had denied Bouron's claim that he was the father of her daughter, and that he should pay her a 'reasonable sum' in child support. Finally, she had refused to take a blood test when asked to do so by the Los Angeles Court, and her paternity suit had been dismissed. But this woman remained one of the most mysterious people in his life. Three years later, on 30 October 1973, her body was found in the boot of a car parked in a supermarket parking lot. She had been beaten to death with a claw hammer. The North Hollywood detectives assigned to the case noted in their official report that her daughter Stephanie 'appears to be of strong Negro blood' and that 'friends of the victim state that she would often pick up men at bars and restaurants'. Her killer was never found.

Grant formed one or two new attachments. In 1971 he met Maureen Donaldson, a young English gossip writer and former nanny whose father was a London fireman, and they started to be seen together in Malibu and Beverly Hills. His friends thought he might want to marry again simply to show that he could provide a stable home for his daughter, but the romance with Donaldson seemed to fluctuate too much for that. His daughter preoccupied him. He was still fighting to keep her as near to him as he could. At the end of his month with her in the summer of 1971 he had even filed a custody suit alleging that her mother had been living in Europe and New York and had ignored his requests that she should come back to California and settle down. Meanwhile Dyan had hired a van with padding inside so that she would have somewhere to scream when she was away from her home in Malibu. But nothing much happened between them until the following March when he heard that Dyan had agreed to star opposite Burt Reynolds in the new Columbia film *Shamus*, which was to be made in New York. Four years after their divorce, the story of Cary Grant and Dyan was still being argued in court.

This time, however, the hearings were held in private. Judge Jack T. Ryburn even ordered that the small windows in the court's doors should be sealed up so that no photographers could snatch a picture, and allowed Grant and Dyan to remain in the court during lunch to avoid being photographed, although they did not eat together. Grant lunched in the court itself while Dyan sat in the jury room.

Cary Grant claimed that he should be allowed joint custody of their daughter so that if his former wife went away Jennifer could stay with him. He also asked that if Jennifer did stay with him he should not be forced to pay his former wife $500 a month for a nanny and that his maintenance payments to her, reduced at the previous appeal to $1,500 a month, should be halved to $750. Throughout the hearings Harry Fain repeated the claim that he had first made in court four years earlier that his client 'loves his daughter and is keenly concerned for her welfare'. He also said that Grant was prepared to devote all his time to her. It was absolutely true.

Dyan, however, feared that her former husband's meanness and his obsession with their daughter might well ruin her life. That was why she had decided to bring the petition to let her take Jennifer with her to New York, even though the six-year-old had started at the Malibu Montessori School only the previous year. She thought the child should stay with her, but Judge Ryburn did not agree. He ruled that Jennifer should stay in California, although her father should take her to New York on at least two visits.

Grant was jubilant. It looked as though he would finally be given joint custody of Jennifer, and he could plan to spend every evening waiting for her to come back from school, every weekend showing her how to ride. Within eight weeks he had sold the rights to his last films with Universal for more than $2m. *Operation Petticoat, That Touch of Mink, Charade, The Grass is Greener* were all included, as was *Penny Serenade*, the only one of his earlier films to which he still retained the rights. There was nothing left for him in the movie business. He even disappointed George Barrie, who had found a script that would have suited him down to the ground and which he wanted his new Brut Productions to make. It was to be called *A Touch of Class*. But Grant simply said: 'If the script had been given to me ten years ago I'd have made it in a second. I thought about it but I realized I was too old for it.'

He continued, however, to protect his business interests. In April 1972 he issued a suit for $1m against Twentieth-Century Fox for including a scene from *Monkey Business* in their film *Marilyn* without his permission, claiming it lessened his 'professional status and earning power as a motion picture star'. He invested in a property development in Malaga in southern Spain, and another near Shannon in Ireland; he thought Jennifer might like to stay in one or other of these places when she grew older. He also joined the board of MGM but concentrated on the company's hotels, not its films. But principally he devoted himself to Jennifer.

Now she really was the only woman in his life. On 22 January 1973 Elsie Leach had died quietly in her sleep in her Bristol nursing home, less than two weeks before her ninety-sixth birthday. The small fierce woman, whose deepest affection her son had tried and failed to win and who had always refused to come to the United States had finally left him. Cary Grant went back to Bristol to bury her next to the other man she had never made happy. Elsie and Elias Leach had not been together much, but he wanted to reunite them now.

'She never smoked, she never drank, and she ate very lightly,' he said later. 'But even in her later years she refused to acknowledge that I was supporting her. One time I took her some fur coats. I remember she said: "What do you want from me now?" I said: "It's just because I love you." And she said something like, "Oh you . . ." She wouldn't accept it.'

When he got back to Los Angeles after the quiet funeral, he declared: 'With the past now gone, I have the future ahead with my daughter.' But it was more than six months before he could bring himself to go back to Bristol and begin the painful process of sorting through his mother's belongings and selling her house. 'To do it any sooner would have seemed like hurrying her away.' Eventually he took back most of the smaller mementoes to Beverly Hills, and added them to the others he had accumulated over the years. Whenever he could he would retire into the fireproof vault, shut the door and look back over the past. There were photographs of his parents, his wives, and Jennifer; records of his life in Bristol, his time in vaudeville; old marriage certificates and divorce papers; passports and press cuttings; presents from Noël Coward and Cole Porter; his father's watch and his mother's rings – all neatly labelled and meticulously kept.

In general, his life continued much as it had always done. He divided his time between Malibu and Beverly Hills. Maureen Donaldson was still the most frequent of his companions. There were servants to look after him, he travelled a little for Fabergé, he supervised his investments, he went to baseball games on Monday evenings. If he thought about getting married again, he could never quite forget that every one of his wives had left him. As he was to tell the *New York Times*: 'I don't know why, they got bored with me, I guess, tired of me. I don't know. Maybe I was making the mistake of thinking that each of my wives was my mother, that there would never be a replacement once she left. I'm not at all proud of my marriage record, but I have wanted a family for years. I finally have this one child, and I will do whatever I can for her. I want Jennifer to give one man love and confidence and help. It has taken me many years to learn that, I was playing a different game entirely. My wives and I were never one, we were competing.'

Offers to return to the movies kept on coming in. MGM wanted him to do a remake of *Grand Hotel*, any number of books and scripts arrived for him to look at, Warren Beatty tried for weeks to get him to appear in his film *Heaven Can Wait* for any fee he cared to ask, but he refused, just as he refused Joe Mankiewicz's suggestion that he appear in his film version of Anthony Shaffer's thriller *Sleuth*. As he turned seventy all he wanted to do was to live to see his daughter become a woman.

All around him the Hollywood he had known was dying. Cole Porter, Leo McCarey and Noël Coward were gone already, and in April Howard Hughes died on his way back to his home in Texas. The stars of his generation were retiring. Fred Astaire preferred to go to the races now, James Stewart was working less and less, and so was David Niven. Irene Dunne was not working at all, and neither was Loretta Young. Howard Hawks was not making movies. George Cukor was not working regularly, and neither was Hitchcock. Only Katharine Hepburn seemed indefatigable.

Cary Grant was afraid of death. He had resisted a hernia operation for some time in case he might not survive the operation, and in June 1977, when he could not put it off any longer, he insisted on having only a local anaesthetic so that he would know what was happening. He also insisted that no women should be allowed into his room. He shaved himself in preparation for the operation, and allowed only men to look after him. He was still, after all, one of Hollywood's original romantic stars, and he saw no reason to risk being seen in an undignified position, or to have his image tarnished in any way.

On one of his earlier trips to London for the annual Fabergé sales conferences he had met a young public relations officer, Barbara Harris, at the Royal Lancaster Hotel overlooking Hyde Park, where the company usually held its meetings. His affair with Maureen Donaldson had been drawing to an end, and he had always enjoyed the company of beautiful young women. He was attracted to the brown-haired, rather sensible-looking girl with her calm expression and open face. She had been born in Tanzania; she was forty-seven years younger than he was. Her father had been a member of the British colonial service, but had returned to England from Africa with his family in 1963, and Barbara Harris had lived there with them since.

When he had returned to Beverly Hills Grant telephoned the serene-looking girl every week, trying to persuade her to come to California. For the next two years he telephoned and flew over on visits, always charming, always courteous, as perfect a suitor as he had been in his films. They went to small English pubs together, had quiet dinners, and she introduced him to her mother. Finally, in the summer of 1978, she agreed to go back to California to live with him.

'I was absolutely terrified of the age difference. Before I went, I thought – at great length – about the possibility of being without him. But I decided to go through with it because, otherwise, you don't enjoy the time you do have, which is precious.' Barbara said about the man who was fifteen years older than her own father had been when he died. 'He is a complex man, extremely kind and intelligent. He has a wonderful humour in him. But I think, sometimes, when people are dominant it is out of shyness or not feeling at ease in a situation.' Unlike Dyan, Barbara did not feel overwhelmed.

For his seventy-fifth birthday, she baked him a cake for the quiet celebration that they had together, no-one had done that for him for a very long time. She seemed happy to have done it, just as she seemed happy to answer the telephone for him, to arrange his trips, to drive his car, to answer his letters, and to organize the renovation of the house in Beverly Hills; and she was not afraid of his moods, or of the memories which he kept in the fireproof vault hidden behind the secret panels. Now, instead of being nervous about it: 'I think of us as being the same age.'

In May 1979, however, Cary Grant had cause to remember that he and Barbara were not the same age. His former wife, Barbara Hutton, had been taken to the Cedars-Sinai Medical Centre in Beverly Hills with pneumonia, and he was worried. Even though she had married four times after their divorce, he had been the only one of her seven husbands she had kept in touch with regularly. She had spent the past six years living barely a mile away from him, in a magnificent permanent suite at the Beverly Wilshire Hotel. They had talked incessantly on the telephone over the years; he had helped her whenever she needed it, and had comforted her when Lance had been killed in a plane crash in 1972. She had always said: 'I loved Cary the most. He was so sweet, so gentle. It didn't work out but I loved him.'

On Friday, 12 May, only a week after she had been released from Cedars-Sinai, Barbara Hutton died suddenly of a heart attack at the age of sixty-six. She had died alone. He did not want to die alone, in a strange city surrounded by servants like his old friend Howard Hughes. He could hardly bring himself to acknowledge his second wife's death. He preferred to remember her as she had been, frail, sloe-eyed, and constantly fascinated by the world.

Cary Grant disliked being reminded of the past. He went to the American Film Institute's dinner to honour Alfred Hitchcock, but only with reluctance. That part of his life was behind him. He had not set foot on a sound stage in front of a camera for more than a dozen years, and he told one interviewer: 'I not only will not view any of my own pictures but I rarely go to any other movie unless it is a Disney film that my daughter wants to see. I don't read most novels either. I enjoy reality too much. I can use the time learning more French, being with Jennifer, doing a lot of riding, a little swimming and tending to business.' It was also part of his tradition: a star should appear briefly from time to time only at private parties for the elite of the movie business to be accorded the deference due to one of Hollywood's aristo-crats, and then disappear again leaving them waiting for more. A star should never mingle; a star should always remain aloof, above all attempts to persuade him to give television interviews, for example. 'I'm not selling any-thing,' he would explain, 'not running for office, I don't really care to be in the limelight.' Exceptionally he made a brief appearance in MGM's compilation film, *That's Enter-tainment II*, but he had done so principally as a favour to MGM's president, Kirk Kerkorian, and he did not relish the occasion, any more than he particularly relished going to the Cannes Film Festival.

He was sick of the rumours that seem always to pursue a star. In September 1980, the film comedian Chevy Chase, whom he had never met, had accused him on the tele-vision show *Tomorrow* of being a homosexual, and had des-cribed him as 'What a gal' on the air. These smears were not new, but they still upset him enough to make him file a suit for slander and claim for $10m in damages. As he said some eighteen months later, however: 'I guess anyone that's publicized is not allowed to be a fairly decent individual. Whether it's for envy or whatever, it perpetuates itself. At my age, though, it doesn't matter. Every dinner table is filled with gossip. True or untrue, I'm old enough not to care.'

In 1981, at seventy-seven, Grant knew that he did not want to live alone and he decided to marry for the fifth time. He had discovered that if a couple had lived together for three years they did not need a marriage licence and could be married secretly by a judge, something that appealed to his sense of privacy. So, he asked Jennifer, now fifteen: 'Look, how would you feel if I asked Barbara to marry me? I'm

317

getting on. I need her.' Her eyes clouded with tears, and for a moment he wondered if she thought he was doing the wrong thing. But when the tears came it was only because she was happy.

'For goodness sake,' he told her, 'don't say anything to Barbara. I might not have the courage to ask her.'

'We were mixing with a lot of married people,' he said later. 'I felt we enjoyed each other's company. It was I who approached her, not the other way round. It took me a long time to decide I wanted to get married again.'

On 15 April 1981, which turned out a soft spring day, Cary Grant married again. Barbara Harris, happy but still composed, stood beside him in front of a judge on the terrace of their house looking out across Beverly Hills, and agreed to become the fifth Mrs Cary Grant. She had no bridesmaids and wore a simple cream silk dress. The only witnesses were her new step-daughter, Jennifer, Stanley Fox and his wife, and Grant's butler and his wife. As soon as the brief ceremony was over the newly married couple led the small group inside for a wedding lunch which the bride herself had prepared that morning because she did not want to 'let our secret out'. That afternoon the new Mr and Mrs Grant left for a short honeymoon with Frank and Barbara Sinatra on their estate in Palm Springs.

Epilogue

'Is it possible to succeed without any act of betrayal?'

Jean Renoir

So many are gone. Gable, Cooper, Bogart and Flynn have followed Valentino, Chaplin and Keaton into the myths of Hollywood's past, beside Harlow, Garland and Monroe. Only a handful of the greats remain. Garbo is still alone, but in New York. Dietrich is in Paris, Colbert in Barbados. Perhaps only Astaire and Rogers, Davis, Stewart and Hepburn shine as brightly in the memory of cinemagoers as Cary Grant.

Few people pause to wonder what is the price these legends have been called upon to pay for their eminence and fame. The tragic deaths are plain enough, the suicides and overdoses, but for those who survive the pressures of stardom never diminish, and they never disappear. To become and remain a star is a unique and painful process. Millions desire it; few understand the reality – in the silent hour before the dawn no-one can conceal the price.

Cary Grant once remarked: 'Everyone tells me I've had such an interesting life, but sometimes I think it's been nothing but stomach disturbances and self-concern.' It is a description that Bud Schulberg recognized in *What Makes Sammy Run*, the best novel ever written about Hollywood, when he said: 'Sometimes I think the three chief products this town turns out are moving pictures, ambition and fear.'

Archie Leach had wanted to become a star. He had wanted to forget the past, to win the affection his mother had never given him, and he had wanted the sense of identity that applause alone could bring. It meant that he existed, that he deserved to be loved. But the price it exacted was a subtle and prolonged torture. Archie Leach realized that he was loved as Cary Grant, and for that very reason it became

321

all the more difficult for him to retain a hold on his own personality. To reveal who he really was might threaten his reputation, weaken his hold on fame.

In Michael Balcon's unforgettable British film *Dead of Night*, made in 1945, Michael Redgrave played a ventriloquist with a strange, haunted dummy. The dummy is Redgrave's own creation; brutal, terrifying yet fascinating and hypnotic. Gradually, as the story unfolds, the dummy takes on a life of its own, more grotesque and terrifying than its creator could have imagined. There is a parallel here with the way in which Archie Leach slipped into the costume and style of Cary Grant. Off the set and back at home, he knew the figure the public loved was not himself, but as that public grew to believe that it was, the creation became, to its creator, ever more frightening. Archie Leach became more and more convinced that he was not real. The ageless dummy that the grown man had created came to dominate the real person who had started out his life as a vulnerable boy in Bristol.

But the desire to remain a star, to sustain the illusion so carefully created on the screen, was stronger than the fears. If the price was depression and insecurity, then so be it. In private, at least, Cary Grant could be Archie Leach, could respect the separation between the two parts of his character. He could try to put the dummy into a case and forget it.

Being a star, however, guaranteed the one thing that being Archie Leach could not – immortality. The tall, dark and handsome figure on the screen became the reality of life, securing his identity, ensuring his place in the world's fantasies as well as his own. His meticulous creation of a screen personality and his determination to remain a star have demanded intense concentration. As one woman friend once described it: 'He agonizes constantly about his interior. Sometimes he hurts people unwittingly because he is so self-absorbed.' Certainly his determined retreat into himself wrecked his marriage to Betsy Drake. 'The marriage was lived on Cary's terms,' she said after their separation. 'It was terribly frustrating to be married to him because he's a very self-sufficient man.' David Niven has recalled that when he and his wife used to visit Grant in Palm Springs at the weekend, 'he'd vanish, and we'd find him hanging from parallel bars, or doing push-ups, or in a trance on the floor mesmerizing his big toe . . . He keeps great chunks of himself in reserve.'

The self-discipline that he brought to his screen career, and the constant worry that it caused him, led him to remain aloof and remote, to protect the separation between Cary Grant and Archie Leach by a reticence that fuelled the incessant Hollywood rumours. For in Hollywood rumour is the blood that sustains the beast. It loves myths, but it also likes to be able to say it knows the truth behind the myths. In these circumstances, inevitably, rumour invaded Grant's life, and he came to abhor it.

Of course, much that was said about him was at least partly true. Cary Grant – no doubt about it – is extremely cautious with money. He habitually examines restaurant bills to see that he has not been cheated, and keeps his own hospitality very noticeably within bounds. As director Billy Wilder once remarked: 'I don't know anyone who's been inside his house in the last ten years.' He dislikes owning houses, except as investments. Yet his shrewdness and bargaining ability have made him one of Hollywood's richest actors, probably worth more than $30m if he were to realize all his assets. He was earning $400,000 a picture in 1946, and at the end of his career his income was estimated to exceed $800,000 a year in royalty payments alone. 'I like money,' he once wrote. 'Anybody know anyone who doesn't? You do? He's a liar.' Grant also likes the ambiance of money. He greatly admired Howard Hughes, copying not only his style of life, with its preference for the telephone and intense desire for privacy, but also his dislikes of needless spending. He enjoyed the company of Aristotle Onassis, and is still friendly with Prince Rainier of Monaco. He likes to prove to those less fortunate than himself that he is a success. He once paid for an ex-co-worker from vaudeville to come to Hollywood and took him round in his chauffeur-driven car 'to show him how well I was doing'. It was the action of a man who can hardly believe his own luck, and needs constant reassurance.

Cary Grant has never found relationships with others easy. He has a self-conscious, de-personalized view of himself and assumes that other people regard themselves in the same way. He has usually tried to manipulate the women he has known. Many of them refer to his habit of dictating to them about their clothes, telling them not to wear make-up, to act demurely, and never to talk about him to others. Dyan Cannon used to call him 'The Master', so determined was he that she should obey his commands. Yet he is also frightened of women and he finds it hard to cope with emotional demands.

The Hollywood columnist Sheilah Graham, who has confessed to being attracted to him herself, once remarked: 'He is always embarrassed when I tell him every woman I know swoons for him. In spite of his friendliness he remains aloof. He may confide in you one day, but the next, when you expect more of the same, he will be cool and on the friendly adviser plateau again, and you'd better not bring up the confidences of yesterday. And you know he is still an unsure man, even when he is advising you so sincerely how to live your life.' Archie Leach's fear of poverty has always co-existed with his fear of any woman who might come to replace his mother, with his horror at the thought of marrying his mother. For almost thirty years he deliberately chose girls who were blonde and blue-eyed, the very opposite of her in looks. Perhaps more than any other, it is this contradiction which lies at the heart of his extraordinary appeal on the screen. There he seems both frightened of women and fascinated by them. Like his ambivalence about many other things, it lies at the heart of his personality.

Women have certainly terrified him, and he has sought out the company of men on many occasions. He preferred to live with Randolph Scott at the start of his career when other eligible young bachelors were living alone; and that too fuelled rumours about him. Hollywood has reported for years that he has had bisexual leanings, and on occasions he has answered back. Once he told the *New York Times*: 'When I was young and a popular star I'd meet a girl with a man and maybe she'd say something nice about me and then the guy would say, "Yeah, but I hear he's a fag." It's ridiculous but they say it about all of us.' The implication of bisexuality in a leading man in Hollywood today carries nothing like the stigma, or the danger of ruin, that it did in the days of Adolph Zukor or Louis B. Mayer, when the faintist hint of any such scandal could ruin an actor's career. Yet even today the movie industry prefers its stars to hide their vices from the public gaze, and they have no option but to protect themselves as best they can. Grant's pending $10m slander suit against the comedian Chevy Chase for accusing him of homosexuality has still not come to court, even though the proceedings were announced in October 1980.

One of Grant's defences has been to take great care to avoid the suggestion that he is in any way feminine. He has usually refrained from wearing make-up on the set, preferring to rely on his perpetual suntan, and he has always seemed less than happy in films like *Bringing Up Baby* or *I Was a Male War Bride* which called for him to perform in women's clothes. Pauline Kael has commented: 'He is never so butch – so beefy and clumsy a he-man – as in his female impersonations.'

His experiments with LSD did harm his reputation to some extent. Some people maintain that they harmed him physically too, affecting his mind, impairing his memory, and making his retirement inevitable. Certainly his experiments with the drug puzzled some of his friends. David Niven maintained that they were half horrified and half made envious by what Grant had willingly subjected himself to, and went on to say: 'It seemed to the rest of us a most hazardous trip for Cary to have taken.' But Grant has remained unrepentant about it.

'My intention,' he said recently, 'was to help make me happy. I suppose everything we do in life, or should do in life, is a consequence of a search for happiness. A man would be a fool if he looked for anything else. LSD's not a drug for addicts. No self-respecting addict would take LSD. The nightmares come out of you.' His experiments with the drug, and his enthusiasm for it, clearly represent part of the battle between the character he created on the screen and Archie Leach. Indeed it was during his experiments with LSD that he tried to reconcile the two halves of his personality, for as he himself said in 1963: 'I have spent the greater part of my life fluctuating between Archie Leach and Cary Grant, unsure of either, suspecting each. Through the drug,' he said, 'I discovered that I had created my own pattern and I had to be responsible for it. I had to forgive my parents for what they didn't know and love them for what they did pass down. It was absolute release.' It also encouraged Archie Leach to think that he could co-exist with Cary Grant, but the contradiction and the separation between the two characters has never disappeared.

Cary Grant has always dressed elegantly in public, but is uncomfortable in formal clothes at home. There he habitually prefers jeans, and open-necked shirts. In recent years he has taken to wearing kaftan tops that his fifth wife, Barbara, has made for him, with white jeans and black velvet slippers.

The director Richard Brooks has long said that 'Cary finds it difficult to accept anything from anyone, gifts, compliments or even love, because he feels the moment you accept anything you are obligated.' It is a reaction he shared with his mother. He can also be extremely generous. He has a habit of buying his friends sudden and unexpected presents – he bought Dyan Cannon a sable coat after their acrimonious divorce, and there are other instances of this trait. He maintains that his reputation for meanness is undeserved. 'I'm sure I have that reputation because I don't gamble or go to nightclubs or give huge parties,' he once explained 'and because I don't believe in giving gifts at Christmas. I give presents when I feel like it.' He refused to tell his daughter Jennifer about Santa Claus because he said, 'I don't see any reason to perpetuate unrealities.'

Less than most people does he like being taken for a ride.

His friend Robert Arthur, who worked with him in his last years at Universal, has said: 'Cary's anger becomes almost a phobia when he thinks he is being taken advantage of because he is Cary Grant.' A most curious and comical instance of this occurred when Grant was staying at the Plaza Hotel in New York. He had ordered coffee and English muffins to be sent up to his room for breakfast. When they arrived there were only three half-slices of muffin, not four.

'I asked the waiter why, and he didn't know. So I called the head of room service, who also didn't know. I went up the line, assistant manager to manager.' No-one could explain. So he telephoned the hotel's owner, Conrad Hilton, in Beverly Hills, 'but his office told me he was in Istanbul.' Undeterred, he then telephoned Hilton in Istanbul to ask why he had only been brought three half-slices of muffin at the Plaza in New York when the menu clearly stated 'muffins'.

'Conrad,' he recalled later, 'knew the answer. It seems a hotel efficiency expert had decreed that all guests left the fourth slice of muffin on their plate. As a plate cleaner-upper, I was appalled.' And he proceeded to tell Hilton that he should immediately alter his menu to read 'muffin and a half'.

'It cost me several hundred dollars in phone calls,' he added, 'but ever since I have always gotten four slices of muffin at the Plaza.'

The same obsessive strain led Grant to take swimming lessons late in life because he wanted to swim 'perfectly'; to take riding lessons to ensure that once he had started to ride he should do so 'perfectly'; to try and dress 'perfectly'; and to look for perfection in his wives. As David Niven put it: 'Cary's enthusiasm has made him search for perfection in all things, particularly in the three that meant most to him; film-making, physical fitness, and women.'

His dislike of cadgers, and of those who want something for nothing, has lain behind his life-long battle with auto-graph hunters. He claims that he is 'only rude to rude autograph seekers', but he does not deny that he does everything he can to avoid giving autographs, particularly to those who fail to show him a proper politeness. On one occasion a fan whom he refused, asked, 'Who the hell do you think you are?' and was told coolly: 'I know who I am. I haven't the vaguest idea who you are, and furthermore I don't care to know.' While on the set of *Operation Petticoat* he even charged for the autographs he gave and donated the money to motion picture charities with the comment: 'Paying makes people aware of the value of what they're getting.'

His privacy is paramount to him. As he told the *Washington Post* when he was honoured by Ronald Reagan in December 1981 for his contribution to the performing arts: 'I'm very self-conscious about being on display. Now on a movie set, that's different. That's all right. That's your office really, and there was no intrusion there by outsiders.'

Almost the only myth about himself which he has not minded being perpetuated is his reported reply to a magazine editor's telegram in the early 1960s which asked: 'How old Cary Grant?' He is reputed to have replied, 'Old Cary Grant fine, how you?' 'That story,' he told his friend Roderick Mann a few years back, 'has been attributed to various people over the years. I wish I could say it was true, but it's not.' Instead he comments: 'I'm actually rather dull, for all I do is relax. I was an idiot until I was forty – an actor, a bore, wrapped up in himself.'

Whatever Archie Leach's private fears, Cary Grant's reputation as one of the screen's most brilliant and nonchalant comedians, whom the director Frank Capra once called Hollywood's greatest farceur, is undimmed. In the aristocracy of the movies he has a stature all his own. Mae West could say to him in 1933, 'Why don't you come up some time, see me?' and thirty years later Audrey Hepburn could say, 'Won't you come in for a minute? I don't bite you know, unless it's called for.' As the critic Pauline Kael has put it: 'Everyone likes the idea of Cary Grant. Everyone thinks of him affectionately, because he embodies what seems a happier time – a time when we had a simpler relationship to a performer. We could admire him for his timing and his nonchalance – we didn't expect emotional revelations from Cary Grant, we were used to his keeping his distance, which, if we cared to, we could close in idle fantasy. He appeared before us in radiantly shallow perfection, and that was all we wanted of him . . . We didn't want depth from him; we asked only that he be handsome and silky and make us laugh.'

It is a judgement echoed by almost every performer who has ever worked with him. James Stewart described him to me as 'a great comedian, a nice man, and a loyal one', and went on: 'I didn't know him awfully well but I liked him.' Katharine Hepburn once described him as 'a delicious personality who has learned to do certain things marvellously well.' And more recently she told me: 'He was great fun to act with and laughter reigned around him – a wonderful comedian and always a lively approach to the material. I did not really know him socially,' she added, 'as neither of us were much on going out. I think he liked working with me. He just could catch the ball and run with it. Too bad he quit. A lovely talent. I learned a lot from him.'

Doris Day explained to me: 'He looks into your eyes not into your forehead or your hair, as some people do. He can make love to me on the screen when he's ninety.' Laraine Day described him as 'A marvellous man to appear with,' though 'in the evenings it was like you were with a different person,' and Samantha Eggar said: 'He taught me a lot about comedy, he was marvellously professional.' Yet she too found him 'an elusive pimpernel'.

David Niven has called him 'the most truly mysterious friend I have. A spooky Celt really, not an Englishman at all. Must be some fey Welsh blood in there someplace. Gets great crushes on people, like the late Countess di Frasso, or ideas like hypnotism. Has great depressions and great heights when he seems about to take off for outer space.' Deborah Kerr regards him as 'one of the outstanding personalities in the history of the cinema.'

Before he died the director, George Cukor, paid tribute to

Grant's talent by saying: 'He really is the great exponent of a very subtle kind of human comedy, having learned the most difficult thing in the world, light comedy. For it to work it must have human appeal.' And speaking for a younger generation of directors, Peter Bogdanovich said: 'What made him so desirable as a player and so inimitable was the striking mixture of a comedian's talents with the looks of a matinée idol. When all the elements are right, his presence becomes an indispensable part of a masterpiece: Cukor's *The Philadelphia Story*, Hawks's *His Girl Friday*, Hitchcock's *North by Northwest* and *Notorious*. The ideal leading man, the perfect zany, the admirable dandy and the most charming rogue: except perhaps in his earliest years at Paramount, he was never allowed to die at the end of a film, and with good reason – who would believe it? Cary was indestructible.'

Stanley Kramer told me: 'Cary Grant has no peers in comedy or suspense. His reputation is the highest in the history of Hollywood – one of the *legitimate* Hollywood "greats".'

The producer Robert Arthur, who shared a bungalow with Grant at Universal and still sits at his desk at home beneath an oil painting of the actor, also gave me his view. 'Cary always represented quality,' he said, 'and because he made everything look so easy we've tended to underestimate him.' Like many of his oldest friends, Arthur is protective of Grant, conscious of the impact that invasions of his privacy have had on him over the years. 'He's always been a very private person and wanted to remain one.' It is a view shared by another of his old friends, Lord Bernstein, who calls him 'a very private man'.

Robert Arthur explains his friend's retirement by saying that 'Cary had always almost preferred the business of making films to the acting, and the old Hollywood that he had been brought up in was slowly dying around him. He was fastidious about everything, and he did not want to make what he thought might be "tasteless films".' None of his close friends sees any contradiction between his directorships of Fabergé, of which he is a large shareholder, or

MGM, and his career in films. As the writer Sol Saks put it to me: 'He always knew the grosses of his films, and he was proud that he had made very few flops.' Grant is also proud of the fact that twenty-eight films of his have opened at the Radio City Music Hall in New York, and between them have grossed more than $12m, making him the most popular performer in that cinema's fifty-year history – considerably more popular, in fact, than either of his nearest rivals, Katherine Hepburn or Fred Astaire.

Unlike some other Hollywood stars of his generation, like Henry Fonda and James Stewart, Katharine Hepburn and Claudette Colbert, Grant has never been tempted to return to Broadway and the stage. He has persistently turned down approaches to do so, and maintains indeed that he hardly goes to the theatre, just as he seldom reads novels or goes to the cinema now. What he values above everything else, he tells people, is his time. As he told Roderick Mann in 1978: 'I doubt if I have more than seventy thousand hours left and I'm not about to waste any of them.'

But his friends are prepared to admit that 'He is another person behind that movie star exterior'. José Ferrer, for example, is convinced that 'behind that joking elegant exterior there lurked tortured emotional depths that would have led to fine serious acting', and adds: 'Obviously the fear of failure, or some insecurity about his ability, or just plain indifference to such a career prevented him from extending his range.' Grant once told him: 'They won't accept me in serious roles, Joe, they want me to make them laugh.'

That was a tragic waste for the film industry. Grant's pursuit of his particular type of stardom meant that the potential of Archie Leach as an actor was never truly fulfilled. Only Alfred Hitchcock really ever came near to capturing part of what might have been possible in two of his four films with Grant, *Suspicion* and *Notorious*. Archie Leach's fears and insecurities had to be hidden if the world was to admire Cary Grant. Only his wives would ever see the contradiction at close quarters.

The actor who told Ingrid Bergman in *Notorious*, 'I've

always been scared of women – I'll get over it,' put his trust in his wives. It was not misplaced. Virginia Cherrill, who now lives in Santa Barbara, California, with her fourth husband, offered to appear as a character witness for him during his divorce from Dyan Cannon. Barbara Hutton remained devoted to him until the end of her life. As he was to say, 'We always stayed in touch, I was the only husband who never took a dime from her.' Betsy Drake has also never said anything critical about him since their separation. Even Dyan Cannon, who said after her divorce, 'I was looking for a Daddy. I married Daddy. He even looks like my father,' has re-established a reasonably cordial relationship with her former husband. He rang her after his fifth marriage in 1981 to suggest it was time she too got married again. He has never spoken critically of her. In this he has shown himself more forbearing than some of his friends, many of whom blame her for the fracture of his public image and feel that, whatever his private failings, she caused him unnecessary unhappiness.

Both Grant and Dyan Cannon are proud of Jennifer, now nearly eighteen. 'Jennifer is very well adjusted when you consider what she has had to put up with,' one of Grant's friends told me. 'She has enormous common sense and hasn't been overwhelmed by the war that seemed to be constantly going on between her parents over her custody. She is more secure than either her mother or her father.' In spite of Hollywood's appetite for younger and younger leading ladies, Jennifer Grant has shown no sign of wanting to become an actress.

His determination to provide a secure home for his daughter transformed Cary Grant's life, for it made him settle down. Now he takes her to the Magic Castle, a Hollywood club given over to magic and magicians and one of the few public places where he feels at ease, and he sometimes takes her with him to baseball games on Monday evenings with his wife, Barbara. His business trips are always carefully planned so as not to curtail the time he is allowed to spend with her.

The actor who told Ginger Rogers in *Monkey Business*, 'You're only old when you forget you're young,' has seldom had a day's illness. He swims a little, rides a little, and rests carefully. He and his wife live happily and calmly in their white-painted house, looking down over Beverly Hills, which still has the perimeter wall that Howard Hughes created for it. They play a card game together called 'Spite and Malice', which Grant maintains is 'a great way for getting rid of your hostilities', and they watch television. He avoids meeting strangers. 'I prefer to stay at home with my wife,' he says firmly.

One American children's performer, Soupy Sales, with whom celebrities often appear for the sole purpose of having a custard pie thrown at them, heard Grant was a fan and the producers rang to ask him if he would appear. Grant, now nearly eighty, told them: 'Gee, I'd love to, fellas, I watch the show all the time, but you know I never do television, so . . .' The separation between the public man and the private world is studiously maintained.

In the years since the public experiments with LSD brought the voice of Archie Leach to the surface, that voice has been quietly but relentlessly suppressed. Only some of Archie's characteristics remain: his fear of disorder and determination to remain in control; his tendency to wash constantly as if cleansing an almost forgotten guilt. The years of fretting over scripts, arguing over contracts and billing, worrying about performances are long over. As he puts it: 'Archie Leach, the dropout-runaway from Bristol, studied men like Noël Coward, and became Cary Grant.'

Once Archie Leach had stepped through the looking-glass to become Cary Grant, there was no going back. What had begun as a sacrifice for fame, affection, wealth and an identity had become a compulsion to remain the ageless, immortal star. The small, vulnerable boy from Bristol had been replaced by a perfectly created music-hall dummy that had no more need of its ventriloquist. If the voice of Archie Leach whispered in the night, only his memories would hear.

333

Filmography

Cary Grant appeared in the following films:

This Is the Night	Paramount Publix	1932
Sinners in the Sun	Paramount Publix	1932
Merrily We Go To Hell	Paramount Publix	1932
Devil and the Deep	Paramount Publix	1932
Blonde Venus	Paramount Publix	1932
Hot Saturday	Paramount Publix	1932
Madame Butterfly	Paramount Publix	1932
She Done Him Wrong	Paramount Publix	1933
Woman Accused	Paramount Publix	1933
The Eagle and the Hawk	Paramount Publix	1933
Gambling Ship	Paramount Publix	1933
I'm No Angel	Paramount Publix	1933
Alice in Wonderland	Paramount Publix	1933
Thirty-Day Princess	Paramount Publix	1934
Born To Be Bad	United Artists	1934
Kiss and Make Up	Paramount Publix	1934
Ladies Should Listen	Paramount Publix	1934
Enter Madame	Paramount Publix	1935
Wings in the Dark	Paramount	1935
The Last Outpost	Paramount	1935
Sylvia Scarlett	RKO Radio	1936
Big Brown Eyes	Paramount	1936
Suzy	M-G-M	1936
The Amazing Quest of Ernest Bliss (U.S. title Romance and Riches)	Grand National	1936
Wedding Present	Paramount	1936

335

One Night of Love	Columbia	1936
When You're In Love	Columbia	1937
The Toast of New York	RKO Radio	1937
Topper	M-G-M	1937
The Awful Truth	Columbia	1937
Bringing Up Baby	RKO Radio	1938
Holiday	Columbia	1938
Gunga Din	RKO Radio	1939
Only Angels Have Wings	Columbia	1939
In Name Only	RKO Radio	1939
His Girl Friday	Columbia	1940
My Favorite Wife	RKO Radio	1940
The Howards of Virginia (U.S. title The Tree of Liberty)	Columbia	1940
The Philadelphia Story	M-G-M	1941
Penny Serenade	Columbia	1941
Suspicion	RKO Radio	1941
The Talk of the Town	Columbia	1942
Once Upon A Honeymoon	RKO Radio	1942
Mr Lucky	RKO Radio	1943
Destination Tokyo	Warner Bros	1944
Once Upon A Time	Columbia	1944
None But The Lonely Heart	RKO Radio	1944
Arsenic and Old Lace	Warner Bros	1944
Night and Day	Warner Bros	1946
Notorious	RKO Radio	1946
Without Reservations	RKO Radio	1946
The Bachelor and the Bobbysoxer (U.K. title Bachelor Knight)	RKO Radio	1947
The Bishop's Wife	RKO Radio	1947
Mr Blandings Builds His Dream House	RKO Radio	1948
Every Girl Should Be Married	RKO Radio	1948
I Was A Male War Bride (U.S. title You Can't Sleep Here)	20th Century Fox	1949
Crisis	M-G-M	1950

People Will Talk	20th Century Fox	1951
Room For One More	Warner Bros	1952
Monkey Business	20th Century Fox	1952
Dream Wife	M-G-M	1953
To Catch A Thief	Paramount	1955
The Pride and the Passion	United Artists	1957
An Affair to Remember	20th Century Fox	1957
Kiss Them For Me	20th Century Fox	1957
Indiscreet	Warner Bros	1958
Houseboat	Paramount	1958
North by Northwest	M-G-M	1959
Operation Petticoat	Universal	1959
The Grass is Greener	Universal	1961
That Touch of Mink	Universal	1962
Charade	Universal	1963
Father Goose	Universal	1964
Walk Don't Run	Columbia	1966

He also made brief appearances in a number of short films, including

Singapore Sue (as Archie Leach)	Paramount Publix	1932
Pirate Party on Catalina Island	M-G-M	1936
Road to Victory	Warner Bros	1944

Acknowledgements

The search for Cary Grant took me to Hollywood and to New York, back again to England, to his home town of Bristol, and then to London. In the process I interviewed more than two hundred people and spent months researching in libraries in Britain and the United States. To all those I talked to I owe a vast debt of gratitude for their courtesy and patience, and for the help they gave me in piecing together a picture of one of the cinema's most intensely private stars.

It is, perhaps, invidious to pick out particular individuals from so many but I feel I must especially thank James Stewart and Katharine Hepburn, Doris Day and José Ferrer, Samantha Eggar, Moray Watson and Laraine Day, to name only a few of the distinguished performers who shared Cary Grant's career. Of the producers, directors or writers who worked with him Robert Arthur and Pandro S. Berman, Stanley Kramer, Delbert Mann and Sol Saks were especially kind; while in the Hollywood studios I received a great deal of help from Vernon Harbin, and John Hall at RKO, Andy Leigh at Universal, and Kellam de Forest at Paramount.

I am also deeply grateful to every single member of the staff of the library of the Academy of Motion Picture Arts and Sciences in Los Angeles, who not only helped me sift through a vast amount of material but also gave me access to two of their special archives: the George Stevens and Hedda Hopper collections.

I owe a similar debt to the staffs of the American Film Institute Library in Hollywood, and the Film Libraries of the University College of Los Angeles, and of the University of Southern California, and to Dr Bob Knutsen of USC who allowed me to delve into the Warner Brothers archive there.

In England I must also warmly thank the staff of the London Library, the British Film Institute Library, and Public Records Office in London, and a series of newspaper libraries in Fleet Street.

But there is another group of people who contributed enormously to this book but whom I cannot thank publicly. These are the men and women, co-stars, friends and acquaintances of Cary Grant who agreed to talk to me on the understanding that I would not reveal that we had spoken. In consequence I can only offer them all my profound, humble, but strictly private thanks.

Finally I must thank my editor Rivers Scott, my friend Giles Clark, my agent Leslie Gardner in London and her associates Joy Harris in New York and Ken Sherman in Los Angeles, my publishers Robin Baird-Smith and Gill Gibbins at Collins and Harvey Ginsberg at William Morrow, and the incomparable Leslie Halliwell for checking my film accuracy. This book could not have been completed without the support and encouragement of Coutts Bank, in whose debt I shall be forever, and whose faith in the project almost rivalled mine.

Most of all, the book could never have been written without the help of my wife, Jan, who not only worked as a research assistant and typist for eighteen months, but who also put up with my obsession with Cary Grant without the slightest complaint.

No one should be held responsible for my conclusions, however; those are mine alone.

Geoffrey Wansell

London, June 1983

Index